Other books by A.A. Gill

TO AMERICA WITH LOVE

A. A. Gill

Simon & Schuster

NEW YORK   LONDON   TORONTO   SYDNEY   NEW DELHI

Simon & Schuster
1230 Avenue of the Americas
New York, NY 10020

First Simon & Schuster hardcover edition July 2013

SIMON & SCHUSTER and colophon are registered trademarks of
Simon & Schuster, Inc.

For information about special discounts for bulk purchases,
please contact Simon & Schuster Special Sales at
1-866-506-1949 or business@simonandschuster.com.

The Simon & Schuster Speakers Bureau can bring authors to your
live event. For more information or to book an event, contact the
Simon & Schuster Speakers Bureau at 1-866-248-3049
or visit our website at www.simonspeakers.com.

Manufactured in the United States of America

10 9 8 7 6 5 4 3 2 1

Library of Congress Cataloging-in-Publication Data is available.

ISBN 978-1-4165-9621-9
ISBN 978-1-4391-0044-8 (ebook)

To Wendy Ewald, the American cousin

Acknowledgments

First and last I must thank Amy Turner, who wrote every word of this book and researched a great deal of it; also my editors Alan Samson and Celia Hayley, who plied their necessary craft, sometimes like Chinese embroiderers, sometimes like abattoir janitors; my minder agents Charlie Campbell and Ed Victor; and those who offered lodging, advice and occasionally derision along the way: Dave Macmillan and Bella Pollen, Christoph and Katrin Henkel in Colorado; Luke Janklow, Christiane Amanpour, Jamie Rubin, Graydon Carter and Dana Brown in New York.

Contents

Give me your tired, your poor,
Your huddled masses yearning to breathe free,
The wretched refuse of your teeming shore.
Send these, the homeless, tempest-tost to me,
I lift my lamp beside the golden door!

—Emma Lazarus, 1849–1887

TO AMERICA WITH LOVE

1

Cuttings

My father told me about the family buffalo over breakfast. He was writing the autobiography, rifling through the attic of his life. The words were mostly accounting, settling up and settling down, exhuming and laying to rest. He'd stop like a man climbing a spiral staircase, and turn to whoever was behind him and hold a memory up. Most often it would be from the war—that was always going to be the biggest thing in any life that lived through it. The buffalo made its bucolic and brief appearance as an aside, a hoofnote, and ambled over the toast and marmalade, a ghostly ruminant. Apparently someone had killed the thing—an uncle, removed and some way back—on the great grasslands of the Wild West, had the head flayed and refilled, and donated it to a museum in West Yorkshire—the town where he'd grown up. The uncle, not the buffalo. Dad said I should go and see it: "You like that sort of thing," and that was it. The headless buffalo departed without leaving a track in the butter.

We don't go in for ancestors in our family, we're not hereditary folk. It's not that we don't have them, it's just that we don't think they're what's interesting about us. You are what you achieve, what you do, not what some blokes you never met did in the back of behind. The whole ancestor business comes with the sort of baggage we would feel embarrassed carrying through life. All of us have exactly the same number of antecedents. We all of us go back to the *Mayflower*, the conquests, the pharaohs, the Flood. Birth and death ought to be utterly egalitarian, unexceptional. The one thing every human on earth shares is predecessors. Sifting an unearned social advantage out of the ossuary is ridiculous and demeaning. The autobiography writing in itself was odd, cut against the grain. My dad didn't even go in for monograms. We were the tomorrow people, all our best bits were to come. Life stories were only reflections in achievement, certainly not retrospective diaries of self-justification. So he was the first of our scattered, anonymously unresurrected tribe ever to write a memoir. I excused it by thinking of it as the hobby of old age, although we didn't go in for hobbies much, either. And then he died, and left a volume of an early life that finished before I arrived. It was published just as he departed.

He left me two other books. Although he was a lifelong atheist of unshakable conviction and faith, there was a toe-breaking family Bible. On its flyleaves, exuberant with a reverential, barely legible copperplate, were lists of births, deaths and marriages stretching hand to hand back to the 1700s. And then a scrapbook, a blue hard-backed thing sold specifically for the purpose, with a royal coat of arms on its opening page, and the instructions "A ready reference receptacle for scraps of print from our chief sources of knowledge: the newspapers. With patent, alphabetical index and spaces for marginal notes, made by Marcus Ward and Co," who had offices in London, Belfast and New York. At the end of the nineteenth century someone had collated and pasted random errata in the thick, wrinkled volume that splayed its rigor-mortisly brittle pages, which contained a sepia collection of obituaries, alderman's reports, murders long past their salacious pleasure, whimsical asides and the comic observations that might have been used by after-dinner speakers. There was news from abroad that mocked foreigners, invitations to weddings and municipal balls, there were birthday cards and cards of remembrance, cartoons of a leaden, comic seriousness, and photographs of awkward, middle-class Victorians trying to live up to their starch and lace. And although by its nature the book is serendipitous and aimless, over time it evolves a plot.

It revolved around two poles, two sets of lives: the probity of Batley and Dewsbury in West Yorkshire, where my grandmother's people lived, and distant, staccato reports from America, mostly in the form of press cuttings and cards that hoped they found you as they left us. There are photographs of cowboys, relaxed in their big-brimmed hats and waistcoats, and there are pages of pressed flowers sent from Colorado. They are poignant and fragile, now the color of old skin, the twigs and folded petals and the crumbling leaves are caught in the split gutter. This book is a memento of a family drifting apart, a list of names. The good wishes, the weddings and funerals, the dead bouquets, hope and fondness, the concerns and rituals of a family are like ink dropped into water.

How quickly roots are separated. How fast new ones grow. The cuttings book is the paper chase of following disappearing runners, the view of a receding future collated by the people who stayed behind. For over 400 years, moved by brave and fearful reasons, Europeans were drawn to America, pushed out or pulled away by the eternal imperative spurs of hope and despair. The hardship and the terrors of the New World were monolithic and relentless, but then so were its promises. And whatever lay out there, at least they knew it wasn't home. It wasn't the immovable, ancient, carping certainties of Europe. When asked if he thought that the French Revolution had been a good thing, Zhou Enlai famously answered that it was too early to tell, which is trite about the Terror, but it would be true about America. It's too early to tell. If you take a timeline from the first settlements in the 1600s to the present, and compare it with the foundation of modern Europe from the end of the Roman Empire, at the same point in *our* history the Vikings are attacking Orkney, and Alfred is the first king of bits of what will one day be England.

I have often thought that Europe's view of America has been formed and deformed by the truth that we are the ones who stayed behind, for all those good, bad and lazy reasons: because of caution, for comfort, for conformity and obligation, but mostly I suspect because of habit and fear. We didn't take the risky road. This book is the next volume to the ancestor cuttings. It is the view of the New World from the Old. It is a look back at the people who went forward and the country they made out of millions of cuttings taken from the roots of millions of families. They formed an America that grew to become the best and finest creation of Europe, the culmination of all its deepest aspirations, the fruit of rue, of wisdom and experience, but a creation that Europe can take no credit for.

My father's family were farmers and mill owners, working water-and-steam-driven woolen mills in the early Industrial Revolution. They made shoddy, taking old yarn, unpicking and reweaving it, and they made a jangle of change in their day. Particularly out of the Crimean War—all those cheap balaclavas. A pair of brothers and their cousin left the farm and the business for America. There wasn't enough work or worth left in the old place after some uncle drank most of it before he was thirty and then crawled, yellow and shaking, to the chapel where he signed a pledge and lived for the rest of his life in a gritted, grim and guilty sobriety. The cousins took what they could and went to test what was left of their luck out in the Rockies at a place called Arickaree, where they bred horses and kept livery stables. They weren't the first to come, they followed a man who'd gone out for the '45 to pan for Californian gold, who then stayed to run a general store, and someone else who'd made some sort of fortune. There are family anecdotes that sound like the script for a silent cowboy movie—Buffalo Bill is said to have lived next door. The Yorkshire boys—the Batley Cowboys—were plagued by rustlers, shysters and grifters, and unreliable help, all probably as keenly desperate as they were. And then one of them got gutshot over a poker game, and the next day his siblings found him left for dead on a rubbish heap, but he didn't die—he was from Yorkshire—and they moved to Detroit instead.

They did well in Detroit, though there was a scandal pasted into the scrapbook. There's the unmistakable pursed disapproval in the cuttings. Despite that, you can sense between the lines the unspoken shadows of the immigrant sun rising, as the old home family genteelly and stiffly subside. The New World failures may have been greater, the disasters more excessive, the consequences more brutal, but there's a bounce in every fall, a spit on the palm's new start for every setback. In Yorkshire there is only the impetus of decline; the farms, the woolen mills, the dairy rounds wither, unravel and turn sour. The family wears out, stumbles politely, tripping over drink and ennui and a genteel surrender to the momentum of underachievement. The scrapbook comes to an end midsentence, a handful of pages left blank as if they can no longer be bothered. Maybe whoever was responsible died or moved on, or married. I always imagine it was a woman who kept and collated it: it's women who unpick and reweave the shoddy of families. Maybe they were just so sad they couldn't bear it. The unintentional narrative arc is a log of profit and loss, the transfer of hope and luck from an old account to a new, from Europe to America. My grandparents left Yorkshire for Kent. My grandmother's brother followed the train west to Detroit, returning only to leave a leg, postbellum. My dad wrote in his autobiography that his uncle had invited him to America with a view to emigration. He was a young man with little to keep him in a battered and exhausted postwar Europe. Everything about America was the place to be, but he didn't stay. He too was both pushed and pulled—pushed out and pulled back. I expect, contrarily, it will have been the comfort and the cornucopia that repelled him, the prospect of the rubble and the pity that called him. He never mentioned this encounter to me—or perhaps he did and I wasn't interested. But now I try to imagine what it would have been like if he had gone. What our life would have been, what I'd have been like if I'd grown up in Grosse Pointe, where the family were now selling Chevrolets.

I'm writing this in Colorado. In front of me on the table is a glass jar with a fistful of wildflowers wilting in the inky water. The little, elegant, hardy blooms of high meadows. Beyond the vase, through a window, a valley falls away. Fields of purple, yellow and white, thick and fetlock-deep, rest like plum salads between hanging red-stone walls, flocked in aspen and fir whose leaves flicker like pale sequins in the wind. A dirt road marks a circuitous river that races past cabins, corrals and grazing horses, and then dies into the overlapping fan of herringboned hills that steeple the middle distance. Behind them, riding above the tree line, are the stacks of sawtoothed mountains; still, in this hot and heady July, they are flecked with slivers of snow. And above it all, that histrionic sky of the West, building the dreaming temples of freedom out of clouds, elevated in the summer heat, boiling up late-afternoon thunderstorms. Buzzards curl on their thermals. This view is familiar before you ever see it. It is the frontier. It is the wilderness, and I feel no particular connection with this place other than being here with my children on holiday. The Batley Cowboys haven't lent or marked it with a sense of belonging for me.

What with the book, the Bible and Dad dying, I'd been scratching the ancestors, and the buffalo returned to haunt me, as the Indians always say it does—Tatanka, the ghost of the prairies. Death lends everything a metaphoric imperative. Mundane objects become fetishes when the departed no longer need them, and breakfast conversations grow runic and wise from behind the shadows. The buffalo returned, a dream totem, my father's familiar, and my quest.

The Bagshaw Museum sits like an ornate and squat toad amid the tight and unattractive little cul-de-sacs of Batley. This is a place that has always grown out of industry and parsimony rather than aesthetics and exuberance. The museum was originally a mill owner's house, erected as the stubby monument to his money and the twelve-hour days and six-day weeks of his child laborers. The memorial to their amputated fingers, broken heads and deafening exploitation. It is a Gothic brass band of boastful brick, and despite its thumbs-in-waistcoat-pocket, portly, mercantile intentions, it turned out to be the embodiment of that Yorkshire cautionary schadenfreude: clogs to clogs in three generations.

The mill boss spent the staggering figure of 25,000 mid-Victorian pounds on his house, and his grandchildren sold it back to the council for five quid. Some years later a local aristocrat donated the land for a public park, and the council turned this empty temple into a museum. Its first and most eclectically vigorous curator was Mr. Bagshaw, a local philanthropist who, in the Edwardian way of things, collected indiscriminately and rigorously, with the global kleptomania of empire and the desire to own, calibrate, measure and stuff everything possible, to put all of creation into its place, and place as much of it as possible in glass cases. The house had briefly done for the ambition of one man what the museum did for Batley. There was an entire Egyptian tomb displayed here in the old drawing room. There were cases of ethnographic flotsam and jetsam and novelty. Added to this municipal treasury, the pillage of imperialism, a great-aunt of mine donated the buffalo.

But museums as indiscriminate collections of ethnic curiosity and snobbery have had their day. The sun has finally set on their patronage. They are academically useless, morally dubious. So when I called to ask if there was any trace of my buffalo, the district administrator told me that the museum was closed for refurbishment and would open at some later date, "exhibiting collections that were more in tune with the educational and cultural needs of the local community." All the old stuff had been put in storage, and she would call me back. And then, the damnedest thing happened. She did. They'd found a reference to the buffalo. It had been donated with a decorative calabash of South American origin, and an eagle's foot. The talon had gone to a school's nature table, but the buffalo was apparently still there somewhere, along with the other embarrassments, locked in the attic. "It may take some time to find," she said. But then the next damnedest thing happened, and they found it, and they told me, and asked if I'd like to see it.

Batley is just off the M1, part of that municipal sprawl that was once the West Riding and is now called Kirklees. The agricultural and craftsman communities have blended into each other. Dewsbury, Heckmondwike, Cleckheaton, Gomersal, Birstall, Soothill, Kinsley, Ossett, Crackenedge, names that sound like what they were, that mimic the bash and grind of industry, that sound like pub jokes. Now you'd only know that you'd arrived in any of them because the road sign tells you to drive carefully, and that they're twinned with some other postindustrial stain on the Ruhr. The museum was surrounded by what must have once been an impressive garden, but now the deep herbaceous border has been stuffed with variegated laurel—the gardening version of a nylon dust sheet. I looked out over the soft landscape, the park, the old mill chimneys, the brick warehouses, terraced streets, the hedges and fields that my family must have husbanded, called in the cows for milking, and tried to wish a connection, a retrospective belonging, some dusty chime of homecoming. But there was nothing. I felt no more connection to this place than I did to the high country of Colorado. Inside the museum, the succession of corpulently, darkly self-satisfied empty rooms swagged their fancy plaster and paneling, and showed off exuberant, varied marbled mantels with surprisingly mean little fireplaces. That really is the spirit of the West Riding—showy on your mantelpiece, parsimonious with the coal. At the top of the building, in the old servants' quarters, the mad attic is crammed to the eaves with the Edwardian museum, a staggering jumble of tat and curiosity, shelves of ethnic craft and gimpy taxidermy. Escaping from under plastic sheeting, piled on sagging shelves, are handles and feet, beaks and ormolu casters, rattan and lacquer, bamboo, china, mud, bone and teak all lying hugger-mugger with a dingy disregard. The curators look at this Tourette's collection of brac-and-bicker with a weary irritation. These things will never be shown again. Museums appear to have an air of permanence, of being the repositories of immortality, but they are just as prone to the whims of fashion and the sliding eye of public interest as a Harrods window. The Bagshaw collection displays another truth about these corrals of culture: more often than not, an exhibition is merely a misplaced object. These things would be mundane and unremarkable in the places that created them. They were exhibited first of all for being curious in this context, and then discarded because the curiosity waned. They now hang in this administrative Hades, a shadow Kafka-world beyond help or home. They can't be sold because they belong to the people of Kirklees who don't know about them, or want them, and they can't be thrown away because this is a museum, and for a museum to discard anything would be an act of philistine, fascist vandalism. But then, to exhibit them would be insensitive, colonially imperious, so they languish here like the old, ugly, deranged children in an orphanage.

I was led upstairs and down corridors to the last room, and there on the table was the Batley Cowboys' buffalo. Correctly, their bison. His face points to the sky. His dark eye stares straight at me with that stoical peevishness that is the species' resting expression. No one has ever been able to surmise what a buffalo was thinking, their faces held low, pulled back into the protection of their massive shoulders, an impassive minotaur head with just this gimlet eye. He is huge—far bigger than I expected. I suppose because I am most used to his most distant English cousin, the domestic cow. His great, woolly head implies a hidden, woolly body behind it, galloping up through the floor, about to heave him through the roof. The head is attached to an ornate and embossed yoke, a brass shield that makes him more decorative than zoological. He lies amid stacks of spears, arrows, knobkerries and clubs, and a pensive pheasant and a rather fine great bustard, like heraldic supporters. The prosaic birds of English copse and heath.

The buffalo has lost his other eye and the sheath of one horn. The injuries make him look more majestic, with a patient dignity. Taxidermy inhabits a half-life, an underpass between life and death. He is oddly vital, still possessed of an animating force, not as defunct as a corpse yet still nowhere near living. A talisman trapped between escape and dust. Where I have felt no particular tug or connection to Batley and these family-familiar dales, or to the pines and meadows of Colorado, I do feel something akin to this dark head, trapped in flight, held in these airless, silent eaves, shrouded in the dust and decrepitude of uninterest. I imagine him spending years on the wall in a modest but sturdy farmhouse, inglorious and oversized, a talking point, an anchor for paper chains and mistletoe above a sideboard in a dining room, with brown furniture smelling of beeswax and ham and vinegar and folded linen, with hunting prints on each side, a beveled mirror on a chain, the bone-handled carving set in its blue velvet–lined box, the slow tick of a grandfather clock, the sticking drawers lined with the yellowing pages of the *Yorkshire Post*, neat with saved candle ends, comic bottle openers, plated silver pickle forks, a box of England's Best matches, a stained recipe for Guards pudding, a china anchovy paste pot containing the charmed and silver three-pences for Christmas puddings. Perhaps they gave him a name, a Yankee name from a penny dreadful Wild West story: Tex, or Doc. Perhaps an Indian name: Sitting Bull or Geronimo. More likely, with ponderous Yorkshire humor, the name of someone he reminded the family of—Uncle Alfred, Witless Wilf. And back before that, when his name was of his own bellowing, I imagine him being picked out by a man from this valley in Yorkshire, their threads converging as the man stepped out on his long journey to the West. First the dogcart to the station, then the train to Liverpool or Southampton, the ship to New York—in comfort, I imagine, not a stateroom, but not steerage—then a long, slow, rocking journey out west on that astonishing marathon of civil engineering and endurance, a transcontinental railway, to get off in some lone, blown and gritty rural town beneath the mountains, picked up by his cousins, who now look quite different, taller in their slope-heeled work boots, darker, rangier, broader, chest-out confident, with broad hats and bandannas, and I expect they suggested a trip to hunt buffalo, to spend a night out on the prairie, sleep under the stars, eat pork and beans, drink whiskey, talk about home and the new life out here in this new soon-to-be state.

It won't have been difficult to kill the buffalo. Over 100 years, from 1800 to 1900, around 75 million were slaughtered, mostly by hunters hired by the railway to feed laborers, or by skinners for their hides: little else was used. And shooting buffalo was the attrition to move on and assimilate the Indians. The naked corpses of the great herds were left on the plains. There were not enough carrion eaters to tidy them away. It was a glut, unexpected and unknown to nature. They leached slowly back into the poor, thin earth, their white bones visible for years as a warning and a threat. Our buffalo won't have been hard to find as he trundled in the diminished herd. They cut off his head and maybe took a few steaks, just to say they tasted it, "a bit like beef, but tougher." And then, months after the man's return to Batley, when he'd all but forgotten, the station master must have rung to say there was a packing case standing on the platform: a pine box with a painted address, the chalk marks of customs and shippers, fragile labels and papers. And they got it back and searched for a chisel and a hammer, and pried off the lid, and there, wreathed in hessian and sweet woodchips, with a faint smell of rot and perhaps the turpentine of wild sage, the buffalo would have looked up at him.

And so it hung: a totem in this museum, not just to the open territorial West, the vanished herds and the tribes, but also this departed and dispersed family. To the vanished millworkers and extinct family farms of the West Riding. The totem head that has outlived the museum. This town is now Asian, Punjabis who came here in the sixties to work the end of the wool, and have stayed to make their own communities. There is a faint and smiling punning irony that in the great urban flow of migration this buffalo from the lost herds has contrarily found himself at long, long last once again at home amongst the Indians.

Outside the shuttered Bagshaw Museum there is a rhododendron-and-azalea walk that has unlandscaped itself and is evolving back into woodland, its rockery paths barely traceable. The ornamental bridges collapse over the poetically meandering rills, choked with bramble and briar, bluebells and banks of pungent wild garlic. A local boy was beaten to death here a few months back. A small dog zigzags past, snorting the tilth, followed by a fat jogging woman in all-day sweatpants. This would all have been planted as a romantic allegory, a setting that would have mimicked Byron and Scott, and late-Victorian paintings and Gothic doggerel. It is a parody of the real, boundless and unwritten wilderness that the Batley Cowboys went to find. Here it hides a defunct place, has grown over the people and things and ways of life that have long gone west. In the oak and beech dapple a clarion of spring birds sing of nests and mates and living room, and mock the earth.

The story of my family, the forgettable, episodic saga of moving on, is not uncommon. Many—maybe most—European families can tell something similar. Cousins, brothers, uncles, aunts, sisters, daughters, sons waving goodbye, promising to write, to send back for others when they'd made the bridgehead, to return money when it was made, to return themselves when they'd made it. There will be photographs and diaries in most attics, stories and fading memories in every household. Emigration is perhaps the most familiar plot in the Old World. In 400 years a trickle became a stream, then a torrent of immigration to America. From 1800 to 1914 more than 30 million Europeans immigrated to the New World: one in four Irishmen, one in five Swedes, 3 million Germans, 5 million Poles, 4 million Italians. There is not a country, a community, a village or household that wasn't affected by the lure of the West, but we don't talk about it much. We're far more familiar, more comfortable with the returning echo from the other side, the view from the New World looking back. Americans are the ones who tell the creation story of a nation. In Europe it's an exodus told as the historical and statistical footnote to the much older and slower-plotted saga whose cast is beyond reckoning. Emigration as part of the Highland clearances, the potato famine, the persecution of Huguenots, ergot blight, the collapse of the southern Italian rural economy, Polish military conscription.

In America, immigration is the story of hope and achievement, of youth, of freedom, of creation. But all entrances on one stage are exits elsewhere. In Europe it is loss. Every one a farewell, a failure, a sadness, a defeat. It must have been such a relentless woe, such an awful repetition of rending, the gut-clenching finality of separation, the absence of love. In the decade preceding it, more Europeans left for America than the 16 million who died in the Great War. Though these are not comparable—these aren't the dead. Occasionally, like my cousins, they brought over their relatives. Some did return, rich and replete, to retire and complete the circle, but most didn't. They hugged their mothers, drank a toast with friends, promised to write, took a last look at the old house, patted the counterpane on their childhood bed, patted the dog, picked up a parcel with a favorite lunch—cheese from the pasture, ham from the chimney, apple from the orchard, the pie with that particular scent of hearth—and they pulled the door shut with a sound that was familiar and final and would stay with them a lifetime, and they walked out and down the street through a thousand-year landscape, and their brothers and sisters would walk with them until they could go no further, and on they'd go, individually, in pairs, in groups and clans, whole villages, classes from schools, congregations.

And mostly, the people who left were the ones who could be spared least. Like a biblical curse, the biblical land called the young and the strong from Europe: the adventurous, the clever, and the skilled. The story of emigration told from America is a moving toward freedom and land and riches, toward opportunity, a clean sheet, a new start. Sweden and Norway, Finland and Iceland lost 14 percent of their population—most of them young. They took with them their stern religion and an astonishing capacity for Sisyphean toil. Also self-absorption that absorbed loneliness. On their backs they carried bags of their homeland's hardy wheat, and with all of that they made something astonishing and memorable. The Irish would attend their own wakes at home, so their families could keen over their departing. Emigration was a death to avoid death; the Atlantic, a Styx.

2

"Stupid"

"Stupid, stupid. Americans are stupid. America is stupid. A stupid, stupid country made stupid by stupid, stupid people." I particularly remember that because of the nine stupids in one paragraph. It was said over a dinner table by a professional woman, a clever, clever, clever woman. Hardback-educated, bespokely traveled, liberally humane, worked in the arts. A clever woman who cared for things. She gave money for their relief, shed tears for people she'd never met and would have been unable to speak to if she had. I can't remember specifically why she said it, what evidence of New World idiocy triggered the trope. Neither do I remember what the reaction was, but I don't need to remember. It will have been a nodded and muttered agreement. Even from me. I've heard this cock crow so often I don't even feel guilt for not wringing its neck. Among the educated, enlightened, expensive middle classes of Europe, this is a received wisdom. A given. Stronger in some countries like France, less so somewhere like Germany, but overall, the Old World patronizes America for being a big, dumb, fat, belligerent child. The intellectuals, the movers and the makers and the creators, the dinner-party establishments of people who count, are united in the belief—no, the knowledge—that Americans are stupid, crass, ignorant, soulless, naive oafs without attention, irony or intellect. These same people will use every comforting, clever and ingenious American invention, will demand its medicine, wear American clothes, eat its food, drink its drink, go to its cinema, love its music, thank God for its expertise in a hundred disciplines, and will all adore New York. More than that, more shaming and hypocritical than that, these are people

14

who collectively owe their nations' and their personal freedoms to American intervention and protection in wars, both hot and cold. Who whether they credit it or not, also owe their concepts of freedom, equality and civil rights in no small part to America. Of course, they will also sign collective letters accusing America of being a fascist, totalitarian, racist state.

Enough. Enough, enough, enough of this convivial rant, this collectively confirming bigotry. The nasty laugh of little togetherness, or Euro-liberal insecurity. It's not just another lazy, thoughtless prejudice. It's embarrassing, infectious and belittling. I once asked a lawyer who specialized in hate crime, racism and intolerance if he had come across a case of an American claiming discrimination. He looked askance. No. Would he prosecute a case on behalf of an American, or America? "I can't imagine a circumstance where we'd bring a case on behalf of America. The law is there to protect the weak and vulnerable," he replied with the smile of political and social virtue that I've seen over so many plates of ham and melon. Funny, and I thought it was for everyone.

Look at that European snapshot of America. It is so unlike the country I have known for thirty years. Not just a caricature but a travesty, an invention. Even on the most cursory observation, the intellectual European view of the New World is a homemade, Old World effigy that suits some internal purpose. The belittling, the discounting, the mocking of the States is not about them at all. It's about us, back here in the ancient, classical, civilized continent. Well, how stupid can America actually be? On the international list of the world's best universities, thirteen of the top twenty are American. Four are British. Of the top 100, only one is French, and Heidelberg creeps in for the Germans. America has won 320 Nobel Prizes. The UK 117. France 57. America has more Nobel Prizes than Britain, France, Germany, Japan and Russia combined. Of course, Nobel Prizes aren't everything, and America's aren't all for inventing Prozac or refining oil. They have eighteen peace prizes, six for literature (they share Eliot with the Brits). And are they emotionally dim, naive, irony free? Do you imagine the society that produced Dorothy Parker and

Lenny Bruce doesn't understand irony? It was an American who said that satire died when they awarded the Nobel Peace Prize to Henry Kissinger. It's not irony that America lacks, it's cynicism. In Europe, that arid sneer out of which nothing is grown or made is often mistaken for the creative scalpel of irony. And what about vulgarity? Americans are innately, sniggerably vulgar. What, vulgar like Henry James or Eleanor Roosevelt or Cole Porter, or the Mormons? Again, it's a question of definitions. What Americans value and strive for is straight talking, plain saying. They don't go in for ambiguity or dissembling, the etiquette of hidden meaning, the skill of the socially polite lie. The French in particular confuse unadorned direct language with a lack of culture or intellectual elegance. It was Camus who sniffily said that only in America could you be a novelist without being an intellectual. There is a belief that America has no cultural depth or critical seriousness. Well, you only have to walk into an American bookshop to realize that is wildly wrong and willfully blind. What about Mark Twain, or jazz, or abstract expressionism?

What is so contrary about Europe's liberal antipathy to America is that any visiting Venusian anthropologist would see with the merest cursory glance that America and Europe are far more similar than they are different, not just similar but plainly related, and not simply on one or two cultural or political levels, as colonies are to their colonizers. The threads of the Old World are woven into the New. America is Europe's greatest invention. That's not to exclude the contribution to America that has come from around the globe, but it is built out of Europe's ideas, Europe's understanding, aesthetic, morality, assumptions and laws. From the way it sets a table to the chairs it sits on, to the rhythms of its poetry and the scales of its music, the meter of its aspirations and its laws, its markets, its prejudices and neuroses. The conventions and the breadth of America's reason are European.

This isn't a claim for ownership, or for credit. America's robust construction, its filigree of sensibilities, its essential genius belong to no one but itself. But America didn't arrive by chance. It wasn't a ship that lost its way. It wasn't coincidence or happenstance. America grew tall out of the cramping ache of old Europe.

When I was a child, there was a lot of talk of a "brain drain"—commentators, professors, directors, politicians would worry at the seeping of gray matter across the Atlantic. Brains were being lured to California by mere money. Mere money and space, and sun, and steak, and Hollywood, and more money and opportunity and optimism and openness. All the Os but without one-upmanship. And there was ownership, and friendship, and a future. All inconsequential fripperies, according to the Old World: beads and mirrors. People who took the dollar in exchange for their brains were unpatriotic in much the same way that tax exiles were. The unfair luring of indigenous British thoughts would, it was darkly said, lead to Britain falling behind, ceasing to be the preeminently brilliant and inventive nation that had produced the Morris Minor and the hovercraft. You may have little idea how lauded and revered Sir Christopher Cockerell, the inventor of the hovercraft, was, and you may well not be aware of what a noisy, unstable waste of effort the hovercraft turned out to be, but we were very proud of it for a moment.

The underlying motif of the brain drain was that while America might have wealth, performance, production, advertising and consumption, for real cleverness you needed years of careful breeding. Cold bedrooms, tinned tomatoes on toast, a temperament and a heritage that led to invention and discovery. And that was only really available in Europe and, to the greatest extent, in Britain. At the same time the establishment was getting purple-faced about the brain drain, they were encouraging working-class families and single, young, skilled men to become "ten-pound Poms"—take assisted passage to Australia. Nobody seemed to notice that these were exactly the people who had once left for America, the country that could now afford to buy brains. The brain drain was symbolic of a postwar self-pity. The handing back of empire, the slow, Kiplingesque watch as the things you gave your life to are broken, and you have to stoop to build them up with worn-out tools. There was resentment and envy that, while the first half of the twentieth century had spent the last of Grandfather's inherited capital, it had left Britain exhausted and depressed, whereas the war had been the engine that geared up industry and pulled America out of the Depression, and capitalized it for a half century of plenty. It seemed so unfair. All that sangfroid on all those stiff lips, all of Nanny's virtues, were, after all, going to be the only chilly, speechless reward.

The real brain drain was already 300 years old. The idea of America attracted the brightest and most idealistic, and the best from all over Europe. European civilization had reached a stasis. By its own accounting it had grown from classical Greece to be an identifiable, homogeneous place, thanks to the Roman Empire and the spread of Christianity, and then through the Dark Ages there was the Renaissance and the Reformation, and then the Age of Reason, which grew a series of ideas and discoveries, philosophies and visions that became preeminent. But at the moment of their creation, there also came the United States. Europe was reaching a point where the ideas that moved it were outgrowing the conventions and the hierarchies that governed it. So democracy, free economy, trade, speech and social mobility were stifled by the vested interests and competing stresses of a crowded and class-bound nation. Migration to America may have been primarily economic but it equally created the space where the ideas that in Europe had grown too root-bound to flourish might be transplanted. Over 200 years the flame that had been lit in Athens and fanned in Rome, Paris, London, Edinburgh, Berlin, Stockholm, Prague and Vienna was passed, a spark at a time, to the New World.

In 1776 the white and indentured population of America was 2.5 million. A hundred years later it was 50 million. In 1890 America overtook Britain in manufacturing output to become the biggest industrial economy in the world. That is an astounding, beggaring achievement. No economy in the history of commerce has grown that precipitously, and this was thirty-five years after the most murderous and expensive, desperate civil war. Indeed, America may have reached parity with Britain as early as 1830. Right from its inception it had faster growth than old Europe. It also had a very efficient modern banking system—another new idea from the Old World—that sold securities and government bonds, a lot of them to English investors. America was, from the very start, seen as the coming nation. In 1900 its per capita GDP was $5,000. In 2009 it was $46,400, and America accounted for a quarter of the world's economy. It wasn't individual brains that made this worth. It isn't a man with a better mousetrap. It's a million families who want a better mousetrap and are willing to work making mousetraps. It's banks that will finance the manufacture of better mousetraps, and it's a big nation with lots of mice.

Why America? There are other places that Europeans traveled to and set up new nations: Brazil, and in particular Argentina, always promised to be the powerhouses of South America. Both got enormous waves of immigration, had great natural resources, but neither, despite the constant promise, evolved to be anything remotely like the country America became. And there was South Africa and East Africa, North Africa, the archipelago Indonesia, Australia, all the focus of empires and nation building. But none quite transcended their geography, their climate, or the little snobberies and prejudices of their colonizers. America did have the advantage of a very early independence, and of creating a constitution that was peculiarly inspired. So, brain-drained Europeans will swiftly tell you most of it came via Locke, and it may have, but it was applied not in England or in Europe, but in America. The construction of the new country wasn't a replication of eighteenth-century England, although some wished it to be so. It was a testing of many, many European ideas of nationhood and liberty. Alexander Hamilton didn't want a democracy at all, fearing mob rule, the dictatorship of the majority. Instead, he called for a president and a legislature elected for life—essentially the House of Lords. He demanded strong central government that could veto states. It was all very patrician and paternalistic. He even mentioned getting rid of the states altogether. George Washington loathed the idea of political parties, seeing factions as being the cause for strife that would stop men voting with their consciences or in the best interest of their state. He came this close to being George I of America, although he was personally against an elected monarchy. The thirteen individual states didn't want the interference of a central government, but they did want its protection. It was Madison who, with a stroke of genius that would be the benchmark for so much American politics, saw that conflict of interests and faction were not in fact the problem but the solution; that tension would make the strength of the structure. Like the guy ropes holding up the big top, they would sustain and restrain government. He set up the Congress not in competition with the states, but as the protector of individual rights, regardless of state.

The arguments and the heartfelt convictions that would boil down to make the Constitution are fascinating. They set the tone for what has been the mantra and motto of American legislation ever since. The new Constitution barely got ratified. Virginia initially rejected both it and the new nation. It was all meant to be a wide, rural republic, made up for the most part of gentleman farmers with some light industry: Anglophone and well read, reasonable, liberal, fiercely self-reliant. But within two generations it grew to be a nation that not one of its original legislators could possibly have foreseen. And that says a lot for the Constitution's spirit and practicality and grandeur. It expanded without ever losing its shape or its clarity. There is not a stupid word or thought in it.

Soon after it was written, James Madison, insisting that a Bill of Rights be attached, presented ten constitutional amendments that laid down the rights of individuals in relation to the state. Many of the legislators thought this was unnecessary, but they passed them anyway. They include the familiar Fifth, that you take because you can't be forced to incriminate yourself. The Ninth Amendment, which is not often mentioned, was perfectly foresighted. It says the numeration of the Constitution, of certain rights, shall not be construed to deny or disparage others retained by the people. So no future law could be made that would deny or trespass on rights already given to Americans. Finally, the founding legislators sitting in Philadelphia came up with the most farsighted institution, one that in its concept and its principle is plainly European, but had never been instigated in Europe. Indeed it was impossible to imagine in eighteenth-century Europe that a Supreme Court could sit above all. No ancient government would willingly have created an untouchable board of wise men to ratify its own judgment, but the founding fathers of America did, and it has regularly passed that judgment on how laws and individual dilemmas reflect on the meaning and the spirit of the Constitution. It has at one time handed down that the Constitution demanded white and black be segregated, and again that their segregation was unconstitutional. Americans don't see this as a weakness in their founding document, only a proof of its magisterial profundity, and its ability to adapt.

There is one other uniquely American difference in the enlightened version of government in the new United States. In Europe, in the Old World, democracy, parliamentary civilian government, a free and impartial judiciary, are seen as being central ornaments of nationhood. They are evidence of the brilliance of culture and the civility of the people. But thanks not least to a smelly, awkward, contrarian pamphleteer and eternally revolutionary Englishman, Americans understand that all government of any sort is a symbol not of their greatness, but of weakness. Tom Paine wrote in *Common Sense,* the most widely read political pamphlet until *The Communist Manifesto,* that all that is good and noble about humanity is settled amicably between people. It is a sign of their failure of trust and empathy that they need to retain governments. Many Americans still believe that while the presidency is a noble office, government is a shame and a reprimand, government is a necessary caution. You take pride not in the collective, in the work of others, but in the individual. In what you have built yourself.

Still, none of that explains why intellectual professional Europeans are so silkily dismissive and abusive of America. There is, among the great similarities, the tangle of fraternity and cultures, one great thing. A defining thing that separates contemporary America and Europe. In the Old World it is a tenet, a continually agreed truth, that the greatest heights of our civilization have already been scaled. That the most beautiful piece of music has already been written, that no contemporary artist will create a work as great as that which already exists in our museums, that no modern architect will design a building that could fittingly replace the great landmarks of our cities. The most moving poem is already uttered, the most profound thought long ago cogitated. In America this concept, this belief, is incomprehensible. Absurd. Defeatist. Visiting Americans like all that glass-case culture stuff, the ancient, static, curiosity-cabinet sense of place. It is enchanting. What they mostly like about it is something that Europeans don't notice. It's the sight and the sense of time running backward, so that you can stand in a place and see the clock revolve widdershins, the calendar regain lost days. But the idea that this might also apply back home in America is shuddery. Who could possibly believe that the best film has already won its Oscar, or that the greatest rock song or photograph has already been sung and snapped? It would not just be deeply depressing, it would be fundamentally un-American. This is the nation of constant expansion, always new, always improved, always better.

On some unremarked day in the nineteenth century, Europe passed, without noticing, a tipping point. It felt, through a collective pheromone, a synchronicity of loss of nerve. A faint breeze of ennui that now it had more to lose than to gain. The journey had been all uphill, now they stood on the crest and looked at the gentle slope down. Europe is a place that conserves. It maintains, it curates its civilization, protects it against the ravages and rust of other cultures, and the rot of time and intellectual theft. We are a continent where fear of losing what we have is greater than the ambition to make it anew. No one will ever rebuild Paris again, no new Renaissance will come to reinvent Rome. No heroic age will tear up the center of London to put an idol on a column surrounded by lions.

But in America, the future can't come fast enough. Despite all the mad, didactic and infuriatingly competing voices and visions of what that future should look like, there is one agreed patriotic consensus: it won't look like the past. America took Europe's great enthusiasm, its big ideas, its invention, its young, and with that it also took the idea and the belief in a better tomorrow, and this is the most fundamental and profound division between the Old World and the New.

3

Harvest

Walking slowly along the glaucous, shaggy banks of a trout stream through the high meadows of the San Juans in the Colorado Rockies, I am looking for wildflowers, because they take me back to the cousins' book, preserved botany. But I'm also here because there's a woman who does guided field tours of vegetation for city folk and those who feel nature is a stranger who speaks a wild, pidgin dialect they don't understand. She gently but relentlessly repeats the historic, medicinal and culinary uses of shy shards of green that are competing in this bad-mannered traffic jam of herbage. She's slight and purposeful, and comes with a slight and purposeful seedling—a child of about ten, with shoulder-length hair, bilberry eyes and a trout-freckled complexion.

As the mother identifies grasses, I try to identify whether this kid is a boy or a girl. It's called something androgynous and wind-blown, like Aspen, or Lichen. The stands of aspen up here are the biggest living thing on the planet—who'd have thought? Acres of aspen share the same underground artery and vein system, their DNA identical. Branches of this lollygagging übervegetable are all rooted as one. Every time the mother finds a plant, she asks the child what it is. The child answers with a bored nonchalance. The mother is keen to pass on knowledge.

This is the sort of stuff that is supposed to be rote learned: the wisdom of Gaia, the ancient mysteries of the mountain, the folk-lore of the forest is given a gravitas and a veracity because it's spoken out loud. The learning is handmade. Knowledge acquired outdoors always seems to have a greater, hardier wisdom than the stuff you find at a desk on a computer. I like this runic information, the slow pace of the picking, the shreds and spikes of greenery, the rubbing and sniffing, the tentative tasting, the emphatic imparting of my new points of difference, the rhythmic repetition of names, Latin, English, native. It all has the somnambulant effect of nursery rhymes, ancient sagas, the singsong of pleasant words, none of which catch. All of them evaporate from the memory like aftershave, leaving a whiff of blossom and cut grass. This shy leaf will apparently relieve period pains and stave off nightmares. This moss will make bile-yellow dye, and was used to line moccasins. This twig, if boiled, will make an infusion that cures cystitis and depression.

I'm holding a posy of mad fronds, feeling like a backcountry Ophelia. Every plant comes with a homily, an anecdote. This one was given by bear to squirrel when he fell in the gopher's hole, this saved the life of a hiker who broke a leg up on Bald Elk Ridge, this was in Pocahontas's nuptial bouquet. The effect of this stream of nature consciousness feeds into the coarse, survivalist fear of "What would I do if I were marooned out here? Could I build a log cabin, roast a beaver, make a hat, find vegetable Valium in sufficient quantities to calm the hysterical fear and apocalyptic fatalism?" These lists and names make an order out of the terrifying, overwhelming chaos. It is no accident that the first thing Adam did was name the wild: tame it on the tongue. Vowel and consonant award some sort of ownership—at least you could shout at the thing that was eating you.

If you do begin to bring a sense of order to the vast, disordered energy of all this random life, it is still difficult to imagine what awe must have permanently accompanied the first European explorers of this place. The monstrous dimensions of America, the thought of being lost forever in it. There is, in one of James Fenimore Cooper's Leatherstocking novels, a long and mesmerizing description of the forests of the Northeast. He calls them a great sea, an ocean of wood, undulating, rising and falling, relentless and endless, stretching across the horizon. He gives us the sense of men adrift, lost in this alien element, vanishing into its depths, swept away by the huge waves, drowned in its dark, silent deep. It's an eerie and profound description.

Cooper was no woodsman himself; his fieldcraft is all bogus and theatrical, but he had been a sailor and he knew something of the great expanse of nature, the implacable loneliness of the unmade world. *The Last of the Mohicans* was the most widely read nineteenth-century New World novel, loved by Victor Hugo; Schubert asked to be read it on his deathbed. Wilkie Collins said that Cooper was the greatest romantic American novelist, who deserved to be known—pause here for eulogistic effect—as the American Scott. The comparison now sounds comically like faint praise—like being known as the Belgian Starbucks. The Waverley novels are now probably as seldom opened as *The Pathfinder*. Cooper owes the decline and fall of his reputation as much to Mark Twain as to a change in taste. Twain wrote the most perfectly swingeing and malevolently witty disemboweling of Cooper's whole outdoors, pioneers-and-Indians genre. But Cooper does have a particularly romantic and evocative ability to conjure a scene, to fill a space, like a brass band heard in the distance. It was his vision that most city people and most Europeans first came to experience, and see in the great, unending mind's eye what America might look like. To shiver at what it might feel like to be lost in the fathomless green.

As we walk through the Colorado high meadows, the most obvious and lyrical plants are the daisies, all oxeyes: about the only plant I actually recognize. They elegantly punctuate the greensward with touches of eggy jollity. "Aren't these oxeye daisies?" I ask tentatively, and the Green Lady tenses like someone catching a sensitive tooth on ice. "They're not supposed to be here, they're interlopers. An old guy I know remembers when there were no daisies in these mountains, now they're everywhere, more every year. Best thing you could do for America is kill every single one of them." She is looking at this picture and ignoring, with willful censorship, the most obvious living thing in it. Refusing to acknowledge the graffiti on a mausoleum. The daisies are weeds.

The definition of a weed is a flower in the wrong place. "They were brought here by Europeans." She says the word flat, like a clerk at the court naming the accused, presumably to spare my European feelings, and not exacerbate the innate pain and guilt I must be experiencing. "As decoration," she adds. To my European eyes, they are decorative. Decorative—such a European foible: so close to decadent—but perhaps I like them because they're from home. Maybe their familiarity in this alien space is what I cleave to. They weren't brought here for decoration, they were the Old World cure for homesickness. And here at my feet are dandelions. The Back Woods Woman says they were also imported by the pioneers as food. Dandelion salad, a precious side dish in France—they call it *pissenlit* because it's a mild diuretic. The lady doesn't tell us that; perhaps she doesn't know. Perhaps it doesn't fit with the Arcadian pharmacy of her pre-Columbian Eden that she wants to pass on to the omnisexual child.

Plants were the first great gift of the New World to Europe. The Spanish and the Portuguese may have come for gold and silver but it was vegetables that made their fortune. The first Europeans to find America were the Icelanders. Leif Eriksson bumped into Newfoundland by accident. Actually it's difficult to tell how much of Norse discovery was serendipity—running to or running away. Norse society was galvanized by a population explosion that put a strain on inherited farmland and caused a boom in feuds, revenge and vendetta. Everybody was avoiding somebody, and probably hunting somebody else. They had a stoically belligerent attitude to the sea. While the rest of the world was loath to lose sight of the shore, the Vikings regularly lost sight of everything except their greed and anger. They would set out on the steepling hills of unnavigated water. They were supreme sailors—not least because they were willing to accept the exceedingly long odds on never being seen again. On top of all the practical climatic terrors of the ocean they added their own sea monsters, witches, trolls, sprites and kelpies, while living in daily dread of the solid roof of the sky falling in on their heads. If Eriksson called the bit of America he landed on "Vinland" because he thought there were profusions of grapes there, he was dead wrong. Vikings may have been past masters at viciousness, democracy and inventing the narrative arc, but they were crap at botany. Iceland is largely covered with some oddly spongy moss, not trees, but Vinland was a solid sea of forest. Nothing but trees, with barely any space between them. To the Vikings, this free wood was astonishing treasure. They stayed for a season to fell trees and fill their longboats, then returned home. Occasionally they came across natives and killed them out of hand, without much consideration that there might be anything else to do with strangers in a strange land. The natives seem to have felt much the same about the uninvited Vikings.

The Icelanders could never have undertaken the open-ended voyages if it weren't for a single essential commodity. Salt cod. Preserved and easily stored rations that meant a ship could travel huge distances, cod turned out to be the first bounty of North America. Among other things it was a tax on salt cod that precipitated the War of Independence. It has been claimed that in the interregnum between the Icelandic lumberjacks' visits and Columbus's mistaken landing in the West Indies, the Portuguese had already sidled up and begun fishing the Grand Banks. They were the greatest navigators of their age—cod is their national dish, and fishermen are secretive about where they cast their nets. The grab for the riches of Central America began with gold and silver, pirates and privateer; the Spanish Main, gold doubloons, yo ho ho and the search for El Dorado, but when the adventurers and the awkward monomaniacs, the explorers, the buccaneers and conquistadors had departed at the end of ropes or poison arrows or some blackened swelling and hallucinatory new disease, it was the merchants who came to realize that the value of the New World was in the earth, and brought back baskets of potatoes, corn, peppers, squashes, pumpkins, avocadoes, strawberries, tomatoes, sunflowers, vanilla, chocolate, tobacco and turkeys.

The discoveries of the New World didn't just add a few exotic dishes to Europe's menu: it was a group of ingredients that changed the way the Old World ate, and how its society was organized. It caused the greatest upheaval in European life that didn't involve armies or plague. The food included two staple carbohydrates. There are only half a dozen eaten in the whole world. To come up with two new ones is astonishing. But today it's difficult to imagine the African diet without mealy meal, the porridge of ground corn, northern Italy without polenta. Try and taste the Italian kitchen without tomatoes, or the Asian market without chilies. Before the discovery of America there is no hot spice—apart from pepper. What were curries like? But nothing transformed the politics, the economy and the table of Europe like the potato. The tuber from Peru.

None of this stuff was taken to immediately. Working people resist foreign food—particularly working people who are mostly agrarian. What you eat is so intimately tied up with where you live and what you grow, and who you are. Food is national identity. So potatoes were initially grown as flowers, and there was a reticence about tomatoes, because they were thought to be related to poison berries. It was the Italians who ate them first. The French fed corn to livestock until the wheat harvest failed, but it was the potato that changed everything. Most notoriously in Ireland, where potatoes became a monocrop, replacing wheat. Not only did the tuber do well in Europe, coming from the variable climate of the Andes, but it had the particularly added benefit of thriving in marginal land.

The smallholdings of Irish farmers were leased from landowners and split between all the sons. They got to be very small—usually between one and six acres. If he grew wheat or barley, a man could feed an average family for, say, nine months. He would then have to work for the landlord for three months to pay the rent. It was bonded labor—close to slavery. Many Irish farmed part-time or, by tradition, joined the English army. In the nineteenth century, one in three British soldiers was an Irishman. But an acre of potatoes would feed the average family for twelve months. So farms that were below subsistence became sustainable if they grew potatoes. With the addition of a little buttermilk and some bacon, this was not a hearty diet, or a very interesting one, but it was serviceable. You'd live. The great thing about potatoes is that they don't need much maintenance—they're sow and forget. Children could tend potatoes, so a man could go off and sell his labor for a profit.

Potatoes were a blessing and then a curse for Ireland. As they turned out to be for the peasants of Scotland, Scandinavia, Holland and Germany. It is a miserable irony that the potato came from America and sent these people back to America as desperate economic refugees. The Gorta Mor, the Great Hunger, the potato famine, lasted from 1845 to 1851. The crop had been failing sporadically for two decades. The blight—*Phytophthora infestans*— probably came from the east coast of America or Peru, in shiploads of guano. First of all it affected England and the Low Countries, but when it got to Ireland there was no respite or alternative. A million died of starvation, and two million emigrated. A quarter of the country was buried or disappeared. Food is the bottom line of everything. There is no compromise or negotiation with a bare cupboard. Most journeys in all of the world start not with bright expectations, a sense of adventure or a bucket and spade, but an empty stomach. It was the belief in America as the land of plenty, of full stomach and endless fields, or fruit and pastures, that drew so many Europeans.

And still when Europeans visit American supermarkets they are surprised by the gluttonous volume of produce. The edible mountains, the sticky, bright rivers, the sugary pools, the model landscape made of sweet and sour, salt and bitter. Back in the Old World, an exclusive food shop may have a single ingredient in the window. An Italian butcher's will often display a rabbit or a veal chop. For Americans, food is about volume: it is largesse and generosity. In Europe we find the uneatable quantities confusing and distasteful. An American health food chain opened in London and presented shoppers with a typically CinemaScope spread of choice, and the reaction of the ecologically parsimonious and waste-sensitive London women was a sort of anaphylactic shock. The meat undulating in sinewy, bloody fields, the shiny, dewy goodness of the mountains and forests of salad, the fifteen sorts of rice, the dozens of ice creams. It is the same feeling that

Europeans experience when confronted by American portions—the gargantuan steaks, the jaw-disengaging thickness and leaking fecundity of sandwiches. The necropolises of wings and legs, breasts and buttocks, the relentless, tyrannical labyrinth of choice, like a child constantly whining "why?" All the condiments of freedom: Thousand Island, Ranch, blue cheese, Italian, French, steak sauce, chili sauce, gravy, mayonnaise, mustard, salsa, chili butter, nondairy creamer. The breads, the chips, the cakes and buns, the bagels and tacos, the fajitas and mushroom-cloud muffins. The magma avalanche of Eat Me. The unquaffable spigot of Drink Me. The tubs and lakes of cola and coffee, the cultural heritage.

This landscape of food triggers feelings quite, quite different in Europeans and Americans. We are deeply uncomfortable with it. Many would call it sinful. It mocks the famine and rationing, hardship and hunger that are just outside the peripheral vision of our collective memory. Oh, the cost, the waste, the ostentation, the lack of self-control. But in America, in America this view is the promise and the reward. It is the proof of the essential goodness and ripeness, the blessedness of the nation. Born from hard work and ingenuity, it is harvest festival, it's God's benison. In the shop in London it was shocking and intimidating and immoral. When we were all supposed to be frugal and husband scarce resources, we were confronted with this profligacy. Shoppers would emerge clutching a loaf, muttering, "Where will it all go? Who's going to eat it?" In America this is the bounty of a healthy, free and welcoming country. It is hospitality and generosity. They are the descendants of immigrants, this is the promise, the blinding covenant of America. A whole new world in a full stomach. Freedom from want. In 1831, Edwin Kershaw, an immigrant from Yorkshire to Massachusetts, wrote home to his wife, "I never sit me down to a meal but I think of the starving weavers of Rochdale."

The food that came back to Europe from America embodies many of those aspirations and qualities that came to be associated with the New World. Food and nationality are constant features of foreignness and belonging. People become what they eat. Or rather they eat what they become. There is a particular Americanness to American food. And when it travels it takes that with it. The potato is the egalitarian: honest, without ostentation or pretension, plain in form, reliable in function, it'll make the most of hard land and it carries with it an intrinsic decency. A bland, trusty dependency. A potato will feed all classes, treats monarch and pauper alike without etiquette or manners. It is cheap and plentiful, and universal. And chili, the pepper; loudmouthed and a pain in the arse. Corn, the largest grass in the world. And not just corn on the cob, the pup and pootoo of Africa, but also popcorn, an invention that is, by every association, American. A peculiar invention of the nation: a food that is created to have no gastronomic or dietary value. No one has ever set a table to eat popcorn. It is consumed while slouched semidressed, hogged without manners. No utensil is used. It is there to sustain some bovine pleasure while you do something else. Something pleasurably passive—watch a movie, a game. So much of American promise, its leisure, its release, its freedom, is embodied in popcorn. So blissfully, irreverently un-European.

Travelers from the Old World didn't arrive empty-handed of course, although the first attempts to grow cereals were a sorry disaster. The Elizabethan colonists probably weren't much good as farmers back home, but later, good—indeed, miraculous—farmers arrived from Scandinavia and Germany; immigrants who carried bags of hardy, Nordic wheat. And they made one of the greatest agricultural transformations ever. Within seventy years they had turned the great northern prairies into the bread basket of the world. In 1846 the English parliament, after twenty years of arguing, passed the corn laws that repealed the tax on imported grain that protected home farmers and the interests of the old, landed families. Britain and Belgium were the only European countries not to have imposed tariffs against the great cornucopia of American grain.

The early explorers also brought a host of exciting new diseases— almost all of them fatal if you hadn't grown up living with livestock, which of course Americans hadn't. Smallpox and measles, influenza, all sorts of diarrhea. In return, it seems likely that Columbus's crew took back with them the billet-doux of syphilis to Genoa and Naples, from where it spread through Europe, carried mostly by soldiers in nasty little wars, where it got called the French Plague, or the Italian Disease, depending on who gave it to you.

The irony of European life was that it was unsanitary and sickly, but if you made it through the first five years you were probably immune to everything. It is the received truth that Europeans brought a great malaise with them. Ill people suffering not just physically but mentally—sickened by their guilt, their prescriptive religions, their appalling class structures, their entitled arrogance. What they found were two continents—North and South America—barely able to feed themselves. The great mystery of America is not how much food it had, but how very little.

No one can say with any certainty how many pre-Columbian Indians there were, but they mostly plied an existence that hadn't been followed in the rest of the world for three millennia. Hunter-gatherers and marginal cultivators, they were already anomalies, alone on the edge of the world. When the conquistadors of central America marched over the hill and saw beneath them Mexico City, Tenochtitlán, floating on its manmade island in a huge lake, they may well have seen a grandeur that was greater than anything in Europe. But despite the great temples, the sophisticated civil structure, the astronomy, geometry and hellish theology, these meso-Americans had never used a wheel. The reason is simple: they had nothing that would pull a cart. There is in all of America one great fatal absence—a domesticated quadruped. Before Europeans arrived there were no cattle, no sheep, goats, pigs, no horses. Americans still find it hard to believe that the horse is not indigenous, so central is it to the idea of their New World. There is fossil evidence that there was once a small, prehistoric horse, but it seems the Indians ate it.

However sophisticated pre-Columbian society may have been, their food supply was always a weakness. The great civilization of the Maya collapsed before the Spanish ever arrived—possibly because they wore out the land to a barren infertility. The great gift of domesticated animals is not the steak or the ice cream, it's the shit.

In Mesa Verde in Colorado, where the state meets in the four corners with New Mexico, Arizona and Utah, there are some spectacular ruins; a national monument to the abandoned homes of the Anasazi people. These were arid farmers who built houses and grain stores precariously high up in the soft rock of their mesas. They practiced a type of desert farming that is now deeply fashionable with ecologists, utilizing tiny amounts of water. It must have been appallingly wearying and worrying and tedious if you had to eke a living out of it. They grew vine fruits and corn, the little finger corn, and supplemented it by hunting rabbits, birds and deer. The Anasazi had either died out or moved on before the great wave of Amerindian immigration: the Navaho, the Ute, the Apache, arriving from the south.

The Anasazi have a mythic, first-people, Genesis status. They are the Elysian, peaceful forefathers of the later, more rambunctious, whooping Indians. They were farmers living so closely entwined to their difficult habitat that they now embody a hippie, environmental oneness with the rhythms and songs of the earth. Their mystical weaving, corn-milling wholesomeness is a central beam of the Southwest's mythological sense of itself. The houses they built, like aeries, are approached only by treacherous paths and carved footholds which belie a pastoral Eden of mutual hand-holding, and speak instead of defensive paranoia, a wary community. And it seems that as the game was hunted out and the land gave up what little goodness it had, they grew despair instead of corn. It's tough being tied to land without domesticated animals. The Anasazi were kept in their place by their failing crops and their investment in their property. It seems that they regressed to the last available food source. The neighbors.

If you buy a ticket on Mesa Verde and follow the tourist guide around the softly steepling ruins, you will be told in great detail about adobe brickmaking and corn stores, about weaving and the assumed daily life and intimate homogeneity of the social system—their simplicity and their relationship with this astonishing, harsh landscape. And if by chance you ask why these symbiotic, perfectly balanced people vanished, you're met with a bland face and answers that involve the mists of time, the rock of ages and the winds of change. There are competing theories. A long migration to become the Hopi and Zuni people, perhaps. If, in a crassly journalistic way, you press on and ask about the cannibalism, then the reaction is stonier. You are no longer an inquiring pilgrim, you are a contrarian gainsayer. A troublemaker in Eden. There is, they say emphatically, no proof. Some people (an academic) may have written a paper, but it's now thoroughly discredited. There is no evidence. These were happy, hippie, down-with-nature, smiley people. You can feel the hostility of the other pilgrims, radiating with a furious disapproval. It's like you're pissing in a cemetery. They didn't come to hear this.

The reality may be very different. Did the Anasazi become systematically cannibalistic? There are fleshed human bones with butchery marks, not stripped for ritual but left in middens. And then there's the shit. The discovery of a desiccated human turd containing human muscle. That is the Anasazi's smoking dung. As soon as you understand that the inhabitants of these cliff communities were both opportunistic hunters *and* dinner, the effort and danger involved in getting to their little fortresses make sense. But as you're shown around, their ghostly lives are spoken of as a vanished innocence. There is an implacable deaf wall of anthropological correctness and indigenous sensitivity. Cannibalism is a Western, white imposition. A retrospective racism. Tribal memory, collective dreams and wishful thinking should, if not silence, then at least reduce to a tearful academic whisper any attempt to discredit the lives of Indians. Haven't they suffered enough?

And it's understandable. History is always personal—never more so than for those who find theirs is written by the enemy. It strips the defeated and the displaced of their dignity. It is a posthumous insult. But the squeamishness here is really very Western. The last great taboo of cannibalism. It doesn't make the Anasazi bad people, just desperate people. Cannibalism is despair and suicide. It invariably eats the host society. It extinguishes community, reduces humanity to the smallest unit of any, and kills coherent, joined-up existence. Cannibalism is untenable, not least for the practical reason that you can't breed fast enough for lunch.

One of the constant, self-serving prejudices of the later waves of innocents who pushed America west was their incredulity at the obvious truth that Indians had never made more of this huge, pristine country. If you've lived in Europe, then the spectacular waste of land that does nothing but be wilderness is inexplicable and indeed, inexcusable. To be pushed out of your home country by the crush of competition, of politics, of despotism, famine and unfair distribution, to have been wrenched from your heritage and your family and familiarity and to find this place uncared for, unproductive, raw, must have had a profound effect. The confrontation between indigenous natives and immigrant Europeans is so often portrayed in terms of morality, an unequal struggle between simple, good, nature-twinned people overwhelmed by voracious, exploitative, stupid greed. But to the immigrants, the waste of America's possibilities, the vacant kingdom that could offer work and sustenance to so many who were starving, must have seemed deeply immoral—sinful. It wasn't that the Indians and Europeans fought over the same place. They saw two completely different landscapes.

My ancestral cousins, after leaving the farm in Batley and making their way to Colorado, rented government land to start their horse ranch. There is, in the family commonplace book, a clipping from the *Yorkshire Post* from October 1897:

> It was my good fortune to be entertained by the Thomas brothers at their horse ranch on the Arickaree. They had between them 250 to 300 horses, mostly mares, and some fine imported horses, and about the same number of cattle. They have a fine residence worth nearly $2,000, nicely furnished, and they take great pleasure in entertaining their friends, who call upon them. There are several corrales. The boys are wholehearted gentlemen and entertained me with fine vocal music, accompanied by the banjo.

The cows and horses that the Batley Cowboys chased around Colorado were the two immigrant ingredients that immediately became synonymous with the United States. Along with pigs and chickens they transformed American culture. They would grow to feed a nation whose population itself was growing exponentially, and which would become an industrial society. But America would remain—in principle if not in fact—an agrarian country. The perception of itself is as a land of homesteaders, sodbusters, soldier farmers and cowboys. Nowhere else in the world have peasants and agricultural laborers become such a poignant and fundamental icon of national heroism and identity as the cowboys of America. Their short-lived utility, barely two generations, is not an American dream, it's a European fairy tale. The story of an agrarian self-determination for workers who have been forced to live in tiny, rotten agricultural cottages, hoeing medieval strips of land, trudging through mud in clogs, doffing their caps. Oh, to be a workingman with the power, the aesthetic and the élan of nobility.

I stare at the cousins in their browning photographs, posed against the painted backdrop of a Victorian parlor, sitting in their work clothes, bandannas, boots, waistcoats and broad-brimmed hats with rakish moustaches and a pistol stuck in a belt. Already there is mimicry here, a knowingness, a dressed-up irony. I try to imagine their flat, Yorkshire vowels; a particularly indelible accent. They are being photographed for someone else, doing what immigrants do, slipping into the new, filling strange shoes. The *Yorkshire Post* mentions the banjo—a new instrument brought to America by West African slaves, the name one of the few words that come to English from the Gambia. It became such a typically American sound: funny, childish and a protest. I expect they sang minstrel songs, perhaps Yorkshire folk songs, Victorian parlor ballads and probably hymns. The picture pasted in the family book is again surrounded by wildflowers: clematis, Indian paintbrush, evening star, aster, marigold, mariposa lily, and a small posy of pansies stuck in later. The flower of remembrance, a floral pun from the French, *pensée*—"in my thoughts."

Just over the page there is a clipping from the *Ladies' Home Journal of Philadelphia*, 1897:

Uncle Sam's wheatfields are the greatest in the world, our production is usually two and a half times that of India, our closest rival . . . The acreage of this grain is equal in size to Arkansas. If a gigantic scale were constructed and the wheat put in one pan and our population into the other, the weight of the people would be one quarter that of the wheat.

4

The Sublime

Pub quiz question. When was the capital Lancaster and then York in the same year? Not in some kingly, bludgeoning tussle, not the Wars of the Roses, not the north in thirteenth-century England, but in eighteenth-century America, during the War of Independence. Lancaster, Pennsylvania, was the third capital of the thirteen continental states. York, a tiny town on the safe side of the Susquehanna River, was number four. The first two were Philadelphia and Baltimore.

York was followed by Annapolis, Trenton and New York. Philadelphia should have remained the seat of government. It was the biggest city in the new nation, but having been chased around the country by King George's soldiers, the government ended up besieged by resentful American ones, demanding their back pay when Congress ordered that the city governor use the militia to disperse them. He understandably refused, and so the politicians picked up sticks and statutes, took umbrage and their government elsewhere. But not before passing a law that declared the capital of this new federation could never again be beholden to an individual state for its security. The bill stated that a ten-mile radius from the parliament would be under its own jurisdiction. In principle, America's capital could be anywhere. It could be peripatetic. It could move like a big caravan. A lot of states offered to give it legroom. It was the rural South, with its interests in agriculture and slavery, that won out.

Washington was proposed on the banks of the Potomac. It was ready to move into by 1800, with a White House and a Capitol, although the mall and the monuments and the reflecting pool weren't added for 100 years.

The first thing you notice about Washington is how very grand it is: what a vaunting self-belief conceived it. The population of America in 1800 was about 5 million—about half that of Britain. But the aspiration, the presumption of this city, its boastful vanity, is overweening, and very un-American. Everything else about the founding of this nation seems to be wrought with modesty, to be careful, parsimonious even. Human-sized and frugal. Bloated statements of imperial splendor are the stamp of England and the corrupt and degenerate, class-ridden Old World. And then to name it for a general, a still-living general, seems an uncharacteristic act of embarrassing hubris. Philadelphia was a much nicer name: more appropriate, donated by Quakers—decent, simple, humorless comrades. The City of Brotherly Love. The seat of conscience. Having forged and hammered out such exacting ideals in a handmade country, they went for George Washington. For a nation that was so collective, based on rational agreement, how do you imagine that conversation went? "Excuse me, General Washington, we're thinking of naming the nation's capital after you." "How nice. Martha will be pleased." Naming capitals for conquering military men is what despots and megalomaniacs do.

And it hasn't helped that bastard classicism is the architectural shorthand that so many totalitarians came up with after Washington. The statue on top of the Capitol building stands on a base ringed by fasces, symbols of the Roman republic. These simple loads of sticks are a metaphor for collective action and the people. Individually they are easily snapped, bound together they are unbreakable. And they come with that little axe that chops them into the same length. It is a suitably humble icon for the United States, but it was also the symbol of Mussolini's fascists.

Washington is the only city that looks like this in the whole country, bar a few copycat courthouses and domes, and the graph of city grids. There are no imitation Washingtons in America, though there are plenty in Latin America: bellicose and operatically puffed-up burgs that mock the nations that support them. A capital ought to grow from the character of the people it represents, but not Washington. It stands aloof as a symbol of something that was once thought necessary and then turned out not to be.

America was the first of the modern age's colonies to pupate into independence. The founders of the state looked for a model, a template of how to be, of how this new, civic animal should conduct itself. And they saw in the brief, plebeian utopia of the Roman republic all the highest virtues of civic service: justice, freedom, strength and forbearance. The will of a free people was implicit in Rome before the emperors, and the classical implied not some experiment, some newfangled, quasireligious theory of statehood, but a return, going back to basics, to a fairer, sterner time before the decomposition and slow decline of imperial Rome with its obvious mirror in England.

So Washington was built with its familiar, po-faced, uncompromising neoclassical façades. The relentless angles of higher purpose. A city constructed not to house people, but to venerate the ideals that people might aspire to. The parable and the cautionary tale of the architecture is unmissable and unrelenting: the whiteness of its morality, the whiteness of its endeavor, the clear-sighted whiteness of its vistas. There is no letup in its spotless diligence of purpose. And although it's knowingly impressive, there must have been many freedom fighters for an independent federation of free states who found that deafening echo of Rome unsettling. It was just another empire—a subjugator of foreigners. It had been the state that persecuted the Jews, that washed its hands of the Crucifixion, and fed Christians to lions for the amusement of pagans. It kept monopolies on trade. And perhaps more important, this turning again to classicism might be seen as a symptom of an intellectual insecurity—the terrible affliction of the colonial who, despite his bluster, still looks to the old country for culture and fashion and, most gallingly, approval. The classics are the marble plinth of European civilization and intellect. The snobbery and the exclusivity of rote Greek and Latin, a few tags and half-remembered panegyrics were the entry to a closed society that surely was the antithesis of everything that had been fought for at Concord and Bunker Hill. Many New World citizens had wanted for themselves what so many of them had left behind. But there was undoubtedly a cultural insecurity, a cringe in Americans, toward the smiling patronage of the Old World. They bridled at the hint of naked barbarism, of living on a thin sliver of borrowed civility, on the edge of a heathen, untamed, uncivilized nation. So you can see, in Washington, an all-too-emphatic riposte from a nation that was born with a thin skin and has never quite got over the nagging insecurity, or could stop itself being impressed by imported sophistication. And even though Washington is a grand city, an imposing and impressive city, it's not a great city. It has no self-deprecation. It lacks self-knowledge. It's a place that reminds the populi how small they are compared to the ideals that protect and surround them. Washington doesn't flirt, doesn't do jokes, has never stuck a finger up its own bum just to see what the fuss was about, doesn't belly dance in the nude in front of the mirror.

At about the time Washington was being built, William Words-worth found himself in a spot of bother. He was out on one of his interminable, purposefully pentametric walks in the Lake District, and had decided to ascend the side of a steep hill. It was steeper than he reckoned. The walk became a scramble, then a climb, then a cling. He found himself "crag-fast": a fine, gritty word that is both a physical and metaphysical predicament. He stared into the void and couldn't ascend or descend, and then, as is the nature of cautionary anecdotes and nature, things took a turn for the worse. The Lakeland weather drew in, and it began to rain. The howl of thunder and lightning rocked and echoed against the granite crags. The rods of water were hurled with a leaden ferocity, the keening air tried to pry his sodden, frozen fingers from the per-pendicular and toss him to the earth. Shivering, soaked and stuck, bellowed at and blinded by the elements, Wordsworth did what poets do. He wondered what it was he was wondering. And to his thunderstruck surprise, he discovered that he was feeling intensely exhilarated, but also calm. This was altogether a new feeling, an original reaction to imminent death and the fury and grandeur of the elements. The storm abated and things looked different. He found his footing, made it down, walked home, lay in a bath and considered what it all meant to blank verse and rambling. It turned out to be a pivotal moment for the romantic movement. What Wordsworth had stumbled upon and clung to was The Sublime.

In fairness, he wasn't the first. Other people had climbed it. Burke wrote a paper on the origins of the sublime and the beautiful. Kant thought of little else, writing a critique of aesthetic judgment. But the sublime really only got meaning and resonance with the romantics. It was the echo of greatness, of the spirit, of outdoors, out of breath. The sublime is an instinctive, emotional response to the natural world. It isn't awe, which you see in the divine in creation—the face of God in a cloud. It is spiritual without being specifically religious. And, most important, the sublime isn't a synonym for beauty in a garden. Beauty is the construct, the genius of civilization. Only man can fashion or understand beauty. Beauty has an aesthetic that can be taught, a form that has rules and a formula. To be moved by beauty is a learned response. Love is beauty, beauty is love. It is civilized. You can be trained and instructed to make and understand beauty. It is, at its heart, the taming and ordering of the random into harmony and it is symmetry. Burke said that there were two instincts: for the sublime and for beauty. The instinct for the sublime was about survival. The instinct for beauty was sociability.

The sublime is to give yourself over to chaos. It isn't simply a response, it's a stepping through, to recognize a connection with elemental forces. The word derives from the Greek for "lintel"— the beam above a door or window. It implies standing on a threshold, entering another realm. The vital element of the sublime is that it always contains fear. There is a terror, an ugliness in the idea that in heaven there is the possibility of hell, that in nature there is always death. In the uplifting, there is corruption and there is danger, and in love there is mortality that is a searing agony. You don't experience the sublime looking through double glazing, or at a distant electric storm, or watching the sea rage on TV. The romantics searched for it in mountains and torrents. They purposefully flung themselves in harm's way in the Alps and the Hebrides. Romanticism grew addicted to the elemental fix. They swam the Hellespont and drowned in Italian lakes.

But all of that was merely a kitchen garden compared with the vast towering nature of America. This New World is a catalogue of superlatives and extremes. It has always seemed to me that the sublime is the most natural, obvious, honest and open reaction to America, where even in the heart of cities you are never more than a cloud away from a wind that will blow you off your feet. No country is as constantly, as physically insistent as America. You are ever pressed up against the landscape, dumbfounded, terrified. Over the two centuries of mass migration, this place must have seemed overwhelming. To get there, to step off the boat, was to pass under the lintel. Oh, the heart-stopping fear, the wonder, the promise of it.

Washington, its neoclassicism, its ruled edges and pleasing symmetry, the clean shadow of the incised oratory, and above all its inimitable reason, is a noble imposition: a better, new-improved, reborn Old World, made by men who were clever, cultured, cultivated and reasonably modern. But the neoclassical Latin model slides off the New World like a paper hat in a thunderstorm. To see America as the raw material for a new republic, to bring this plaster beauty of classicism to it, you need book learning and schooling. It's the well-mannered vision that comes from under a wig, in a drawing room. To experience the sublime, there is no need of learning or even literacy. It is the emotional response for those with the eyes to see and the yearning expectation of being part of something.

It's always seemed that the sublime has been the effervescent vitality of American culture, that poured almost immediately out of this unmade, unmakable world. The fear and the wonder, the fear and the ugliness, the heartbeat, the life force, the sadness and the optimism. It is the heat and the salt and the joy, and you find the American sublime in jazz, in the beat poets, in Melville and Whitman, in Steinbeck and Kerouac, in abstract expression-ism. In Ansel Adams and Mark Rothko and Georgia O'Keeffe, in Edward Weston and Jackson Pollock, and in Mardi Gras and spring break, in spirituals, rock, rap and country, in modernism, in every skyscraper, Chevrolet and Cape Canaveral launch.

Georges Clemenceau, the French president during the First World War, was a fat, droll and beady manipulator, with oyster eyes and a window-box moustache. He sat through the drafting of the Treaty of Versailles guarding his overweening irritation at the harmonious, reasonable, highfalutin world designs of Wood-row Wilson, the president who brought the full grid and panoply of neoclassical Washington to charitably fix busted, decaying old Europe. Clemenceau wrapped himself in the thick, Gallic coat of amused patronage, hooded like a man who's being sold back his own cutlery, and said over smoky dinner tables that "America is the only nation in history which miraculously has gone directly from barbarism to degeneracy without the usual interval of civiliza-tion." He was a bit of a one for the witty aperçus, was Clemenceau. You can imagine him rolling them miraculously round his froggy tongue as his shirt studs twinkled in the candlelight, and then his deadpan amusement as the table laughed sycophantically. His was the sort of cleverness that the French adore and always mistake for wisdom. He also said that military justice is to justice what mili-tary music is to music, and that war is much too serious a matter to be entrusted to military men. This is an Oscarish, all-purpose line that can be adapted for almost any after-dinner or best-man speech. Money is too serious to be entrusted to bankers, justice to judges, truffles to cooks, law to policemen, God to bishops, and sex is far too serious a matter to be entrusted to your wife.

The jibe about barbarism to degeneracy without civilization has stuck. It still offers a little snobbish smile at haute European tables—particularly French ones. They have always taken the suc-cess of Anglophone culture very badly. How satisfying to assume that, in truth, it isn't really culture at all, just some stripper's mim-icry, not the real thing; electroplated, mass-produced, gaudy and greedy.

One of the most embarrassing things I've ever done in public was appear—against all judgment—in a debate at the Hay Literary Festival, speaking in defense of the motion that American culture should be resisted. Along with me on this cretin's errand was the historian Norman Stone. I can't remember what I said, I've erased it. It had no weight or consequence. On the other side, the right side, were Adam Gopnik from the *New Yorker* and Salman Rushdie. After we'd proposed the damn motion he leaned into the microphone, paused for a moment, regarding the packed theater from those half-closed eyes, and said, soft and clear, "Bebopaloola, she's my baby, Bebopaloola, I don't mean maybe. Bebopaloola, she's my baby, Bebopaloola, I don't mean maybe. Bebopaloola, she's my baby doll."

It was the triumph of the sublime. The bookish audience burst into applause and cheered. It was all over, bar some dry coughing. America didn't bypass or escape civilization, it did something far more profound, far cleverer, it simply changed what civilization could be, and it did it without intellect, and without commiseration, without looking back. It set aside the canon of rote, the long chain letter of drawing-room, bon-mot-received aesthetics. It dashed the politeness and the prettiness. It was offered a new neoclassical, reconditioned, reupholstered start, a second verse to an old song, and it just took a look at the view and felt the beat of this vast nation, and went for the sublime.

There is in Europe another popular snobbery about the parochialism of America, the unsophistication of its taste, the limit of its inquiry. This, we're told, is proven by that favorite canard, the algorithm of ignorance: "How Few Americans Travel Abroad." Apparently, so we're told, only 30 percent of Americans have passports. And whenever I hear this, I always think, my good golly gosh, really? As many as 30 percent. Why would you go anywhere else? There is so much of America to wonder at. So much that is the miracle of a brand-new minted civilization. And anyway, European kids only get passports because they all want to go to New York.

5

Guns

It's a slight, satirical comfort that London's Imperial War Museum is built on the foundations of Bedlam. The madness of war, here it is memorialized and domed in pale stone and glass cases, rising out of a lunatic asylum, an imposing and stately building guarded by priapic naval guns that could once fire shells the size of small cars over the horizon. It is a maudlin and reflective place for old men. On the one hand, a stone box that contains all the myriad mechanics of human failure, vanity and stupidity, and on the other, a sarcophagus of glorious heroism, fortitude and resistance. But that's not the reason it saddens men. It's because it reminds us that we are no longer boys. We don't run in with bright excitement at seeing tanks and dive-bombers. We no longer race through the pyrotechnic gaiety of bombast and bayonet, yelping with the sheer joy of soldiers. Military museums make the old feel old and frightened, and the young young and excited. Which I suppose is why they fight wars. "Young men make wars, and the virtues of war are the virtues of young men—courage and hope for the future. Then old men make the peace and the vices of peace are the vices of old men—mistrust and caution." That's from *Lawrence of Arabia*: the movie, not the man.

Down in the museum's vaults, that are the bowels of glory where the defunct and constipated ordnance is kept and stacked and labeled for doomsday, there is, on the walls of one small locked room, a rack of ancient rifle muskets, unvisited by the public, unnoticed by the staff. Their stocks are cracked and mended with copper wire, their fore-ends worn and bound to barrels, decorated with ornamental studs and nails. These are percussion-cap muzzle loaders. In evolutionary terms, Neanderthal guns. They are the link between the Brown Bess of Waterloo and the Breechloader of *Zulu*. These guns are from the American Civil War, almost certainly from the South, and how they got here is a salutary story. After the capitulation of the Southern states, they were sold by the Americans to the French, who used them in the Franco-Prussian War against the Germans, which ended badly for the French. Badly for Europe, as it turned out. It was the crucible that melded a greater Germany. Bismarck announced the birth of the new, united Deutschland that would be über alles in the Hall of Mirrors at Versailles, and these guns were captured, taken as booty back to Germany, where they were sent to the colonies in Africa—Tanganyika, Togo and Namibia—and given to the askari, native troops. Or, more likely, the irregular African home guard.

Pause here for another thin smear of irony. These guns that had once defended slavery were now in the hands of Africans, who rebored them, took the rifling out, because a smooth-bore musket is easier to make bullets for, and they were once again used in a war. The forgotten theater of the Great War, the long retreat through the bush where a large British force out of Kenya pursued the brilliantly commanded German irregulars through some of the roughest country in East Africa. In 1918 the rifles were captured by the British, and so they ended up here on a rack in a basement, still elegant, still with their fighting figures, their long barrels and their decoration. Still dustily exuding a hint of boyish menace. These stocks might have fitted gray shoulders at Bull Run, or the Battle of the Wilderness. They fired at the black-helmeted cavalry at Sedan, and were carried quietly through the bush on the Sand River and the shores of the Rift Valley's Lake Rudolf. Old guns rarely die, they just hang on walls. Military curators will tell you that the ease of their job is that we don't throw away guns. For all the wishful piety of turning swords into plowshares, we hold on to them. Just in case. We will, if asked, turn pots and pans and park railings into Spitfires, but not ballistic missiles into swings and seesaws. At the Battle of Omdurman, where Churchill fought in the last British cavalry charge against the Mahdi Dervishes, among the dead they found tribesmen wearing chain-mail that had been stripped from Christians on twelfth-century crusades.

The Civil War muskets may well have been manufactured in Britain. The South bought thousands of rifles from the Enfield factory in Manchester. During the Civil War, America manufactured hundreds of thousands of guns, mostly in the North: before Detroit was called the Paris of the West it was known as the Arsenal of Liberty. They made all sorts in the New World: Springfields and Spencers, Henrys, Sharpes, Remingtons, Kerrs, LeMats and Griswolds (manufactured in Griswoldville, Georgia). By the time war guttered to its exhausted end, the country was glutted with firearms, which is why they were selling them to the French. But the war had been a blessing—as wars tend to be—for gun manufacturers.

Samuel Colt has a war story that is repeated over and over in American innovation. He began very young, he went to sea, came home, went on the road with a traveling laughing gas show, but always hankered after guns. He's famous for inventing the revolver, which he didn't. The mechanism had already been patented as a flintlock in England. What he did do was improve and simplify the mechanism, and then crucially, like Edison and Ford, industrialize the process of manufacture. Before Colt, guns were handmade by craftsmen, he mass-produced pistols and went bust; he was saved by demand, in particular by the demands of the Seminole War in Florida, the Spanish-American War, and then the big one, the Civil War. Smith and Wesson, who made cheaper revolvers, came up with a thing called the volcanic pistol, which didn't work. So they sold it to Mr. Winchester, who, along with his engineer Mr. Henry, made repeating rifles, named after each other. The Winchester became the generic name for any lever-action repeating gun. Gun manufacturing became, ironically, cutthroat. Colt spent much of his time in court arguing over patents and copyrights. Derringer, who invented the gun that killed Lincoln, made as much money in lawsuits as he did selling guns.

The real star of ballistic innovation is not in improved delivery, but in a better bullet. The gun is essentially a tube with a hole in one end and a small hammer at the other. It's the projectile that does the business. The rimfire cartridge was the breakthrough. Powered by stable and smokeless fulminates, it is the natural longevity of guns (as opposed to gun owners) that is the jam in the lock of gun-makers. Guns rarely commit suicide, or indeed kill each other. America has a lot of guns—always has had a lot of guns. The militia in the War of Independence owed much of their success against the British and German troops of King George to the Pennsylvania rifle, a spiral-bored thing with a barrel twice the length of an English musket, which, as a patriot wrote to the London *Times*, meant "the worst shot could put a ball into a man's head from 150 to 200 yards," and that officers coming out to America would do well to settle their affairs first.

The reputation for sharpshooting went ahead of the citizens' army, and probably did as much to unsettle the redcoats as their shooting. It became a self-serving mythology about Americans that they were all born crack shots: Hawkeye, from the Leatherstocking stories, Davy Crockett, Sergeant York in the Great War, and the hosts of cowboys and lawmen hitting the mark, splitting hairs, shooting the guns out of the bad men's hands. It's an American birthright, the myth that America's sons are born to the gun. A great deal of what America thinks about itself and its history rolls around guns. Old Europe's history involves rather more guns, we've been firing them at each other and the rest of the world for much longer, but the implements themselves, the mechanics of violence, have never been as important as the uniforms of the men who shouldered them. Guns in America define what people think not just about their country but about each other. They are one of the deep fault lines of a homogeneous, easygoing, individualistic society. Gun ownership and the restrictions on gun ownership neatly mark the line between liberal and conservative, the coasts from the middle. Gun crime and the danger of urban streets, or violent suburban burglary, is at the root of both pro- and anti-political positions; both sides believe that America is potentially a very violent and murderous place. The statistics on this are interesting and revealing. Statistics are only tallied-up lists of numbers and percentages. They don't tell you about perceptions, collective beliefs, pessimisms or expectations. Creeping downstairs to confront a noise in the dark isn't made any less frightening if you're carrying the rolled-up national statistics on violent deaths, but it might be if you were carrying a baseball bat or the most powerful handgun ever made.

Unkind comparisons are often made between Switzerland and America. The Swiss—also a federation of semi-independent states—are even more attached to their guns than Texans, and they have a greater number per capita, but death by shooting is so rare they don't even collate the figures. But you've got to ask yourself, do you feel Swiss? What is the point of shooting a Swiss? There'd just be another one there in the morning, wearing the same gray suit, polishing his rimless glasses.

For what they are empirically worth, here are the national league tables for death by firearms, collated by the UN. I don't think they can include wars or civil unrest, or judicial firing squads. So, this is deaths by bullet per 100,000. In at number one is Colombia, with a whopping 51.8 whacks. Next is Paraguay with 7.4, then Guatemala, Zimbabwe, Mexico, Costa Rica, Belarus, Barbados, and the United States with 2.97—just ahead of Uruguay. So, the US is only just in the top ten. And now compare that with the statistics for murderous death without bullets. The US comes twenty-fifth, the UK is twenty-seventh. And now the overall bullets and no-bullets untimely death rate. The US is seventeenth, below Slovakia and Poland. The UK is thirty-first. Less murderous than peaceful little Switzerland, though just a tidge more maniacal than New Zealand. So, statistically, you're more likely to be murdered on the laid-back holiday haven of Barbados than in America, with or without a gun. There are other ways of looking at this list. Eight of the top ten gun-crime countries are from the New World, and so speak Spanish, the language of inarticulate anger. All are notably religious, and all predominantly Christian, though half-and-half Catholic and Protestant. Perhaps more telling is that all of them were colonies. It might have something to do with that peculiarly schizophrenic relationship that ex–freedom fighters and revolutionaries have with firearms.

North America was born into a succession of vicious little wars that continued in fits and starts from the sixteenth century to the turn of the twentieth. Native wars, wars against the Spanish and the Dutch, tiny wars named after English monarchs—William's War, Anne's War, which may or may not have been rereleased as the War of the Spanish Succession, or the Seven Years' War, or quite possibly the Nine Years' War. It all gets quite confusing because wars in America are often European wars under different names. There's the Seminole War, the war against the tribes of the Northeast, Tecumseh and Pontiac. There was the splendidly named Beaver War, more wars with the French, the Spanish and Cuba, and the West Indies. Then there was the French and Indian War. Perhaps that was the Seven Years' War. There was the big revolution for independence, and again, the War for Canada in 1812 against the British. And there was unpleasantness against the Mexicans, and the massive cataclysm of the Civil War, and then the Indian Wars in the Northwest. And somewhere in the middle of all this, there was a bit of a war with the Mormons. There is not a generation of Americans that doesn't have a direct experience of some sort of emergency or resistance in their own back gardens. Almost all of them were fought at home. No European nation ever fought that many small wars in its own house.

The War of 1812 is possibly the most pointless ever fought by two grown-up countries. Not one person in a hundred, in either America or Britain, could now tell you what it was about. The American Congress declared war on Britain under the catchy slogan of "free trade and sailors' rights." It was by no means universally popular. New England refused to have anything to do with it, and many of the territories were against it. In Britain it was an unwelcome sideshow to the main event. There was the big war in Europe against Napoléon, and in fact, 70 percent of America's trade was with England. But still the trigger was Westminster's unilateral ban on American trade with France, and the stopping and searching of American merchant ships on the high seas, looking for contraband and for British naval deserters, which led to the press-ganging of Americans into the Royal Navy, because it was difficult to tell a British sailor from an American one, and the Royal Navy weren't terribly careful or choosy, indeed they were desperate for crew. There were other objectives—a significant faction of American raptor politicians and patriots wanted to annex Canada because of the fur trade, and because they wanted to expunge the English from the continent. And because Canada looks, on a map, more American than British. There was a general feeling that defeating the thinly populated and defended north would simply be a matter of marching in and accepting the gratitude of tearful Canadians, desperate to throw off the colonial Scots vowels and the wrong sort of bacon, now free to be Americans. Actually, many of the inhabitants had been American loyalists, forced to leave the United States in the ethnic cleansing after the War of Independence, and most Canadian immigrants from Scotland and France had no desire to be part of an expanding American empire ruled from Washington.

And there was the third combatant. The British wanted to set up an Indian Nation in the Northwest. They supplied and helped the Northern tribes. New European settlers in the territories below the Great Lakes were coming into conflict with Indians. The Canadians had always had a more peaceful and liberal relationship with indigenous tribes. Canada grew to be a place of sanctuary for America's displaced natives, as it would be for the Underground Railway and escaping Africans. The war was a dissolute and periodically vicious campaign that was marked by the British burning the White House and blockading ports, including Baltimore, where the lawyer Francis Scott Key rode out to a royal naval warship to represent a friend who'd been taken into custody, and was himself kept overnight for his own protection as his home port was bombarded. All night he listened to the salvoes scream and thud into the protecting keep of Fort Henry at the mouth of the harbor. All the lights in the city were extinguished. The only illuminations were explosions. And as the dark departed, so did the barrage. Scott Key rushed on deck and looked at the smoking fort and exclaimed, "Oh say, can you see, by the dawn's early light, our flag still flying?"

And then there was Tecumseh, the Napoléon of the Indian nations, who rallied the red men, and fought with an intensity and martial skill that astonished and confounded the white men, and was killed. The last Indian confederation of nations fell apart, and though individual tribes and groups of warriors still fought alongside the British, it was the end of a concerted movement for a unified Native American homeland. This, like so many Indian defeats, was merely a footnote for the main combatants. Although, in the long term, it may have been the most significant result of a pretty insignificant war. The conflict came to an end when the two casus belli—free trade and sailors' rights—vanished due to events elsewhere. In 1815, Napoléon was finally defeated, and there was no need for an embargo, nor for press-ganging sailors. And anyway, the war in America had reached an uncomfortable and unprofitable stalemate. With an unseemly alacrity the two sides signed the Treaty of Paris, which put everything back to the way it had been. News of the signing took two months to reach America. A week after peace was declared, the Battle of New Orleans was fought, a resounding if pointless victory for General Jackson and the Americans, who lost thirteen dead to English casualties of two thousand.

The consequence of the war, particularly of the victory at New Orleans and some resounding successes at sea, was a greatly rejuvenated self-confidence in America, which had briefly dropped its head in bad-tempered internal squabbles and uncertainty about the future. The peace did what the war had failed to do—it drew together the states and territories with a sense of mutual pride and well-being. It was also the testing flame that brought forth a real sense of nationhood in Canada. Burnished and independent, the Canadians had in almost all cases defeated or seen off American land forces. They'd defended their vast, white, dull country, and in the process become a real place rather than a collection of ports. In Britain, hardly anyone noticed. The defeat of Napoléon and the immense reorganization of the world that was about to take place at the Treaty of Vienna concentrated everybody's attention else-where. But the Admiralty noticed. The new American navy had been particularly successful at sea. They'd been better trained and motivated as sailors, and commanded by better captains; men like Stephen Decatur: "My country, right or wrong." They had built a new superfrigate, and the Royal Navy found it had nothing in its class that could stand up to it. The War of 1812 led to better ship design, but overall, there was no noticeable aftertaste or animus, no resentment or mistrust. The United States and Canada went back to sharing the longest undefended border in the world, American and British relations continued with a cordiality that grew to a mutual sycophancy as the century progressed. Eighteen twelve is still a model of how to fight a really good-natured war without recrimination. It was like a family squabble between grandfather, son and uncle. And you can still wonder why they bothered. The losers were those who remained where they fell in the silent, fro-zen forts of the Northwest, in the great wastes of pine forest along the lakes, in the steaming Missouri, or who were commended to the deep. And as ever, the Indians, of course.

As the breadth of new land and the throat-tightening prom-ise of self-determination drew immigrants to the new territories of the West, settlers found Indians with guns. Almost as soon as Europeans had arrived in the New World, they traded guns to the natives—guns and horses. What else would they want? Radi-cally, and catastrophically, they altered the social and political bal-ance of Indian life. In cowboy films, the very worst baddies, worse than rustlers, hornswogglers, back-shooters and fifth ace players, were those wicked, venal, money-grubbin' varmints who sold guns and liquor to the Indians. Giving a gun to an Indian was akin to dry-gulching your neighbors' kids. The unfilmed truth was no less unpleasant, but it wasn't quite like that. Clan and tribal life in pre-European America had always been a violent web of alliances and vendettas. Tribes had traditional enemies they fought with and raided. These encounters could be murderous and ingeniously cruel, but they amounted to no more than unpleasant natural wastage. They came within bounds that allowed tribes and family groups to continue with a tidal equilibrium, in much the same way as they always had. The addition of guns to these ancient, implacable and mythologized conflicts made them calamitous. Most Indians were killed or displaced by other Indians. The guns were traded initially for fur, creating a market that hadn't existed in anything like this volume before. So monopoly of beaver rivers became economically lucrative to tribes. Top hats in Paris and London were paid for with genocide along the Great Lakes of the wilderness. It was also in the European traders' interest to support some tribes at the expense of others. As the frontier moved west it found Indian societies already collapsing under the stress of trade and the efficiency of war. New alliances were formed, like the Comanche in the West, a group of Indians that broke from the Shoshone to exploit the market for horses, and became terrifyingly fierce peripatetic rustlers. Guns wiped out the buffalo. The American bison was shot to near-extinction, most often by hunters employed by the railways to feed navigators, but also to deny the meat to hostile Indians and encourage them to continue to move to the margins of this new old country.

The guns of the West are an awful example of how a single piece of technology dropped into a fragile and technologically sparse culture utterly transforms and ultimately destroys it. It was the gun itself, this mechanized lump of modernity, that fell out of the sky into society and shot everything. All the other European stuff was amusing or irrelevant—beads and blankets, mirrors and saucepans. It was the gun that did the work for the settlers, on its own. Before Custer and his cavalry arrived to fight the last of the desperate Plains Indians in the Black Hills, the war was already won and lost, and it gives a lie to the smooth and patronizing conservative truism that it's not guns that kill people, it's people who kill people. The thing comes with a menu and a promise, and new possibilities, none of which were available to a tomahawk or an arrow. The mass-manufactured handgun and the Winchester made death and power different, because they were different. Just as a telephone is not merely an improved letter, a bullet isn't just a better arrow. One of the great lessons of 200 years of American boom is that technology is never neutral. Things come with demands, they have needs and they exploit the environments they find themselves in. America invented technopomorphism, the imbuing of functional tools with sapient attributes. There is no such thing as an inanimate object, they are just resting. But the sad moral is that, despite the havoc and the genocide, the gun was seen, right to the very end, as a remarkable boon, a fantastic blessing, that had improved the life of the tribes. It was a great gift.

The National Rifle Association is one of the biggest pressure groups in America. It donates large sums of money to lobby and support politicians, it uses celebrities and fear and nostalgia. But at heart it's really just a PR group for gun clubs. Take five minutes to read some of its literature or skip through the millions and millions of words of gun-toting indignation on the Internet, and you'll notice a particular tone of voice, a barely contained hysteria. It all seems to be typed by men being held back by their buddies. No other nation in the world gets this overwrought and sentimentally extreme about utensils. The whole gun-owning, -stroking, -displaying bumper-sticker thing, with all the special clothes and accessories and the complete nerdy, hobbyist shenanigan of gun loving at the clubs and the ranges, is ridiculous. Shooting is simpletons' golf. Fat blokes in earmuffs and grim women with peroxide hair.

In Vietnam I went to see the elaborate tunnels that they keep for tourists and which were used in the war to serve underground villages. Along with the little dusty mannequin tableaux of punji sticks and booby traps, I was encouraged to rent an old and wobbly Kalashnikov, or an American M60, and purchase bullets at a dollar each to shoot at targets. An American boy next to me emptied a clip into a cardboard cow and, breathing hard, held the gun in front of him like a fiery cross, overwhelmed by the joy of it. I asked him how it felt. "Oh man," he said, "this is what I came here for. This is so amazing. It's being part of the war." He told me how shooting the gun was a way of paying homage to the men who fought here. "It gives you such a rush, it's like a movie, only it's real." That was in itself a strange projection of emotion, but made more so because he was a first-generation Vietnamese-American, whose parents had escaped Saigon and now had a chain of diners in Florida.

You read the pro-gun antiregulation rants, and you'd think that not to have a gun, not to have a number of them secreted about your person and an assault rifle under the bed, was innately suspect, an un-American act of martial nudity. I said that, at heart, it's about gun clubs and lazy golf. Well, you make your own hole. But really it's nothing to do with guns at all. It's making a place for all the stuff that guns pack with them: the promise, the assumptions, the history, the needs and demands.

And the anti-gun urban liberals are really not that much more evolved. They have an equal and opposite fanaticism about guns—that to own one is to be a latent murderer. But worse than that, it's to be tasteless. There is a raft of assumptions that go with gun ownership. You will be racist, you will treat women badly and patronizingly, you will call them honey when they get angry, you will eat food with infantile, exclamatory names with your fingers and drink from cups that are bigger than your head. Your children will be named after Disney animals spelled by illiterate Eskimos. You will think that football is more important than interior decoration, and you will think nothing for conservation. Your car will be vast, you will burn things recreationally and you will have a flag that's larger than your bed hanging outside your house, or your trailer. Your religion will want to burn homosexuals, Muslims and books, in that order, and your T-shirts will wear opinions, as will your car's backside. Guns are a trigger for a whole magazine of internal snobberies and prejudices that crackle through white European-American society. There is a salutary sentence for these two groups—the gun lobby and the urban liberal. They are two tribes tied together by guns.

That top-ten list of trigger-happy nations has one other element in common. They are all countries with serious drug distribution networks. The guns go with the drugs. The people who are shooting and being shot are not generally the law-abiding religious beer-and-chardonnay-sipping whites, but Hispanic and black gangs involved in some part of an illegal trade. Crack cocaine is the contemporary beaver, an international fad that has radically altered the economics of the poorest, marginal people, indigenous America. The gangs are the tribes of the New World. Those with the most to be frightened of are crack addicts and dealers. A junkie with a revolver is far more likely to shoot a dealer for his next hit than to travel out to your suburb, break into your house, steal your flat-screen TV and candlesticks, go back downtown, find a fence, make a deal, get paid, go and find a dealer and pay for a hit. Cut out the boring bit: shoot the dealer. Get a whole stash of hits. Junkies are sad, bad and mad, but they're not dumb.

On my desk, beside the keyboard and the phone, lying on top of a guide to birds, beside my daughter's silver shoes that are full of pencils, is a gun. It looks like a gun—very gunlike. You don't have to know anything about guns to recognize this as a cowboy Western revolver. It's fully technopomorphic, that's what it is. Dark metal, with an octagonal barrel, a brown wooden handle. It's a Smith and Wesson rimfire, .32 caliber, model 1, second issue. It might have been used in the Civil War, or the Indian wars. It has an embossed metal American eagle coat of arms on the handle, so I expect it sat in the drawer of some civil servant or bank guard. There are lots of other things on the desk, books, papers, plugs, small votive statues, letter openers, spectacles, shells, pre-Columbian pottery shards, a tin whistle, amethysts from Madagascar, a Victorian toast rack, a box of statins, kid gloves, five Norwegian kroner, a silver tiger from Calcutta, a magnifying glass, Ethiopian incense, a gold half-hunter pocket watch, an empty Colman's mustard tin. But it's the gun that dominates. The mechanical jib of its outline: it's mutinous. Everything else arranges itself around the revolver. They don't want to turn their backs on it, the books and the wallet, the folded handkerchief, the postcard of Cambodia all know where the gun is. It is the center of the diorama, the vanishing point. It gives the space a tension, intimates a story, a plot. It turns a still life into a memento mori. It is a castrated thing, an emasculated gun. It will ever be mute, with a clumsy, clicking hammer. But still it threatens with the power of its kind. It has a generic stillness, a tense, mechanical panache.

Have you considered the guns in American films? Of course you have. But have you considered the number of guns in British films? French, German, Spanish, Hungarian, Swedish films? You probably haven't, because there aren't that many. Very few. An occasional gun. But a gun in a film is so culturally specific to America. It looks odd in world cinema unless it's ironic. I wonder if there are more balls in English films than guns, more nipples in French films. Guns in America's story are a constant, a plot device, like coffee cups in European films. Guns are Hollywood. They've grown there, an indigenous part of the landscape. All sorts of films can have guns: comedies, cartoons. There are funny guns, science-fiction guns, big plastic flashing guns. Guns evolve an aesthetic, own a fashion sense in their habits and display. The movement of guns becomes balletic: this year we will hold guns like this, not as we did five years ago. The body language moves on. You may imagine this is because actors make conscious decisions to do things differently, but it's far more likely that the guns are holding the actor at arm's length. They have the power. Everybody looks at them. The guns are manipulating the flickering light. Their hero is only an extension of the power. Guns in American screen culture may be the result of a constant, right-left tension that exists about firearms. They may be the visible evocation of fear in American cities. They may be a legacy of a frontier past. Or it may be that the guns are adapting, mutating, colonizing another environment like industrial parasites going legitimate. The gun doesn't want us dead. Dead people don't own guns. Dead people don't want guns. The guns want us aware, they want us fearful, they want us to want them. Already in America, there are more American guns than there are Americans.

6

Speeches

The last word Abraham Lincoln ever heard was "sockdologizing." It's a particularly cruel salting of Southern vindictiveness for a man who made so much out of words to have to go to the choir ambrosial with a word that ugly ringing in his ear. It's from a line delivered by the actor Harry Hawk, playing Cousin Asa in *Our American Cousin,* which was the great hit of 1865. And the big laugh line, that always got a huge hoot from an audience, is "Don't know the manners of good society, eh? Well, I guess I know enough to turn you inside out, old gal. You sockdologizing old man-trap."

John Wilkes Booth, who possibly founded the fashion for hyphenated thespians—actor-director, actor-writer, actor-waiter, actor-assassin—knew the text. He knew that the secret of tragedy, like comedy, is all in the timing. So he waited in the dark behind the president for the laughter, and shot Lincoln behind the left ear as the audience howled.

It's an odd word, "sockdologizing." It's an original New World–ism, and comes from "doxology." In a church service that's the final response in a prayer. It's a malapropish spoonerism that came to mean the last word or the final put-down. Buffalo Bill used it in relation to a knockout punch. It's a word from a colorfully slanging vernacular that spent a lot of time in church. The play was a light comedy, a sort-of story that was popular in America right up to the films of the forties: hick but honest American finds he's kin to decrepit English aristocrats. It's a plot that is culturally envious but also mocking. The play has a character called Lord Dundreary, who gave the name to a fashion for long side whiskers.

You might wonder what Lincoln was doing there, really, at the end of a war. Everything about his assassination is odd, unlikely. I don't mean the conspiracy theorists' coincidences that grew popular in a would-you-believe-it way after the shooting of Kennedy, the ones that whispered, "Both men had vice presidents called Johnson," "One was taken from a theater to a warehouse, the other from a warehouse to a theater," "Both assassins had three-part names." I don't mean any of that stuff. That's not odd, it's just coincidence. The really coincidental thing about coincidences is that they happen so constantly and predictably. Everyone involved in the tragedy of Lincoln's assassination was sort of odd. Two things I should perhaps mention first. Lincoln is the greatest American who ever lived. He is probably one of the greatest people who ever lived. And second, when he died, he was a year younger than I am now. It is in the nature of greatness that we are drawn to measure ourselves against it, and that that tall, rough-hewn figure was all done before he reached sixty is straitening. I can't get any distance from the event. It always seems a present calamity, such a despairing, desperate shame. Lincoln had done the great work of his life saving and binding the Union, but it wasn't so much the war as the unresolved, unmade peace that dissected and distorted America for the next 100 years. It was at the moment of his departure that his particular tone and toughness were needed the most, to win the peace as he'd won the war.

Still, the circumstances of that evening and the players who took part in it, this play outside a play, are odd. There is the terrible, gimcrack comedy and the fact that nobody wanted to go with him. You'd have thought that if the president asked you, any of you, to the theater, you'd say yes. You wouldn't mention that you couldn't find a babysitter, or unfortunately had a previous dinner party, were a bit under the weather. But the Grants did. The general and his wife were supposed to go but they made their excuses. Apparently Mrs. Grant and Mrs. Lincoln couldn't bear each other. So, in the end, the president took a young staff officer, Major Henry Rathbone, and his fiancée, Clara Harris. She wasn't just his fiancée, she was his stepsister. And her dad was a senator. When they married, Henry's stepfather was also his father-in-law. Later, he would be made America's representative to Hanover, where he would go mad and kill Clara, and end his days in a German asylum for the criminally insane. He was buried next to her in a grave that was grubbed up in the fifties because nobody cared. Their son became a member of the House of Representatives.

Booth was particularly incensed at the halting of prisoner exchanges between North and South. He had first planned to kidnap the president. Then he decided to keep it a plan of single syllables. He wanted to kill Grant too. But he wasn't there. So Booth got into the box and no one noticed. There was supposed to be a soldier outside the door, but he'd gone to the pub with a coachman. Some see a conspiracy in this dereliction, but it looks like he was just a soldier who'd rather have a drink than sit in a hall in a theater. Waiting for his moment, listening to the inane play romping on, possibly noticing that Harry Hawk wasn't terribly good in the role, Booth waits his cue and steps out of the shadow, holds the Derringer to the back of the president's head and pulls the trigger.

Now, that's odd. Why a Derringer? A little one-shot squib of a thing? A gambler's fifth ace. The loose ladies' desperate rape alarm. One shot, up close, that's all you get. What if the soldier had been on the door? Booth also had a knife. He was planning to stab Grant—why not take a bigger gun with more bullets? Shoot everyone? As the president slumps in his rocking chair—hold it again just there: *a rocking chair?* Who goes to the theater and asks for a rocking chair?—Mrs. Lincoln screams, and Henry Rathbone goes to grab Booth, who slashes his arm and then stabs him. The audience looks up at the presidential box, with the flag of the treasury swagged underneath it. Some of them think this is part of the show. Booth leaps to the stage, the spur of his riding boot catching the flag. He lands heavily on his left leg, fracturing it. So there he is onstage, in a packed theater. You think he can hop off? He's an actor, of course not. He faces the audience and shouts, no, he *declaims* with a gesture, waving the bloodied knife, "*Sic semper tyrannis!*"—"Thus always for tyrants," the state motto of Virginia.

Latin, in this neoclassical city with all its columns and statues, dates and incised wisdom. Latin picks him out of the bloody melee of common-or-garden cutthroats or deranged obsessives in this nation, which has seen so much close-up gore. Oh, we know who he thinks he is. Of course we know. With his Latin and his gory dagger (nice touch, the dagger), he's the American Brutus.

As he delivers the line, Major Rathbone shouts, "Stop that man!" and the confused crowd realize what has happened. Audiences think collectively. Booth exits, pursued by history.

There are, it turns out, three doctors in the house. The first to get to the door of the box, which Booth had wedged shut, is Charles Leale, an army surgeon. He's seen a lot of gunshots. He came to the theater not for the play but to watch the president. He'd asked for a seat where he could get a good view of Lincoln: that amazing head, the astonishing face that's still striking, still makes you pause when you see it on a banknote. They lower Lincoln to the floor. Another doctor, Dr. Taft, is shunted up from the stalls into the box. They first look for stab wounds and then, cutting off Lincoln's collar, see the clotted bullet hole. A third doctor, Albert Freeman Africanus King, arrives. He was born in Bicester, became an obstetrician in Washington in later life, and was one of the first doctors to make the connection between mosquitoes and malaria, suggesting that the city of Washington have a big mosquito net put round it. They laughed at him. The next doctor who mentioned it got the Nobel Prize.

Lincoln is carried out to a boardinghouse opposite, where he is laid diagonally on a bed, too tall to lie straight. He gathers more medical men. In the end there are eight. Government ministers arrive, and soldiers in a fluster as the news spreads like blood. The government is set up in a next-door room. Messages are sent, orders given. No one knows if this is the beginning of fresh insurrection, other troops, more assassins. Mrs. Lincoln is the only woman there. Inconsolable, sobbing, surrounded by these grim-faced purposeful men in their long-coat suits, stiff collars and blue uniforms. They've seen battle, seen plenty of death, lost friends and brothers, sons and comrades. They are men on men's business, ferocious and resolved. Men with duty to do, and purpose to do it. She is merely a woman, heartbroken, bereft: her life's duty and purpose lies on this little cot. A man shouts irritably, "Take her out of here," and the president's wife is hustled into another room, where her wailing won't spoil the somber and dignified tableau of the death of a president. Lincoln never utters another word. He lives on till seven in the morning. When he finally dies, his wife won't be with him. Charles Leale stays for nine hours. "I held his hand firmly to let him know in his blindness that he had a friend."

Booth leaps on a horse—as well as you can with a broken leg—tied up outside the theater, and hightails it out of that burg. On the turnpike he meets fellow conspirator Herold, who has been helping to try to kill the secretary of state, William Seward. That attempt failed, though an awful lot of people were stabbed on the way. Seward will later buy Alaska from the Russians and get a town in the chilly north named after him. The men stop off at one Dr. Mudd's house, so Booth can have his leg splinted. Mudd will be jailed for this act, and it causes an argument about the higher calling of doctors, to help all, irrespective. In truth, Mudd was probably also a conspirator, and he has lent his name to an expression: "His name is Mudd." Booth and Herold gallop on south, dodging the hue and cry. They end up cornered in a barn. Herold gives himself up; he'll hang later. Booth won't. The soldiers, in good cowboy form, set the barn on fire. One man creeps around the back, and through a crack in the wall sees Booth and shoots him. Boston Corbett. He was an odd chap. Born Thomas Corbett in the East End of London, he came to America and worked as a milliner. Called himself Boston, got religion, and he too went bonkers, probably due to the mercury used in preparing top hats—hence "as mad as a hatter." Boston cut off his own testicles with a pair of scissors so that he wouldn't be bothered by lustful feelings for prostitutes. Afterward, they said, he ate a meal, went to a prayer meeting, then took himself off to the doctors. He was an imposingly frightening-looking man. He'd been captured in the war and imprisoned in the notorious Southern camp at

Andersonville, where he'd been released in the prison swap that Booth had wanted to maintain.

The bullet hit the actor in the spine, instantly rendering him a quadriplegic. They dragged him out of the barn and laid him on the porch of the house. He lived a couple of more hours. Booth's last words were "Useless, useless," sometimes seen romantically as a recognition of the futility of his crime, but probably because he asked the soldiers to hold up his paralyzed hands so that he could see them, since he could no longer feel them. He was talking to his fingers. Boston Corbett was arrested for disobeying orders—they wanted Booth alive—but he was released and given a $1,500 portion of the $40,000 reward. He went to Minnesota, dug a hole, and lived in it. He died in a forest fire.

Walking up the steps of the Lincoln Memorial, the first thing you feel is its vastness. It is a huge thing. And then you see the statue of Lincoln sitting pensive, wise, an evocation of Solomon asking North and South to cut their baby in half, and you think, that's life-sized. This was a huge life, and this is about the size of it. Most great men are made great by their times. Events and the crest of history lift them up, invigorate them: Churchill, Napoléon, Washington caught their waves. And then there are very, very few who are great and whose greatness makes the time they live in. Lincoln was one of those. A towering inspiration despite the Civil War, not because of it. On the side panels of the memorial are two speeches. The Gettysburg Address he made on the dedication of the battlefield that had seen the largest continuous slaughter of men ever, not to be outdone until the trenches of the Great War.

He didn't think much of that speech. Indeed he wasn't even the main speaker—that was one Edward Everett, governor of Massachusetts, onetime plenipotentiary ambassador to England, and a famous after-dinner raconteur. Everett spoke for over two hours. Of the dead he said, "You now feel it, a new bond of Union, that they shall lie side by side till a clarion louder than that which marshaled them to the combat shall awake their slumbers," and a lot more of that sort of tumpty-tum stuff. After he'd finished, the crowds began to trail off, go for a drink, something to eat. Lincoln got up and spoke 270 words in about the time it takes to broadcast a commercial break. The Gettysburg Address finishes with: "and that government of the people, by the people, for the people, shall not perish from the earth." It's the greatest speech ever made. Theodore Sorensen, who was Kennedy's speechwriter and composed the 1960 inaugural address, said that this was special because it uses short words. It has none of the book-learned flamboyance of Everett. It isn't a performance, it is altogether a new thing, pared down, stark and vivid. It is the foreword of modern times. Only afterward, as it was disseminated in print, read out loud on street corners, in factories and barns, in prairie dormitories, around campfires, in bars and from pulpits, across the dining tables and soup kitchens and school desks of the fractured nation, did it grow to be the best-known speech ever given. To go alongside Lincoln's best-known political rubric: "You can fool all the people some of the time, and some of the people all the time, but you cannot fool all the people all of the time." On the opposite wall of Lincoln's memorial is a rather less universally well-known speech, the second inaugural address, delivered over a sea of mud in 1865, just up the road.

In a cupboard hidden in the side of the monument there's a little souvenir shop. I bought a postcard of this speech. I keep it on my desk, somewhere under all the traffic jam of disposable words. It says:

> Both parties deprecated war. But one of them would make war rather than let the nation survive, and the other would accept war rather than let it perish. And the war came . . . Both read the same bible and pray to the same God, and each invokes his aid against the other. It may seem strange that any men should dare ask a just God's assistance in wringing their bread from the sweat of other men's faces. But let us judge not, that we be not judged.

It ends:

with malice toward none, with charity for all, with firmness in the right, as God gives us to see the right. Let us strive on to finish the work we are in, to bind up the nation's wounds, to care for him who shall have borne the battle, and for his widow and his orphan, to do all which may achieve and cherish a just and lasting peace among ourselves and with all nations.

It's difficult to dissect oratory without first killing it. But the top quote is as simple and succinct and satisfying as finding a jigsaw piece. The short, staccato sentences: "And the war came." The war is a third element in an argument. It is a storm, a judgment, a curse. And then, that phrase, "wring their bread from the sweat of other men's faces." No image in Marx or Europe's glib socialist literature touches that awful vividness. And finally the summing-up that sounds so familiar—trite even—because it's the template, the well-thumbed crib for a hundred hundred politicians and press spokesmen and secretaries. It, or something paraphrased from it, has become the oratorical rubber stamp of official comment. Lincoln is the jigsaw piece in a picture that, at his death, hasn't yet been made. Such a transcendent orator, not simply due to his commitment or his conviction, his country lawyer's ordering of arguments, but because of his uncertainty. It is his struggle with competing beliefs and ideas. Lincoln doesn't declare for the defense or the prosecution: uniquely for a wartime leader, he is rarely adversarial. His words are worried, humane and concerned, encompassing intractable demands and elbowing needs. In all his great speeches it's as if he has taken the back off a conflict. You can see it working—the tension, the emotion—and he leads you through to a conclusion that, while inescapable, is never easy or necessarily straightforward. It is Lincoln's struggle not with compromise but with fairness, charity and humanity. He feels his way to a sticking point. Every word is weighed against the weight of that great conscience. The brilliant, elevating phrases, the elegant rhythms, the great simplicity, without decoration or embellishment, are load-bearing beams and joists that hold up purpose. His prose is sturdy and firm. He is without peer.

On the steps of the Lincoln Memorial, Martin Luther King Jr. had the Dream, and made a speech of compassion, conciliation and struggle that drew as much from Lincoln as it did from the pulpits of the South. It was on these steps that Marian Anderson sang to and for a nation, invited by Eleanor Roosevelt after the Daughters of the American Revolution had refused to give this black woman a platform in 1939. You suspect it was her talent and beauty that frightened them. They wouldn't have minded if she was handing out towels in the ladies' room.

Standing here, looking down the long road to the Capitol, I wonder what it was that came together to make America such a rhetorical nation. Look at any book of great speeches and the first half will all be classical, then a thin slice of Peel, Pitt and Churchill (who was himself half Yank), and the rest will almost all be American. Right from the get-go, they've had a talent for whittling the language into ringing exclamations, the telling euphony. Americans have always liked to talk, and they also like people who don't talk, the mixture of speedy tongues and taciturn understatement. They seem to form a coalition of listeners and salesmen. The explanation for why arguments are so polished and natural over there is a gift of the Constitution, freedom of speech. Not just the right to say what you want, but the obligation to exercise that right. And then there's the belief, the pulpit and the lectern, the long Low Church tradition as opposed to the rote, repeated litany, the rhythms of Methodism and Nonconformist ranting combined with the rhythms and circumlocutions of the King James Bible, that is in turns bare observation and courtly Hebrew syntax. There is also the style of voice that comes from Irish to English, and Lowland Scots to English, and there's English spoken as a second language, as it was for millions of immigrants, from Europe and Africa. The importance of the declaimed word surely must have grown out of a population that read little—if at all—in English, who had to listen carefully.

And so there emerged a tradition of straight talking with elegant phrasing, with humor and hyperbole, and it developed an accent almost immediately. People commented on the American style of talking, typically with the stress on vowels above consonants, as opposed to standard English, which shrinks vowels and beats time on consonants. It is in the consonants that we keep instructions, orders and directions. But emotions are displayed and imparted in vowels. The vowels are color, consonants black and white. The American accent has more access to emotion than English. You're more likely to sound like a friend than a public information announcement. On the other hand, standard English is more trustworthy, being less emotive. American accents sound more partisan. It is a voice that has grown out of debate, out of long seasons with little company and no more entertainment than the sound of voices.

Look at American television, and marvel at how much of it is just talk. Whole channels, whole days without drawing breath—devoted to arguments. There's the importance and the influence of shock jocks, commentators and preachers. America talks constantly, and it is immensely fluent. I'm always amazed at how erudite the vox pop interviews on TV news are. Simply stopping people on the street and asking for an opinion. Everyone is practiced. Everyone's born knowing how to speak into a microphone. Audiences are eager to air opinions. When Americans talk, they talk with ease and confidence. They seem more comfortable in their own mouths than the English do. That's rather intimidating. We practice a mumbled reticence. The ways of talking, the rhythms and the language of black and Hispanic speakers, the people of the Northeast and the Southwest, of legislators and lawyers, evangelists and direct marketing TV presenters, of secondhand car dealers' forecourt radio ads, all have their own particular argots, jargons, punctuation, slang and rhythm, their own color and tones. Everything—newsprint, novels, theater, billboards—sounds out.

The great distinguishing feature of American writing is that it almost always sounds like a voice in your ear. Words on the page are spoken. Most European writing—all English English writing—is about writing. It's silent, and cerebral. It has never been said out loud. It's never meant to be heard. But read Twain or Steinbeck, Mailer, Hemingway, Updike or Wolfe, and you can hear it. It's constantly repeated that we are countries separated by a common language, but that doesn't sound right. What is more likely is that the Old World's English is a written language, and the New World's a spoken one. Back in the Old World, there are regular and vitriolic complaints about Americanisms, the invasion of Yankee pronunciations, usages and, particularly galling, syntax. Tellingly, these complaints are almost always made in print, with the offending words and expressions written phonetically, with hyphens and italics, and quotation marks. All the paraphernalia that Old World English writers use to patronize. But it again shows the difficulty of finding a voice in English English. You have to jump the dictionary to inflict some pantomime approximation, to tip the reader the wink that this sentence is said by an Irishman, or a West Indian, or an American.

The arguments for resisting American usages and pronunciations are as stupid as they are vain. It isn't about language, it's about a thin-skinned cultural insecurity, a sense that we may be the unfortunate warblers, feeding an arriviste cuckoo. Anyone trying to arrest mispronunciations or add written instructions to a language, to put up warning lights or cage the thoughts in others' heads, is patently absurd and embarrassing. New World English is spoken by more people than Old World English, and it's more energetic and creative. It's not respectful of language, because language doesn't need or want respect. You don't need to whisper round English, it isn't a library, except in England. American English is a power shout of expostulation and invention. It's the language of power and business, and it's the language of the powerless and the poor. Stand on the steps of the Lincoln Memorial and consider that Washington and London both looked back to Rome for their intellectual political culture. London took writing, Latin grammar, form, rules and rhythms, and America took oratory, and straight off wrote the finest, grandest thing ever said and ever written. The Declaration of Independence. But it is a declaration, not an essay, not a paper, a missive, a memo, a Magna Carta. It is to be declaimed, it sings out of its ink with a clear voice that has shouted round the world: we proclaim these truths. It is from a spoken language.

There are lots of great, memorable American speeches. I particularly love this one, that wasn't delivered in English. In fact, it was in a language no one speaks, made by Chief Seattle, and is said to be faithfully and simultaneously translated by a white man, though I think that's unlikely. It sounds too much like *The Last of the Mohicans.* Seattle was a Good Indian, they named the city for him. The backstory of this speech is the usual blood-and-feathers of reneged treaties, the pressure on land and the sad and fatal move to reservations. His speech was made to his people and the government on signing a treaty that would move them far away. It was not the speech of a new nation's growing pains and coming of age, but of an ancient, frail nation's demise. Whether it is Seattle's or Dr. Smith's, between them they came up with something intensely moving:

The very dust under your feet responds more lovingly to our footsteps than yours, because it is the ashes of our ancestors, and our bare feet are conscious of the sympathetic touch, for the soil is rich with the life of our kindred. The noble braves, fond mothers, glad, happy-hearted maidens, and even the little children who lived and rejoiced here for a brief season, and whose very names are now forgotten, still love these somber solitudes and their deep fastnesses, which at eventide grow shadowy with the presence of dusky spirits. And when the last red man shall have perished from the earth and his memory among the white men shall have become a myth, these shores will swarm with the invisible dead of my tribe. And when your children's children shall think themselves alone in the fields, the store, the shop, upon the highway or in the silence of the pathless woods, they shall not be alone. For in all the Earth there is no place dedicated to solitude. At night, when the streets of your cities and villages will be silent, and you think them deserted, they will throng with the returning hosts that once filled and still love this beautiful land. The white man will never be alone. Let him be just, and deal kindly with my people. For the dead are not powerless.

I was at the Mile High Stadium in Denver at the end of the Democratic convention in 2008. People—most of them young— queued for three or four hours in the sun to hear Obama speak. Finally, after the warm-ups and the flattery, the veterans of previous campaigns, the endorsements and the promises, he walked onto the field and, separated from the crowd only by a sheet of bullet-proof glass (Lincoln and Kennedy's legacy), he was greeted with a great exhalation of praise, a cascade of applause that washed round and round the stadium, slapped and eddied back and forth. They raised up their voices. The noise they made was a feeling. It made you part of something huge, gave them this long, open-throated echo, the ululation of people going somewhere. Obama smiled his easy, midwestern smile, and said thank you. Thank you. Over and over. I've looked it up. I think he said thank you thirty-three times. It became a mantra. The speech itself was workmanlike, smooth, and sounded like the work of a committee ticking boxes, pressing buttons. He has a marvelous delivery, terrific natural timing, a very attractive beige voice that's light and warm like a summer cashmere sweater. At the time a lot of Democratic weather makers were comparing Obama to Lincoln, off the record, just as background, unattributed. There was the oratory thing, and Illinois, both were down-home lawyers. But they're not the same. The shiny, satisfying bits of Obama's speeches—"We are the ones we've been waiting for. We are the change that we seek"—the headline-quotable tweeting stuff, like champagne flutes from boxes of plastic peanuts, was too glib. Too handsome, too keen, too damn needy. Lincoln was ugly and awkward and reluctant, and a Republican. And he'd never have said thank you thirty-three times. What was impressive, what was moving, was that 80,000 young Americans would come to hear a politician make a speech. They could have watched it at home on half a dozen more comfortable mediums. They came because, still, there is something indelibly, throat-catchingly American about a crowd and a man raising his voice. Here are a few political quotes from across the spectrum. They're not the best, or favorites. Just plucked out.

"We need men who can dream of things that never were."

"People are just about as happy as they make up their minds to be."

"If anything in this life is certain, if history has taught us anything, it is that you can kill anyone."

"I have often said there is nothing better for the inside of a man than the outside of a horse."

"Fear is the path to the dark side. Fear leads to anger, anger leads to hate, hate leads to suffering."

"A fellow ain't got a soul of his own, just a little piece of a big soul, the one big soul that belongs to everybody."

"Doing well is the result of doing good—that's what capitalism is all about."

Kennedy, Lincoln, the Godfather, Reagan, Yoda, Tom Joad from *The Grapes of Wrath*, Ralph Waldo Emerson.

7

Sparks

We need to talk about Topsy. There's no nice way of putting this. Topsy's dead. Topsy was an Indian elephant—four and a half tons of dead elephant. She was part of a circus at Luna Park on Coney Island at the turn of the twentieth century, and she killed a keeper—well, three keepers, but over three years. One keeper a year on Coney Island seems pretty abstemious for an elephant. The last one, Topsy's final keeper, had been a drunk who fed her a lit cigarette. I expect his last words were: "Hey, wanna see what happens when you feed an elephant a Camel?" Yeah, *that* happens. It makes a sort of infuriated noise and stands on your head. They decided that Topsy had to be put down. Three strikes, and your feet are cocktail cabinets.

This is where it gets weird and uncomfortable. And I have to say, weird and uncomfortable in a particularly American sort of way. This guy comes along and says he'd like to kill the elephant. Well, lots of people want to kill elephants. Theodore Roosevelt did a $2 million safari killing everything he could find, and you could go and shoot an elephant in Texas next week if you have a mind to. But this guy didn't want a trophy, he just wanted the elephant dead. He didn't care what she'd done. Guilt wasn't an issue. What was important was that she was big. Elephantine. And *how* she died. That was the most sweatily, dry-mouth, itchy-palm thing. She couldn't just cash in any old how. She had to die in a really special way—a way he'd invented—and he wanted to film it.

Now, at this point we have to ask ourselves, if this was our decision—to let him, to say yay or nay to the bespoke murder of an elephant—what would we have done? It's a test. How good an

American could you be? Well, of course you said yes. Not just yes, but Woo, Yes! Youbetcha! Let's sell tickets! We can pay to watch Thomas Edison electrocute an elephant. For it was he, the wizard of Menlo Park, as Edison was fondly known, who wanted to do it.

He had copper shoes fitted for her. The Society for the Protection of Cruelty to Animals did get queasy, and insisted that Topsy be fed arsenic-laced carrots first, which she apparently appreciated more than the cigarette. And they let her out into a field, and she stood there. It's difficult to tell what an elephant's thinking, but she seemed pensive in a taciturnly pachydermish way. There was no evident jolt or shock, no curling of the trunk or trumpet, or final, Cagneyish defiance, no ear-waving semaphore intimating that she regretted nothing, she'd stomp the bastard again but bore no hatred for the rest of you weird, snub-nosed melonheads.

Her feet began to smoke. The copper shoes were burning. Elephants have very sensitive feet. They can't jump. They have four knees and no elbows. Topsy toppled forward, fell and lay on the earth. The film was a big hit all over America. People paid their two bits to see the elephant die by the miracle of the modern age. So, Mr. Edison, what made you think of running 6,600 volts through an elephant? Was it starting with the cats and the dogs that gave you the taste for it? Then the cows? Edison killed hundreds and hundreds and hundreds of animals without a second thought. He did it for capitalism. It was strictly business.

The current wars are still arguably the most extreme commercial race and black propaganda contest in all of capitalism's bright history. They were fought between Edison's General Electric Corporation and Westinghouse. It was a fight to the death (as it turned out, many, many deaths). Business often uses the language of battle as a metaphor. This wasn't a metaphor, it was about whether America should use Tesla's alternating current, or Edison's direct current. Tesla had once worked for Edison and they'd fallen out. The argument came down mostly to how much copper wire you had to use to carry the stuff from generator to lightbulb. AC is more efficient, cheaper and adaptable. On every level that you care about, AC is the way to go, but that really wasn't the point. Edison had patented and invested in direct current. He needed DC to win. So he put it about that AC was more dangerous.

There was a general nervousness about electricity. Even in my lifetime, my grandmother, like Thurber's, thought it could leak out of the sockets and might kill her in the night like gas. In fact, it's surprisingly difficult to die from an electric shock. Mostly, the energy in electricity burns. It can give you very nasty burns. A whole lot of electricity can burn your offal, but to kill you it's really got to stop your heart beating. Your heart has to be on a direct line between the source of the electricity and the earth, which, from electricity's point of view, is home. It doesn't want to kill you. It is disinterested. It wants to get out of you as soon as possible; you're a nuisance, a waste. You're resistance, and resistance is kryptonite to power. And an alternating current, it's true, is marginally, minutely more likely to oscillate at a rhythm that will fibrillate your heart. But there's really nothing in it. Still, Edison was the better showman and more deadly. He saw an opportunity to terrify customers and influence governments. He employed one Harold Pitney Brown to electrocute animals all over the country with AC current. Brown would get them to walk onto metal mats, then bang! Edison chose Brown because he'd written a letter to the *New York Post* describing in touching detail the death of a boy who'd brushed an AC wire. Brown already had a failing DC electrical goods company. He took to offing animals as negative advertising. I can see him in a truck full of strays and a generator, perhaps a banner and some bunting. He'd stop in little community town halls, churches, schools, kill a couple of cats, finish with a dog. And then one day he had this large Newfoundland cross that was only agonized, not actually dead. And the SPCA stepped in again and stopped him from having another go at it. This was the first creature ever to have its electric execution commuted, though not for long. He finished it off in the next town.

You get the feeling that Brown was an efficient man. He was Irish, born in India, his father had been a naval officer. Brown Junior ended up as a professor of electrical engineering at Harvard and MIT, and a lifelong cheerleader for the metric system. But what gives him the place in America's index is that he built the first electric chair. It wasn't designed by him, it was designed by Alfred Southwick, as an act of civic devotion and proactive modernity. Southwick was a dentist. Most of us understand that there is something intrinsically unsavory and weird about dentists. We suspect that apart from riding Harley-Davidsons in bandannas on weekends, they also sniff underwear and talk dirty to strangers on the Internet in the guise of fifteen-year-old Belgian girls. It's all there in their manner—the pain, and being forced to stare up their noses. It was Southwick's profession that gave America the electric chair and not the electric stool or doormat. If he'd been a psychiatrist, it might have been the electric couch. They did toy with the electric swimming pool and the electric yoga mat, but the dentist chair turned out to be, well, more appropriate.

It's often thought that Edison came up with the idea of the electric chair: like everything else he came up with, he didn't. But he certainly paid for it, and insisted on having it made. The idea might have sprung from his keenness for killing cats and dogs, but it was the brainchild of the efficiency movement. They were a pressure group that wanted to rationalize and improve all sorts of public businesses, from elections to work practices. Executions were old-fashioned and—worse—Old World. Hanging was what the despotic, corrupt nations of Europe did. They also used axes and guillotines. They strung good workingmen from lampposts. The America of the new, efficient age needed a new, efficient American means of ultimate judgment. Something that was clean, simple, humane and "now," that showed America in the bright, crackling arc of the new. The way murderers were dispatched would be part of an industrial process of justice.

The efficiency movement came from a sector of social politics that is peculiarly American: modernizing, technocratic conservatism, the belief that technology and innovation is the natural and ethical way to preserve and promote traditional life. Efficiency is godly. Many aspects of life came under the scrutiny of the efficiency movement. Political reform, education, taxation—all examined for improvement. Efficiency was an evangelical social crusade that was itself part of a broader Progressive Era that spanned the turn of the century and dissipated into the Depression. Its great success in terms of its social engineering was Prohibition, which also turned out to be its greatest failure.

The Progressive Era and efficiency recruited people who felt strongly that America was born to be a prescriptive nation with a strong common purpose, that was God-blessed. A nation that had a responsibility to be very different from the others, particularly from Old Europe. A new Chosen People. It was impressed with a house of new isms and ideas. Science, business, technology were opening the back of life, so that we could see how everything worked. The progressives loved Fordism for instance—based on the rigorous and not altogether pleasant politics of Henry Ford, who believed in the conveyor belt but, more important, in paying his workers well because, as he said, "They should be able to afford the cars they made." Progressivism wanted fair taxes so that the rich paid more than the poor. They wanted electoral reform and wider suffrage. And they had a Low Church faith that education was the key to everything, including heaven. They championed the Wisconsin idea where the state legislature used the state university as a research and legislative bureaucracy, so that clever people would suggest reform and draft law, and think about problems in an academic manner, and use learning as a tool not just for the individual, but one that could be utilized by the community.

One of the heroes of the efficiency movement was Frederick Winslow Taylor, a man who embodies so much of the intensely single-minded, relentlessly convinced proselytizers who have both harried and hounded America with their monotone convictions. He was a mechanical engineer who worked at Bethlehem Steel on the production line and then as a manager. He grew convinced that most businesses were innately inefficient, that all elements of work should be minutely examined and rationalized. Every job could be broken down into individual actions, and wherever possible a machine or mechanical process should be used. Workers ought to be continuously monitored by a succession of managers who would then cross-check and relay their findings to more managers. In this way, the random nature of work could be reduced to predictable and measurable actions. Workers were the least efficient parts of the process.

Taylor fell out with the other managers at Bethlehem after deciding that the optimum shovel-load for men doing manual labor was 21½ pounds, therefore shovels of different sizes should be used for each material shoveled, to allow a uniform and consistent shovelful. Having been fired, Taylor naturally wrote a book, and lectured in an inspirational manner to managers. He didn't claim there was an innate nobility in labor, but an innate dumbness. Memorably, he said, "I can say without the slightest hesitation that the science of handling pig iron is so great that the man who is physically able to handle pig iron and is sufficiently phlegmatic and stupid to choose this for his occupation is rarely able to comprehend the science of handling pig iron." His methods, he said, were good for workers, maximizing their efforts and therefore wages. He said the Taylor method would make unions irrelevant. Everything a workingman needed would be arranged by scientific management.

Taylor and his Taylorism must have been one of the great comic characters of America—observing the infinitesimal movements in other people's lives without ever considering the absurdity of his own. His photograph shows a face utterly bereft of self-awareness, indeed, impervious to internal inquiry. Taylorism could be applied to everyone but Taylor. His teaching, though, went around the world. Taylorism and Fordism were particular favorites of both Lenin and Stalin, who tried to impose them on Soviet factories, with rather more rigor and harsher consequences than in America. In the end it was a typically bolshy French academic who pointed out that according to Taylor's book every workingman needed to be constantly answerable to several managers, and that hardly seemed a practical, economic, efficient or sensible way to go about making rubber ducks. Though, coincidentally, that is how most French industry is now organically organized.

Taylor's time studies also impressed Frank and Lillian Gilbreth, and they did much the same thing with movement—adding the two ideas together to get Time and Motion Studies, a fad that kept corporations perplexed and workers infuriated for half a century. Between them they were the prophets of bullet points, Venn diagrams, the whiteboard, the box you think outside of, and the loop you're kept in. Frank and Lillian were good at this efficiency stuff because they had twelve children, two of whom wrote a book called *Cheaper by the Dozen,* which has been made into two Hollywood films starring Clifton Webb and then Steve Martin. Actually, one of the children keeled over dead early on, but they didn't mention that in the book because it would have spoiled things. *Cheaper If One's Dead* doesn't sound quite as snappy, and it would have wrecked the efficiency of the concept.

So, in line with the principles of efficiency, Alfred Southwick the dentist—who sat on the splendidly directly named Electrical Death Commission—approached both Edison and Tesla to offer them the glory of powering up the dentist chair at the end of your world. Tesla and Westinghouse declined. Edison, with a characteristic brilliance, leaped at the chance, and insisted on using an AC current, so the chair would be powered by Tesla. He worked assiduously to get New York State to accept it, and when Westinghouse refused to supply his patented generator to power it, Edison had one ordered in the name of a university, and had it shipped via Latin America. It cost $700. The Electric Death Commission got a really special demonstration from Mr. Brown. He zapped a cow for them, and then, as an encore—just to show this was no freak show—he lit up a horse. They were impressed. Who wouldn't be?

New York got its electric chair, and then had a look round for someone to sit in it. And they got William Kemmler, who'd hit his girlfriend, Tillie Ziegler, with an axe. His lawyer appealed the hurried death sentence on the grounds that the electric chair was a cruel and unusual punishment. Westinghouse supported the appeal. William was put in a suit, had his head shaved, said, "Good luck," to the audience who had come to see the New Age.

The problem with what follows is that no one knew what was actually supposed to happen, except Mr. Kemmler, who calmly said that he was going to a better place, and to the executioner,

Edwin Davis, that he should do it properly, and that he was in no hurry. Edwin, who had been practicing on lumps of steak, said "Goodbye, William," and threw the switch. The current passed through the man for seventeen seconds. Just pause, look at your watch, and hold your breath for seventeen seconds. A doctor pronounced him dead, but the audience noticed, dead or not, he was still breathing. Another doctor, a Scotsman, concurred. There were still vital signs, and there was a call for more current. But they had to wait for a charge to build up. The second time, William's blood boiled, and his veins burst. There was smoke and sparks, and a smell of burning flesh. People tried to get out of the locked room. The entire process took eight minutes. It was horrific. As the *New York Herald* boomed the next day, "Strong men fainted and fell like logs on the floor." The oxymoronic State Commission for Humane Executions stated, "It was the greatest success of the age." I suppose that depended on what you wanted or expected from the future. Southwick, the killer driller, who naturally was in the stalls, said, "We live in a higher civilization from this day on," which must rank as one of the most astonishingly disconnected, contrarian observations ever made out loud by a dentist.

William Kemmler did posthumously decree a new word: electrocute, the portmanteau truncation of electric execution. And America got, for the best part of a century, the most modern means of execution that was less efficient than stoning to death. People make very bad conductors of electricity. They need to be hairless and wet, not too fat or stout-hearted. The electric chair got nicknames, and became a macabre folk image. Mississippi had a mobile one, "like a chair you might see on a porch," someone said. Andy Warhol made it a multiple. The chair joined the ghoulish items in arcade horror dungeons, and like most things that seem futuristic and prescient, it speedily became immensely dated, looking crude and ancient and cruel, as crass as a guillotine or gibbet. But in one sense it fulfilled the remit of the Electric Death Commission. It was, and is, utterly American. It became a symbol of American justice, of class, of race, of the cussed independence of states, of poverty, guns and frontier law. Winston Churchill said in 1944 that if Hitler were captured alive, he should be summarily killed in the electric chair, it was the death for gangsters, and then added that they'd probably be able to get a chair on lend-lease. But the electric chair is also the one piece of American culture that failed to travel. Only one other country ever used it—the Philippines. And it didn't even do what it was designed to do. Not kill people: it killed hundreds of people. It didn't kill AC current.

In 1893, despite fearsome lobbying, just three years after the death of William Kemmler, the Niagara Falls Power Company chose to go with AC current to feed the industry of Buffalo, which became briefly known as the electric city of the future. Every new generator and electric plant followed suit. By the sixties, the only places still using DC were bits of Stockholm, and Beaufort Street and Commonwealth Avenue in Boston, where it regularly blew up domestic appliances—most often Mr. Edison's record players.

Almost immediately after the Niagara decision, Edison bought up a competing company that used Tesla's alternating current. That, after all, was the smart capitalist choice, the modern choice. And anyway, Edison was privately, personally, against capital punishment. But this was business. He didn't have a particularly proselytizing animus toward murderers or cats and dogs, though the one successful thing that came out of this bizarre corporate battle was Harold Brown's peripatetic pet executions. Today, this very day, 319,178 pigs will walk onto the electric yoga mat and be electrocuted with an alternating current—humane, clean and efficient.

But here, finally, is the really odd, the really mental thing. Topsy was executed in 1903—ten years after the argument was lost. Edison was already making money out of AC current. Why did he do it? Why electrocute an elephant in copper shoes? Because he could? Because old habits die hard? Because it was there? For a bet? A dare? Or just because he wanted to make an elephantine snuff movie? Maybe he was bonkers. There is, in America, a thick, rich seam of bonkers. Bonkers people and things. Bonkers ideas and beliefs. Bonkers that goes beyond the merely eccentric, and that we guiltily recognize back here in the Old World. It has a familiar expression. That American, mono-obsessive, driven loopiness is ours—principally Northern European. And I'd go out on a limb and suggest actually most of it comes from East Anglia. Although most immigrants were economic or political or opportunist, there were also a disproportionately large number of men who were on missions—pilgrims with new visions and secrets, formulas and plans, with diets and purges, men with personal maps for apocalypses and the code for salvation, men with universal cures.

Europe is, for the most part, a hugger-mugger continent that works best on the consensus of inertia and precedent. Those who have dogmatic and contrarian beliefs can cause disproportionate ructions and ripples in our overcrowded and hierarchical communities. America is the place with the space and horizons for the really committed, swivel-eyed, self-appointed prophet. So the boats for the New World would attract a fair number of itinerant, frothing Prosperos, and they have sown a contrarian furrow in American life, an expectation of inspired madness. There is a theory that bravery and intrepidness and extreme risk taking are all sorts of madness, and that only one person in 1,000 or 100,000 is born without the normal safety rail of self-preservation, the pressing need to turn around and go home when it's dark, cold and frightening. A few humans are actually drawn to the edge, and as a species we need them. They are the innovators and the explorers, the decorated heroes. They are also, more often than not, prematurely posthumous. The loonies, the visionaries and the fearless have a much higher mortality rate than, say, the writers who memorialize them. In fact, a considerable number never make it past adolescence—they fall out of trees, into rivers, they crash bikes and overdose. But they are humanity's pathfinders. We need them to see what's on the other side of the mountain, to set up the rope bridge, to navigate the rapids, to fight the bears, to find fire. It is the bonkers who hold the Prometheus Gene, and a significant number of immigrants who came to the New World had it. It leads to Lewis and Clark, to Custer and Daniel Boone. It also leads to Ted Bundy, Billy the Kid and Charles Manson, as well as Teddy Roosevelt and Carnegie, Morgan and Edison. The

Prometheus Gene gave America its entrepreneurs and inventors, the railway navigators and polar explorers, and a great many insistent voices in the dark of the night, promising a proprietary brand of God.

America, built on religious contrarianism, has incubated a far wider and more exotic range of votive beliefs than anywhere else on earth, with the possible exception of India. And without wanting to disparage anyone's fondest faith, America's big sky and bigger spiritual yearning has led to some truly eye-bulging and belief-suspending premises for salvation. It's difficult to imagine that the golden plates engraved with the book of Mormon could have been found anywhere but in the New World, or that L. Ron Hubbard would have found a congregation for Scientology. The fervor of religious experience has been a constant throttle and brake on American life, from the witch hunts of seventeenth-century Massachusetts to the New Age pantheistic hedonism and self-help of twenty-first-century Arizona.

There are Aspinalls in the family. I don't quite know where they fit. Everyone else on my father's side are Taylors or Thomases. But the family Bible from the eighteenth century has the records of the hatching, matching and dispatching of Aspinalls, and some of them turned up in America, and then in the commonplace book of cuttings that's beside me as I write. Bethel Aspinall came to America with a small fortune. Before he could spend his money he went to travel the country. He stopped in Memphis, Tennessee. He pressed the button for a lift, stood under the lintel on the edge of a great new world. The door opened. He stepped over, and fell to his death.

8

Skyscrapers

The international measure of impatience is generally agreed to be the time between pushing the button for the lift and then pushing it again, in the animistic unbelief that the blind machine somewhere above will hear you and understand your irritation, glean that you're in a hurry, ignore other pushed buttons on other floors, and descend to your needs. But here's a funny thing. The first lift shaft was built four years before the first lift. In 1852 Peter Cooper was constructing the Cooper Union building in New York with an elevator shaft, in the sure and certain knowledge that if he built it, the lift would come. That isn't an act of impatience, it's an act of faith, and it is, archetypally, the act of an American.

The first lift actually went into the EU Horton building on the corner of Broome and Broadway in Manhattan. Installed by Elisha Otis, whose name you still see on most elevators and escalators, the lift is still there, still carrying people to the fifth floor.

But, unfortunately for the story, this isn't the first lift, and Otis didn't invent it. Archimedes invented some sort of lift, and there have been cages worked by pulleys and cranes operated by men or animals for thousands of years. Coal mines had lifts that descended hundreds of feet. There were already hydraulic lifts, cylinders helped by counterweights that would push up cages using water or oil. They couldn't go very far because you needed a hole under the building as high as the shaft in the building, and as my poor Aspinall relative discovered, those weren't very safe—not safe enough to make living on the sixth floor a carefree proposition. What Elisha Otis did invent was the safety lift—an automatic stop before you hit the bottom. A sure-thing, bet-your-life brake.

And, in traditionally Yankee showman style, he demonstrated it at the World's Fair of 1854 by having himself hoisted. And then with a roll of drums, the rope suspending the cage was cut. The box shuddered, stumbled, but held fast. It was what cities had been waiting for. Elisha hadn't invented the lift. What he had invented was the walk-up. That poor thing—the filing cabinet of failure and depression—the apartment block without mechanical ascension.

Otis later made a special lift for the Cooper Union out of gratitude for the faith it had shown. Peter Cooper had imagined that lifts would be oval. They turned out to be square, but Otis generously built a bespoke one. The Cooper Union was, and still is, a school. Peter Cooper was a self-taught entrepreneur who believed with a fearsome fervor that education should be free— as free as water, as free as air—to all classes, colors, races and sexes. Which was quite a radical open house for the middle of the nineteenth century. His school was an academy of practicality and invention. In its hall, Abraham Lincoln made a speech that became known as the Cooper Union Address, in which he laid out why federal land, the territories to the west that were not yet states, should be free of slavery. He said of the South's refusal to compromise, "You will rule or ruin in all events." And he finished with the clarion phrase "Let us have faith that right makes might," a thought that could be the motto on a dollar bill. Since Lincoln, Presidents Grant, Cleveland, Taft, Roosevelt (T.), Wilson, Clinton and Obama have all spoken here, as have Mark Twain, Salman Rushdie and Hugo Chávez.

Peter Cooper once ran for president—it's a very rich-American thing to do. He made his money from glue. His wife, Sarah, put fruit in the glue and invented Jell-O. Being in the just glue, not just desserts business, they sold the recipe and it was sold again, a few times, until somebody finally had the bright, new-American idea of marketing Jell-O by sending out hundreds of salesmen with recipe leaflets, thereby coming up with something called mass marketing, as well as the sublimely named "congealed salad." Jell-O is powdered gelatin with a fruity flavoring. You add hot water and then chill it. To this you might add chopped things, fruit, vegetables, eggs, marshmallows, pretzels. The list was as long and impressionistic as Friday night vomit. Typically, the Jell-O would be poured into a circular cake mold. A lot of German immigrants would have brought those with them, so you'd have a circle of tomato jelly, and in the middle, perhaps Russian salad or coleslaw, maybe pickled fish. These were cheap and festive and easy and turned out to be particularly popular at communal meals and potluck lunches. Presumably because you wouldn't have to eat them yourself.

This coming together of young mothers and neighbors in societies and clubs was symptomatic of immigrant people eager to dig foundations, join in new communities, make friends. Jell-O reverted to its origins—it was the glue of small towns and new suburbs, and has risen to the acme by becoming the official snack of Utah, where you can eat it in any one of the Chuck-A-Rama chain of home-cooked buffet diners. There is not much to say about Chuck-A-Rama, except that it was named by Don and his son Dwayne Moss as a nod to the chuck wagons of the pioneers, and Don's passion for Scout-O-Rama, whatever that is. And once, in the Tailorville outlet, a couple on the Atkins diet were asked to leave after visiting the roast meat stand twelve times. Later, Dwayne apologized.

Obviously I only mention Chuck-A-Rama because it is head and shoulders the worst name for a restaurant ever written in ten-foot-high letters on a freeway billboard, and is an example of a particularly American ability to come up with consistently dreadful names for new things. Just as there is an inspiring national talent to invent stuff and to think forward, so there is an equal and opposite imaginative black hole when it comes to naming the stuff: the conflation and truncation of words, adding extraneous vowels and hyphens to the portmanteau. Here, in one story, we have the wonderfully appalling examples of Jell-O, congealed salad and Chuck-A-Rama. There is even a kind of Jell-O called D-Zerta. But just to walk down the central aisle of prepared goods in an American supermarket is to be assaulted by a big top of infantilized clowns' names: the mincing, mangling and mutilating of language to simplify and cretinize. Aristotle devoted his life to the naming of flora and fauna, and Carl Linnaeus labored to codify the strata, layers and classification of all living things with the luxury of both a Latin and a common name. Just think of the gallimaufry of beautiful, evocative, witty and onomatopoeic appellations that ordinary folk have rolled over their tongues for hundreds and thousands of years, to familiarize and encompass and know the stock of the world. And then consider what the American advertising and promotional industry has invented, that hideous, discordant, sugary earful of exclamatory graffiti: Friskies, Cheez-It, Chips Ahoy, Kool-Aid, Softsoap, Wonder Bread, Cling Free, Cheez Doodles, Twinkies—they sound like the inglorious dead on a memorial to street mimes.

Thomas Edison was a graduate of Cooper Union. Like Otis, he is principally famous for things he didn't do. He didn't invent electricity, or the lightbulb, the phonograph or the movies. These misappropriations didn't bother him much: he didn't correct folk. What he was good at, what he really knew, was patents. Between 1860 and 1890 there were 500,000 patents registered in America. Monopoly is the story of nineteenth-century fortunes. Edison was bombastic, driven, ruthless, litigious and popular. He became the archetype of an American businessman—brash, brilliant, mendacious and public. He and Otis both created enormous multinational companies—General Electric is still the biggest publicly traded business in the world. But it was another man who stands between Otis and Edison, who arguably made a greater impact on the rise of America in the nineteenth century. Ladies and gentlemen, a big hand and a big thank-you for Frank J. Sprague. Not a name that rolls off the tongue—barely gets over the teeth. But Frank Sprague left the cities of America American. The places that we know, even if we've never traveled to them.

Born in 1857, he joined the navy. He was a naturally inquisitive engineer and installed the first system of electric bells on a naval ship, the USS *Lancaster*. He was the only American judge for pumps and generators at the Great Exhibition in the Crystal Palace, and then Edison lured him from the navy to come and work at Menlo Park, New Jersey, the first commercial laboratory of invention in the world. Edison had a real knack for discovering bright sparks. He'd noticed that the laboratory was very wasteful of effort—experiments were haphazard and merely inquisitive. Edison, for instance, tried out thousands and thousands of materials to find a filament for the electric lamp: human hair, coconut. Sprague used mathematics to rationalize expected outcomes and, while Edison was obsessed with light, he was more interested in electric engines. He left the laboratory to work on his own, apparently without making a lifelong enemy of Edison, which was unusual.

In quick succession Sprague came up with things that, put together, didn't so much change the American city as free it up to become itself. His great gift was to make electric motors efficient. He discovered a way to reclaim power, to pay it back to the main supply.

He didn't, in fact, invent the electric lift. That was done by the Siemens brothers, or more precisely, Werner von Siemens, while he was in jail in Germany for coming second in a duel. He also invented a new way of electroplating silver and gold, and was furious when he was pardoned, as leaving his cell deprived him of peace and quiet. But the Siemenses were more interested in communications, that was their thing. So they abandoned the lift and Sprague used his new motor to make it much, much more efficient, both in its power and its use of space. He had trouble selling it. Hydraulic lift companies did their best to stop it being introduced. Finally, Frank Sprague managed to sell a couple to the post office, but only when he'd agreed to install hydraulic ones when his own failed. They didn't. And he went on to invent the overhead trolley pole; his improved motors had the traction to get up one-in-ten hills. It was a huge improvement on cable cars like the ones that climbed up San Francisco. The first town to invest in the immense infrastructure of trolley buses was Richmond, Virginia, in 1889. By 1890, there were 110 in production or planned. Sprague sold his motor company to Edison in 1895 after getting orders to build forty-nine lifts for the Central Line on the London Underground.

He sold the elevator business to Otis and then took his electric motors and put them in train carriages—one to each coach—that were all linked and could be driven by a conductor sitting in the front or the back, which meant that you could run a railway without an engine. Chicago was the first city to buy it—it became the elevated railway, the "L"—then Brooklyn, New York and Boston, and finally he improved his lift so that you could run two lifts independently at different speeds in the same shaft, thereby saving even more space. He sold that idea to Westinghouse.

Sprague's inventions—mass transit and safe, efficient elevators—made the modern American city function, with their distinctive pace and look. Today in Manhattan, just over 30 percent of households own a car. In central London, just over 30 percent don't. Efficient mass transit meant that people could work further from where they lived. He invented daily commuting. But, most dramatically of all, the electric safety lift is the yeast that makes skyscrapers rise. No other single thing is more emblematic of America—its power, its aspiration and its people—than these god-bothering fingers.

It's not exactly quite precisely true that the lift invented the skyscraper: there was another element—the steel or concrete armature that you can hang a building on. There is a limit to the size a masonry or brick-built building can grow before it can no longer sustain its own weight, though until the twentieth century the tallest and largest buildings in the world were masonry built. The cathedral spire of Ulm was the tallest building until the Eiffel Tower, and the Jetavana Dagoba Stupa in Sri Lanka is the largest brick building. But in practical terms, they're not much use as mixed-use office and residential with retail opportunities at street level. For something that is quite so totemically American it's odd that nobody really knows what a skyscraper is. Well, we all know one when we see one, but there is no official classification or definition of skyscraperness. And, most un-Americanly, there is no minimum height, no lower limit for the number of floors. The name skyscraper is originally nautical. Skyscraper is the tiny, triangular sail flown from the top of the mast.

There is an argument about which building was actually the first skyscraper. The likeliest candidate is the Equitable Life Insurance Building, 120 Broadway, New York. It was 130 feet tall and had eight floors. Six floors is the usual limit for pedestrianized properties. Like a lot of Manhattan buildings it had a partial iron frame. It burned down in 1912. In 1884 the Home Insurance Building in Chicago was constructed with a steel frame on which the floors and the walls were hung. It was 138 feet and ten stories high. Neither building looks terribly distinguished in the context of their cities. No one today would point at them and say, "Look at that skyscraper." They are nineteenth-century offices with a couple of more floors. In 1888 an architect predicted buildings he called stratosphere-scrapers, that would reach an unimaginable twenty-eight floors. He was mocked. Then in 1890 Louis Sullivan and Dankmar Adler put up the Wainwright Building on Chestnut Street, St. Louis. It was instantly recognizable as something new. It leaped a decade and became a predictor, a talisman for the new century. It left behind all the accessories and frills of European architecture. It makes no reverential references to Gothic or baroque. There is no mannerist decoration or robber-baron commercial insecurity about its façade. It is all-American: clean, clear straight up, imposing. It could have grown out of no other earth. It belongs to no one's vernacular but its own. Sullivan wrote: "The skyscraper must be tall, every inch of it tall. The force and power of altitude must be in it, the glory and pride of exhilaration must be in it. It must be every inch a proud and soaring thing, rising in sheer exhilaration that, from bottom to top, is a unit without a single dissenting line." That's a pretty good definition.

The high towers and the lift invented a new space, a new etiquette for being close to strangers, with minimal eye contact, no conversation and no farting. Lifts are small, mute dramas full of tension, loved by filmmakers and slapstick comedians. The lift became a photo booth, a minute theater, a little scene from your own daily soap opera. It added a new sensation to city life: the pleasurable stomach lurch of ascent, and sometimes the popping of an ear. The lifts in apartment blocks became small parlors of polite inquiry, staccato conversations of neighborliness and the overfriendly, waspish niceties directed at Hispanic doormen. They also inverted the hierarchy of space. For 3,000 years the most sought-after rooms were on the first floor—or the second floor if you're an American. The piano nobile, the grand first floor, was for animals or the shop. One flight up was the master bedroom and reception rooms, and the further up you went, the lower your status. Scullery maids roosted like swallows in the eaves. But the lift brought us to the penthouse to live with the angels, the glass walls, the silent buffet of the wind, the hiss of climate control. And beneath the great, blinking panorama of the city, wall evaporated into air. No art or bookshelf could compete with the view of omnipotence, the sense of living on Parnassus, a double-glazed Valhalla. And a view suddenly had a value—real estate agents could sell something they didn't own.

Skyscrapers have remained a quintessentially American vernacular. Everyone else seems just to get them plain wrong. In Europe they were seen first as ugly civil engineering, a cheap mop bucket for slums where low-level poverty could become vertical poverty. The streets in the skies that socialist councillors boasted about in England were stinking, frightening alleys. The miraculous lifts were drunks' lavatories, stairwell shooting galleries and bordellos for lotharios who were still living with their mums. In Europe, the packs of high-rise public housing are familiar from the outskirts of cities. The old centers were preserved with a cultural conservatism. The reason that skyscrapers don't really work in the Old World is architectural snobbery: even the most ordinary Victorian terrace is preferable to anything a contemporary aesthetic can dream up. And there is still the nagging resentment that the modernist tower was so obviously American. Europeans should not be importing their sensibilities from over the Atlantic. Skyscrapers work in America because they are loved and valued, not as cheap packaging for a messy underclass but as pinnacles of aspiration. Their symbolism is completely different. They are the axis mundi. The rod around which the world spins. The point of the compass.

There are other high-rise skyscraper cities—mostly in the developing world. They are homages to the mercantile muscle of New York. They are built as an omen to lure wealth. New York is the start of the modern, and right from the beginning there was a race for the top, and for most of us, forever, the Empire State Building will be the tallest in the world. Like the racing cars of the fifties that still look properly fast, the Empire State Building looks like what the tallest building in the world should look like. Ever since the race for height left the United States it has become ever sillier and uglier. As I write it rests with the Burj Khalifa in Dubai—a city that is an idiot's cartoon version of America, a place that bought the look like a label-obsessed bimbo without bothering with the ethos. The Burj Khalifa tower soars without meaning or interest. It was opened at about the same time a thirteen-year-old climbed Everest. The effort for highest has become devalued to chump change. But the sight of Chicago or New York still astonishes. The old, four-story assumption that skyscrapers are essentially alienating and antihuman, that they reduce the majesty of mankind to specks, to grist in the machine, is patently untrue. We are a species that is used to living with things that are bigger than us: mountains and forests, rivers and seas, deserts and steppes. In fact, almost everything is bigger than us. We walk down the avenues of Manhattan and feel elevated by the buildings. Skyscrapers have a collective, panoramic power. They are again evocations of the sublime. They rise up to make us aware of the accomplishment and the brilliance of our clan—collectively and individually. And that was one of the great tautologies, the triumphant contradiction of America, that e pluribus unum—one people out of many. But it was also one *person* out of the many. Frank Sprague invented one other thing: the electric lift call button—the measure of New World time and aspiration.

9

Stories

When the Thomas brothers' dude ranch in Arickaree, Colorado, didn't prosper, they did what so many would-be pioneers and new-again agrarians did. They packed up the cart, had a sale in the yard and sold the bits and pieces to the next sucker with soft hands to come and try his luck. They headed out, waving goodbye to the neighbors they'd never see again. Perhaps it's easier the second time. After the first cut of leaving home, does that scar make it lighter to move on? Is it a learned accommodation, a reason that Americans still seem to find their roots are so shallow, so easily transplanted? This peripatetic gene, the default of renaissance, the permission and the ability to walk away was the great new deal of America. To be dealt a whole new hand has the constant reprieve of optimism. Fitzgerald's mordant observation that there are no second acts in American lives sounds like a poignant dying fall, but is plainly and patently not just untrue but precisely the opposite of the truth. It is in Europe that we are born and bred to a single role. America is populated by second acts, encores and revivals.

So, Will and Tom the cowboys left for the city. Quite why they chose Detroit is a mystery. It may have something to do with that Bethel Aspinall who died falling down the lift shaft in Memphis. The report of his death says that he was newly from England and left $100,000. In the family cuttings book there is also a long eulogy for another Aspinall, Joe, from a Detroit paper reprinted in the *Yorkshire Post*. He was apparently the first man to build a steam-powered woolen mill on Hebble Brook in 1807, and then immigrated to Detroit to become one of the founders of the Board of Trade. The grateful members passed a resolution to spend $200 on a portrait of him. Among other things, Joe had a building firm, and I know that the Thomas boys went to Michigan to make bricks. Being in the brick-making business in the 1890s was a smart move. Before Detroit's image and associations were merged with the motorcar and Motown, it was hubristically known as the Paris of the West, presumably by people who had never been to Paris, or possibly the West. The brothers set up Thomas Bros. and according to the *Detroit Free Press* were the city's sole agents for hydraulic-pressed bricks, which were used on the fronts of many of the best buildings. Their tiles furnished many roofs. They made Detroit, and Detroit made them. The Thomases flourished and prospered. A William George Thomas finds himself in the *Denver Daily News* in a marvelously operatic and purple report concerning "a penchant for forging his father's signature in a too-promiscuous manner." William was the city's guest at police headquarters.

He is a comely youth of 19, the beauty of whose boorish face had ne'er been marred by moustache or whiskers. Young Thomas had long posed as a blood. He has been somewhat handicapped by a rather limited supply of the long green, but hit upon a happy opportunity, and being well-acquainted with his paternal relative's signature he sought to imitate it. The smooth-faced youth roiled in opulence. Young Thomas was an admirer of the stage, and mightily worshipped at the shrine of stars whose charms were the attraction at The Olympic—a variety show. Here the boy forger was a prince—nothing was too good. The ladies worshipped him. Either a suspicion that it would be worse for him to migrate, or a sudden desire to investigate the Wild West induced Thomas to bid adieu. At the same time, two lady performers were about to start for Denver. William came along. His father caught onto the dishonest practices his heir was indulging in. He summarily stopped William's promising career by telegraphing Chief Farley to look for the youth. The task of ferreting out the young Thomas was entrusted to detectives Ingersoll and Leydon, and their prey was soon run down. They first arrested the young ladies who were accompanying young Thomas on his

Western tour. They reluctantly accepted the hospitality offered by the prison matron, being held as hostages. He was easily traced and placed under arrest. His capture affected the lad greatly, and tears flowed copiously. While Thomas chafed at his confinement and shuddered at the awful thought of the hereafter, his two ladies compassionately sobbed for Willie. Annie Belle and Maud Lewis were the names of the girls with whom the youth fell in love. They are both pretty, and charming enough to cause cupid's darts to enter the heart of men more sedate than a 19-year-old boy. Annie's principal charm is a wealth of golden hair, and she is as vivacious as a child of 12, and has barely passed 16. Her accomplishments in the Vaudeville line consist in her ability to perform trapeze acts so gracefully that man's admiration is enamored. More sedate than Annie is her companion Maud, but not one whit less attractive, although several years her senior. She too hugely enjoys the novel experience she has undergone. When a news reporter called on the maidens yesterday, Ms. Lewis gravely opened the door asking, are you a detective? Upon receiving a negative reply, both girls chorused, "Come in." Obeying, the twain gave him a detailed recital of her connection with William George Thomas. "He was just awful anxious to pay our fare, and we let him," chimed in Miss Belle: "William was an exemplary young man in his treatment of us until Monday evening, when he came up here with two young men. Then he said something to me that I resented. I ordered him and his friends out of the room, and if he had not obeyed, you bet I would have put them out, for I am rather muscular myself." During this communication, Ms. Lewis sat demurely sewing on a pretty garment in pink, intended to adorn her person. She is rather silent and apparently hugely enjoyed all her lively companion's sallies. She is an artist who skillfully holds her audience with the song and dance act. Both girls feel sorry for their friend, but yet rather glad he is so easily got rid of.

That is just such a brilliant piece of reporting: so vivid that it's not reading, it's watching. Back over the brittle yellow paper, past four generations, I know all these people. I can see the pretty pink garment and I tip a cap to the anonymous hack who wrote it.

And then there was Fred J. Thomas, who, according to the clippings that dot the book, was a good, nice man; blessed and popular. A cutting calls him "the jolly paymaster of the Detroit and Milwaukee railroad, and the happiest man in town, because a month ago a pair of little strangers arrived at his house with the intention of remaining there as permanent boarders," and his fellow employees at the railway presented him with the "handsomest double-barreled baby carriage ever seen in the Northwest." The gift had been ordered from New York. The presentation speech was made by Superintendent Callaway, after which the twins were placed on exhibition and greatly admired. Then, thirty or forty pages on and sixty years later, here's his obituary, with a photograph of a smiling, avuncular man with elegant whiskers. He looks like the most popular, friendly man in the world. It's the sort of face they put on humbug packets or pancake mix. He died of Bright's disease. It doesn't exist anymore—or rather, it's not a diagnosis anymore. It's a severe kidney condition: blood in the urine, back pain, water retention, phantom testicle ache, death through high blood pressure and renal failure. For many years he managed the entertainments given by the Board of Trade for the benefit of the industrial school. He wrote a series of operettas which were produced on these occasions: *The Honest Burglar, Our Mama, A Child for Adoption* and *Border Belles.* You can just hear them—the patter of sentimental ballads, the tintinnabulation of the titles. You can see the amateur baritones with the top hats and the rouge, the coy, white-faced coal-eyed ingénues, the dames in drag, the hallooing of the audience joining in with choruses, the bunting, the declamatory swagger, the embrace of the dénouement. His eulogies are effusive, stuffed with the mordant, Tennysonian clichés of the age: "Frederick W. Thomas has obeyed the summons to join those who move toward the mysterious realm." "In his heart was the pearl of honesty," and what could have been better than to be a respected railwayman, that harbinger and paymaster of the smoking, puffing, indomitable engine of the modern, at the turn of the greatest century, in a wildly optimistic, bursting town? He had four children, all girls, and that's what he looks like: a man who's been surrounded by the love of fussing women.

Women turn out to be the Thomas weakness. There is an unspoken theme in these memories stuck in the cuttings book. Next to Fred's obituary and the black-edged card from the Indian Village Club, there is Albert B. Thomas, a rather different color of Thomas. Here's a drawing of him, a pertly, feebly handsome man, hair neatly parted in the middle, a dandy's moustache, limpid, insincere eyes. I bet he smelled nice. He's had to resign as the secretary of the Detroit Stock Exchange after proceedings were opened for his second divorce in a year. The first Mrs. Thomas cut him loose for extreme cruelty and immediately married her sister's widower, moving to Seattle with their only child, while the debonair stockbroker Thomas took up with Miss Ethel Riminson, formerly of the Telephone Girl Vaudeville Company (here we go again), who had been touring in a production of *The Girl with the Auburn Hair*. In her photograph she looks handsome enough, comely rather than pretty, by the lights of the time. Big, deep eyes, bowed lips set in a round face, not exactly with the dew of youth on her cheek. She sued for divorce within eight months of getting hitched in New York and set down that her husband treated her very cruelly, grasping her by the throat and choking her, using violent and threatening language. Some of his talk, she said, would not bear repetition. He told her to "go back to the low life" he said she'd led before they married.

Besides this report there is another that has been folded over. It says that Albert has been fined $25 or sixty days for hitting a chemist clerk over the head with his cane, cutting him badly. The chap was trying to dun him for a bill of $20. Albert Thomas sounds like an unpleasant piece of work. The cuttings go on to say that he told friends he intended to fight the divorce for the reason that he cared for her and hoped to once more win her affections:

> Mrs. Thomas is at present filling an engagement with Todd's Band, and the first step toward a reconciliation was taken by

Thomas a few evenings ago while the band was giving a concert at Clarke's Park. At the end of Mrs. Thomas' number, she was presented with a magnificent bouquet of flowers. There was no card, but she knew that it had come from her husband, and those who witnessed the little drama say she was completely overcome with her emotions. A nice little note of thanks was sent to her husband and he said the divorce suit will be quietly dropped.

Well, you just know that A. B. Thomas's story is not going to end well. And three years later there is the penultimate ochre sliver of paper from the *Detroit Post*. His story goes from comic to tragic pathos:

Albert B. Thomas, former secretary of the Detroit Stock Exchange, is in jail, accused of petty crimes. He is the victim of paresis. In the opinion of Dr. William Hanlen and Dr. I. L. Polozker, progressive paralysis set in a half dozen years ago. With that has come a breakdown of mind and body. In the paralytic state the victim imagines he has vast wealth and is the hero of great exploits. Dr. Hanlen thinks if Thomas made false pretenses as to his wealth, he fully believed them to be true. "You know, I sold $770,000 of Detroit telephone stock to the Michigan telephone people," said Thomas, "and never knew what would happen to the stock holders till I saw 774 names of telephone victims in the journal. I was educated at Annapolis, and when I graduated at 19, I went with Captain Forbush on the *Marion* to the Japan station. I was a second lieutenant. On the way running back to Santiago de Chile, we were caught in the most horrific typhoon that I ever passed through. I was on starboard dogwatch, and when the captain was called, the guns were lashed and ropes and cables fastened to all parts of the ship. We battened down, and I went up to the bridge to mark her course. It took four men to hold that ship on the frightful storm, and I stood 79 hours on the bridge in full charge. After all was over I slept for 36 hours, and smoked cigarettes all the afternoon in a steamer chair. After we got to Santiago I was assigned to the quarter deck under Rear Admiral Winslow in the

Mediterranean squadron. Then the *Bear* and *Thetis* were given to the government by Great Britain, to seek out Greeley in the Arctics. Lieutenant Commander Schley, as he was then, had two whaling captains under him, who understood the Northern currents. We went up to Point Barrow on the upper coast of Alaska, and then struck eastward to the mouth of the McKenzie. Then we got caught in the ice and drifted westward to the Siberian tundras. And one day, when the men were shooting polar bears for food, we found a piece of wood. More precious then than gold. The word "Probyloff" was scratched on it with a piece of ice. "Problyoff"—miles and miles from civilization. There we found Greeley and 17 of his sailors, out of 600 who'd started out. Frozen and starved, and rotten with scurvy. Oh, it was a pity to see them. They had lived so long up there among those Laps that they had forgotten the English language. Yessir, when we got them down towards the Ukon, Schley's surgeons and doctors brought them round alright, and they had learned English from us. They were a noble-looking lot of fellows. Then I found I was made Lieutenant Commander. After that I went to the embassy at Paris, at Berlin, at St. Petersburg, and at the court of St. James, and came home to the Spanish War. I commanded the *Vesuvius* there and I condemned her. My uncle Will is using the patent of the Earldom of Scarthmore in Yorkshire, England. But I have the crest and seals and own all the castles and estates. I am the Earl of Scarthmore really. That sounds like a damn fool proposition?" He laughed heartily. "I'm nervous about being here. The naval department may shorten my leave, and I want to be well enough to go back. But I can fix it alright." With these, and other wild stories, Thomas has entertained his neighbors in the jail.

Immediately under this story there is a little clipping that says: "AB Thomas dead. July 19 1905. Mr. Thomas was suffering with locomotor ataxia, and his brain became affected. His friends had him placed at Eloise, where he has since remained. He married Dorothy Robinson, an actress. She was suing him for divorce at the time of his removal." There is something Fitzgeraldish in A. B. Thomas. The weakness, the charm, the anger, the failure, the sex and the fantasy. And for him, there was no second act. Beside his death notice there is a small social announcement telling us that "Mrs. Frederick Thomas and Mabel M. Thomas are at Grey Gables, Grosse Pointe, for the summer. Mrs. William Taylor and Miss May Taylor will be the guests of Mrs. Thomas until they return to England in June."

May Taylor was my grandmother, just a teenager. She traveled on the *Lucania* to visit her cousins. It was an immensely important trip. The resonance of it, the poignancy of it, would remain vividly with her for the rest of her life. She would speak of it in a whispered voice, her eyes always looking into the corner of the room. She spoke of seeing Indians, real Red Indians in wigwams. She spoke of the lake, and the space, the country club and the cars, the great houses of Grosse Pointe, the elbow room and the new gentility. America was always a benefactor to her, a haven, a place of wonder and promise, and she passed that on to me. Her brother, Clifford, came over to start his new life: went out to Detroit to work with his cousins at Thomas Bros. in the brick business. They were very close, May and Clifford. She adored him, he always protected her. Their separation was a leitmotif of loss and a cause of pride for her, as for so many immigrants and their families. He grew to be intensely American while remaining solidly Yorkshire, returning to fight in the Great War as a volunteer in the American army. He lost a leg. The family story goes that while being invalided back to England on a troop train, another soldier complained about the terrible smell in the carriage. "I'm sorry, that'll be my leg," said Uncle Clifford, removing the offensive rot with his pocketknife. This last detail may have been added by childishly gory imagination. He sent back money, bought my grandparents a car—this was an unheard-of luxury for the bank clerk my grandfather was—and during rationing he sent food. And with it came the image of America as the redoubt of hope and plenty. In my grandparents' house there were little mementoes of Americana:

the bowl for the cranberry sauce, the board my granddad taught me to play checkers on. They said it came from the original ranch in the Arickaree, and that Buffalo Bill had played on it.

When I was ten my newly widowed grandmother was staying with us. I came home from school to find her crying. I'd never seen an old person cry before; I'd never seen her cry for my grandfather. She sat neat and straight in our sitting room, hands in her lap, holding the small, lace-trimmed handkerchief that lived up her sleeve like a magician's sneeze. She made no sound, the tears streamed soft on her cheek. She was embarrassed to be seen, as I was to see her. I didn't ask. I found my mother in the kitchen and she said quietly that my grandmother was sad because the president of America had been killed. We don't any longer ask people where they were when they heard Kennedy was shot, because now most people weren't born. What I remember, why I remember where I was when I heard Kennedy was shot, is my grandmother crying. I don't think it was particularly for Kennedy—she'd probably have preferred Nixon. It was the sadness. The tears were for America, an empathy with a nation. She owed it her sorrow.

The television news that night had film from the American Embassy in London. There weren't that many Americans in London in the sixties. Students and businessmen mostly—but here they were sitting on the steps in Grosvenor Square, sobbing and stunned, holding their heads and each other. I remember a man punching something inanimate—a tree, a wall. The BBC reporter, with that clipped urgency that broadcast journalists used, asked a little group why they were there, with an incredulous lift before the question mark. I remember a girl—I've made her beautiful, American, limber and straight, healthy with a clear, strong face— but she probably comes from some advertisement. What I do remember clearly is what she said. "We just wanted to be close to our country." Even then, to a ten-year-old, that seemed unbearably touching, as if the country, that vast, hard, rich place, needed the comfort of this girl. We are used to nations being called mother or father, given cartoon embodiments, John Bull and Britannia. But the idea of my country needing me for anything other than to be dressed in khaki at the end of a bayonet seemed unlikely. And certainly this old, smoky, blackened, damp place, that still smelled of coal gas and mince, didn't need a hug or the solace of loved ones. I tried to imagine the English traipsing to the embassy in Washington on hearing of the death of the Queen, so as to be closer to home, and frankly, I couldn't.

It was terribly important to my grandmother that we remained hands-clasped with our American cousins, Clifford's children and grandchildren. We are a small family; the connection was important, and I think she believed that it might again be a lifeline.

Every American family owns stories like the Thomases and the Taylors. They are fascinating because they are so ordinary, so typical. What is astonishing about them, and these newspaper cuttings, is that they are already so completely and unequivocally American. The language of the reporting is instantly recognizable. It is that applied, invisible conflation of the baroquely otiose with the down-home folksy that twangs both colloquial and authoritative. The syncopated sentences with the dabs of color. Already in the middle of the nineteenth century this is its own language, with a confidence that is missing in the strictly formulaic and classically polished English newspaper reports. American stories are not the stories of the Old World. They have the chatty feel of barroom anecdotes. America developed a narrative sense and a style that makes you believe that the plots of their lives, grown out of this earth, are caught in it. American English whittles and molds the stories and parables of the people who come to the New World. They become as familiar as fairy tales.

For years I've asked Americans to pass me their family stories. Usually they're not more than two or three generations old. Personal creation myths, they are worn smooth with telling, but they all have the same elements in them. Whether they start in the shtetls beyond Transylvania, the fjords of Scandinavia, the bogs of Kerry or the indentured poverty of Southern Italy, they are not European stories. They have a vivacity and a purpose that becomes an American story. And they all have consistent elements: first the hardship, the destitution, the despair, the sadness of leaving, the distance traveled, the work of a mythological harshness, the fortitude, the belief. And then there is always, inevitably, something else. The guiding, unseen hand. There's fortune: the luck, the serendipity, the coincidence that leads to the first break, the luck that finds the apartment, the lost uncle bumped into on a street corner, a girl glimpsed on a train or behind the counter of a delicatessen, the fortuitous marriage, the glint in the pan, the silver dollar discovered in the linen, the gift, the piece of advice, the wrong turning that turned out to be the best turning, the heads-up. American stories are made with hard-won fortune and stoic coincidence. There is a sense that these people and the people who came after them were blessed and chosen for a purpose by the dealer, by the turn of the river. There must be millions and millions of stories that withered on the branch; narratives that have no one to tell them, lost in paupers' graves, lonely suicides and sad, grim, chilly lives petering out without remission or payoff. America gave beginnings, dénouements and epilogues to the people who landed on it, and it's these countless odysseys that are the kindling of a culture that grew faster and louder, brighter and stronger, more fluently deep and effervescent than any in all civilization. The lucky truth is that America was *born* as a second act. Once is tragedy, twice is romance.

10

Sex

"They're better." Um, better how? "Better at It." Better than who? "Better than English blokes." Who says they're better? "Every body." Everybody? "Yes, it's a collective fact. Whaddayoucallit?" The received wisdom. "Yes, the received wisdom from the ladies' room is that American guys are better at sex than English guys— Europeans in general. They take it seriously, they get in there, they're enthusiastic. Not really about *you*, but about the sex. You see, that's the big difference, European guys think it's all about seduction and romance and stuff, and that's lovely, but the finale is getting you into bed. With American guys the seduction stuff is corny, the romance is the script from *Friends*, but the bedpost isn't the finishing post, it's the whistle. It's the pitch. I am their Super Bowl. American guys really want to be good at sex. America invented sport fucking. It's possibly America's greatest gift to the world. They train, they do push-ups, they read books, they're squeaky hygienic, they moisturize, they eat well. It's not vanity, it's training. It's no coincidence that Americans talk about 'scoring' with someone. If I don't have a screaming, claws-in-the-ceiling, humongous orgasm, they've failed. They're back on the bench shaving their balls, popping supplements. For an English guy, being good in bed is like being good in a room: they're polite, they're amusing, they have small talk, they know that girls go first, but it's all a sleight of hand. Parlor tricks. They do sexual etiquette, but for them, being good in bed is mostly being tidy, entertaining, and not farting. American boys do it *to* you, not with you. Which is perfect for a Saturday night, a weekend, the sum- mer, but you wouldn't want to live with one. It would be like being on a football field every night. The whole nine yards." That was a thirtysomething professional Englishwoman.

It's difficult writing about sex, because nobody knows anything, and everybody knows everything. They know so much that it's the only part of the body that can go missing. Take the G-spot. The end zone for sexual athletes, discovered and named by a German doctor, annotated, explained with guided tours as the Third Way, by people with leers after their names and sensible spectacles. They have flip charts about G-spots and how to get in touch with them. Then, last year, more serious people in white coats with no-nonsense underwear came along and said it was gone. Vanished, sunk. It never was. Just a wrinkle up the sleeve of fun. The G-spot was mythical. It was the Snark of female gratification. The Frumious Bandersnatch excised. Damn! After all that ferreting about. All those fingers arthritic and wrinkled like pale prunes. All the "Are we there yet?" How can you lose a bit of vagina? It's like being told Belgium doesn't exist, only sadder. That's why you can't write about sex. Because even the people who know everything know nothing.

But you couldn't write about America without sex. It is the V-8 under the hood of the nation. And if America didn't actually invent sex, then it does seem to have reinvented it: repackaged it, reconditioned it, and rewritten it. Given it, in short, a jolly good seeing to. To begin with, they discovered and encouraged the people who could actually have sex: teenagers. They invented them. The whole point and purpose of teenagers is sex. Everything about them is sex. They make music that is the sound track to sex, they pay for a fashion industry that advertises sex. They invented new places to have sex—in cars for instance. No one ever had sex in a car before American teenagers showed them how. They invented events for sex: proms, rock concerts, spring break, camp. America's genius has always been to take something old, familiar and wrinkled and repackage it as new, exciting and smooth. Inventing the teenager as the Third Age was the greatest marketing tool and economic golden calf of the twentieth century. Coupling them with sex invented a raw, intense, sleepless, firm, fit, brokenhearted priapic age.

America's greatest single gift back to the Old World is the blow job. Like so much, they didn't actually invent fellatio: you can find it on Greek vases. But they did elevate it, value it, made it a meal on its own. Rather like they invented brunch: the ingredients were all already there, it was just that no one had given it a name and a time and a place before. The blow job was any time, almost any place. It was gratification for busy people. You do me now, I'll do you later. No fuss, no mess, big grins all round. It was extracted from foreplay and bigged up. The blow job became an event. And the oddest thing happened to girls. They got good at it. American women got competitive, a can-do spirit kicked in. They exchanged tips, wrote semiserious articles and, most bizarrely, got together for self-help blow job seminars like Tupperware parties, where an expert (to begin with, generally a gay man) would teach the finer magic and explain how you build muscle, overcome gag reflexes. What had been a head-pulling, hair-pushing, pleading and bul-lying birthday treat became a girl thing. It was, in a weird, round-about way, about control. Taking back the joystick. This was not something that was done to you anymore, it was something you did to him. That was the theory. And, most important, it wasn't sex. Sex was intimate and precious, and you didn't just give that away. Sex may be only for The One, but a blow job was a trick, a skill, an achievement, and we all heard the American president say under oath, in close-up, in every kitchen, bar and bedroom in the world, "I did not have sexual relations with that woman."

There it was. The presidential seal of not-counting. A blow wasn't penetration. And it was just there, the great triumph of American teenage culture. It broke through into the mainstream, right up to the White House. When kids say politics has noth-ing to do with them, that nobody listens to them, you can say hey, hold up there, young fella. What about the blow job? You kids did that, you took it out of sex, out of the bedroom, out of guilt, out of sinfulness, out of lying to your mum, and you passed it onto the most powerful man in the world. Don't ever say no one listens to you when you talk with your mouth full.

Sex didn't have the best of starts in America. It nearly didn't make it at all. The first English colonists were the most proscriptive, repressed, judgmental and frustrated boatload of onanists in the flat world. The sweaty, self-mortifying black-hat Protestant mullahs of sixteenth-century Massachusetts, with their terror and their original sin, their fear and anger, their lustful loathing of women, the horror of breasts and of the moans in the night, the sweaty, moonstruck dreams of incubi and succubi, and the double-dicked devils, the familiar transforming dogs and cats and goats, sodomizing Beelzebub, all the horror of unlocking that septic well of lust and sperm, the witches' incantations, the cruel seductions and the displacement of the rack, the gibbet, the pressing stones, the birch, the ducking stool and the branding iron, all the sorry, symbolist projection of their thwarted libidos.

America reacted against that with waves of self-expression, self-abuse, liberation, subjugation, openness and voyeurism, freedom of speech and the billboard obligation to ogle. There are, as one American boy said to me, two ways in America to have sex. All the way, or save it for the honeymoon. It's either purity or porn. The constant tussle and tug of American prudery and license can look like the squirming on the sofa of hormone-maddened dry-humping teenagers. It's all spittle and thumbs. Both sides—the censorious and the libertarian—need the other to get off on. They are locked together in a masochistic clinch. This is the nation of checks and balances, but instead of creating a reasonable equilibrium the argument is like two 200-pound men shoving each other in a canoe. The fury and the spite, the murderous righteousness over abortion, contraception, marriage, divorce and homosexuality are hysterical. America pioneered the birth control pill in 1960, but Connecticut had to be forced by the Supreme Court to prescribe it to married couples in 1965. And only in 1973 was the prescription of contraceptives to the unmarried deemed to be a matter of personal privacy. But the righteous, restrictive religious intervention into other people's lives offered the leverage for two of the most memorable, admirable and successful movements of the twentieth century: women's liberation and gay rights. And while neither of these was solely or even primarily about sex, sex was the promise and the engine of both. They were part of what was loosely, and even admiringly or pejoratively, called the sexual revolution. From the fifties on, sex looked, smelled, sounded and tasted different. The smell of sex in the morning smelled like America, and like victory. The sexual revolution copyrighted medicinal sex, sport sex and psychological sex with the happy, self-serving belief that sex was good to you, so you should be good to sex. Indeed, the better you were, the fitter you'd get. Sex looked fit and energetic, muscular and blonde, probably with freckles. And best of all, it was innocent and dumb, like Marilyn Monroe, who wasn't really dumb, and wasn't really blonde. Sex was lights-on, growling jig-a-jig, with a mirror, minty breath, cherry lips, pine pits and peachy, lubricated vagina. Sex was a fruit salad at home, in the kitchen.

From England, American girls looked Amazonian, Elysian, knowing ingénues. They became the astral bedroom fantasy of the world. They were a sexual type that had never existed in Europe, where girls were demure or they were brassy. They could be smart and seductive, they could be cool and forbidding. They could be many, many sophisticated and innocent things, but they were never like American girls. It was an amazing piece of national PR. They were spread over everything American. American girls sold cars and gum and dishwashers, but in a homely, organic way.

My first knowledge of the cornucopia of goodness that was American sex was *Playboy* magazine. My father got it every month, because of the writing, obviously. I never read a word. I looked at it for the astonishing breasts. These otherworldly women, standing astride Harley-Davidsons or getting out of baths, playing with drum kits and skis, and lying on many, many, many beds. Oh, the pneumatic glossiness of them. The heavy, shiny pages of the magazine weren't big enough to hold them. They needed their own, larger sheets to contain their smooth, glowing, undulating pulchritudinousness. They were perfect, ripe. It was like seeing some dreamy fruit at the point of optimum, plumptious juiciness. *Playboy* was the harvest festival of sex: offerings of plenty. As a marketing invention, the centerfold was sublime brilliance. It didn't feel prurient or dirty or seedy to look at these naked women: they weren't remotely like anyone we knew. *Playboy* was the *National Geographic* of urbanity. My mother would snort and say, "They're not real, you know, those girls," and they weren't. That was their joy. In 1960s England our girls weren't even from the same species. We had jolly ladies in *Health and Efficiency* magazine, supposedly produced for nudists, but really for thirteen-year-olds with their vests tucked into their Y-fronts. Or *Reveille*, a newsprint magazine for the armed forces, where the girls were sway-backed, tummy-sucked, with lantern jaws, squinty eyes, a straw hat and probably a judicious beach ball. They were obviously rude, and no better than they should be. But the *Playboy* girls. That was like looking at the next rung of evolution. There was no sense that I, or any of my friends who came to snigger, would ever graduate to having a woman like this, any more than we'd be spacemen or cowboys. It wasn't just that we couldn't imagine what to do with them—we could imagine—but they plainly wouldn't have any idea what to do with us. What we saw at school were girls who played netball, with drippy noses and national health spectacles. These women were like tableaux from High Renaissance mannerist paintings. Cloud-borne goddesses, evocations of justice and victory and charity. They were parables of America in their brilliant pink bodies that had been bred from the promise of fecundity and the harvest of fresh air and space and sun and lawn sprinklers. The dryads of everything, of plenty: plenty of freedom, plenty of orange juice, plenty of recreational fucking.

Every month in *Playboy* there was an advertisement with a headline that went: "What sort of man reads *Playboy*?" It was selling subscriptions. But I always imagined it was advertising the men. What sort of man did read *Playboy*? What sort of man got to mount the foldout women? I was particularly fascinated with them. The picture was always taken in what would probably be called a romper room, or the den, on two levels with cushions and leather armchairs. There was a sense of insouciance, opulence and technocratic ease. Three or four men, all best friends, would be arranged around, say, a piano. One of them would be playing silent jazz, the others holding crystal glasses, laughing. There would be a black one, one with a polo-neck cashmere sweater, one with a trimmed beard, one would smoke a pipe. And draped over them and around them like cashmere duvets would be girls. Great-breasted, wide-mouthed, sleek-limbed girls. The recreation of champions, resting their arms on the men's shoulders, looking deep into their eyes. My dad was a man who read *Playboy*, but he wasn't like this. I was a boy who sneaked looks at *Playboy*. Was there perhaps space for me under the piano, or behind the leather sofa?

I've just bought a book, *The Complete Playboy Centerfolds*. It's taken me some time to get through them, they're a thick read. Or perhaps a thick dribble. They've shrunk. They're now unfolded, staples removed, but it's an extraordinary journey through the postwar social history of American sex, and may well be the most wordlessly eloquent book on American sexuality and taste ever published. As I turned the pages, I would recognize girls. They'd come back to me like old school photos after thirty-five years, some Miss March or November would drag me back. Actually, not like old school photos. They begin in the fifties and the sixties as very odd-mannered tableaux, seminaked in everyday mundane settings, like the second act of a bedroom farce. The watcher can make up little scenarios for them: "I was just cleaning out this cupboard in the nude, except for these toweling pants and a bowler hat," and we just walked in, and they turned to the camera with a look of mild surprise. Not like, "Oh my God, what are you doing in my bedroom?" Not like you were the window cleaner or leery Uncle Wilf, but like, "Oh, my, you're early, hon. You caught me just like this on tiptoes, with nothing on but an artist's palette and a nylon polar bear." We, the invisible men in this little drama, we'd come in with our fishing rod or briefcase, or golf clubs, and she'd be surprised, a nice surprise, she was pleased to see us. "Oh, you should have told me you were going to be early, I'd have cleared away my old lacrosse kit and the balloons. Do you want to cum on my magnificent breasts now, or shall I tell you about my day?"

As they get into the seventies, the pretense, the tiny pretense, of a scenario, of role play, that the viewer can use to slip in, vanishes. They just pout. She gives you a name so that you can grunt something that isn't "bitch." She's a girl on brown satin sheets, whose look says, "What took you so long? I'm hotter than a George Foreman grill set to sear. Get in here and knock one out on these frankly unbelievable breasts." The nineties are the autumn of the *Playboy* centerfold. Not only have the girls reached a level of stratospheric match-readiness, but the airbrushing makes them look as fine and shiny as customized Chevys. These ladies are pimped, and the century ends with a naked troika—wham!—the Dahm triplets.

The *Playboy* centerfold was never arty or cool. It was never chic or cutting-edge. They were rarely ever more than mildly raunchy. All through the decades they appeared behind the curve, and their curves are not negligible. *Playboy* centerfolds are an American trophy. The nation's hood ornament, from the limo of state. Every boy has passed under the shadow of those perfect breasts on the way to adulthood. They looked up and knew that this was the statuesque of liberty. Tom Sawyer messed about in rivers; postwar American boys messed about in garages with centerfolds.

The centerfolds of 1957, from January to December, are June, Sally, Sandra, Gloria, Dawn, Carrie, Jean, Dolores, Jacquelyn, Colleen, Marlene and Linda. In 2007 they were Jayde, Heather Rene, Tyran, Giuliana, Shannon, Brittany, Tiffany, Tamara, Patrice, Spencer, Lindsay and Sasckya. Bunny girls went from being the girl next door to the pole dancer upstairs, and they confirm a particular American sexual trope. This is breast country. Bosoms are American. The rest of the body is really a delivery system for the great forward momentum of Mount Rushmore breasts.

In the great tradition of childish naming of taboo things, there are surprisingly few commonly used American vulgarisms for vaginas. It's a pussy, the anthropomorphic euphemism. Bottoms are tushies, botties, fanny—which over here is a front-bottom. In Europe there are hundreds and hundreds of words for vaginas: funny, fond, disgusting and fearsome. The most commonly used—cunt—is the "nigger" of body parts in America: unsayable in company, even young, liberal, cool company. You can't say "cunt" at table. At least "cunt" still retains a full battery of juice to shock.

It is a votive obscenity. But the embonpoint has been doused with dozens of commonly used slang terms: babbaloos, badoinkies, balloobas, bazukas, bazoomas, bejongas, boobs, boonies, boobsters, boulders. And that, if you hadn't noticed, is just the *B*s. Not even all the *B*s. My personal favorite this week is chesticles: deeply misguided and wrong on every level, from the aesthetic to the biological. But what you can't fail to notice about these names is how toddlerish they are, how utterly infantile. Sound repetitions and visual onomatopoeia.

Breasts are a secondary sexual characteristic. They originally won their shot at stardom when we became bipedal, thereby robbing the bottom of its eye-level uxorious attraction. The breasts were pressed in to imitate the lost bum. The cleavage resembles buttocks, red lipstick mimics an excited vulva (if you've never seen an excited vulva). American fashion, art and popular culture venerate the cleavage, elevate those teetering, heavy breasts. Nowhere else in the world could have invented a chain of restaurants called Hooters. And in the *Playboy* centerfolds you can see how the shape and the style, the semaphore of breasts has changed. In the fifties they have a spectacular, gravity-defying, cantilevered pointiness. In the seventies they fall into braless teardrops. In the nineties they're globular and solid, and every so often there are girls with small—well, small*er*—breasts. Sort of normal-sized, but still perkier than meerkats on coke. But it's merely a nod to sophistication, to the European girls who have petite booballala-boobettes. They are only a pair of placebos from a disappointing month. "Where's the meat?" said Mr. America.

Tom Ford, the designer, has a theory that American design follows the shape of idealized American breasts. The fifties are pointy, echoing the motorcar fins and the sci-fi look of things: missiles, UFOs, the brutalist, mechanical, cantilevered and aggressively questing breasts of optimism. In the sixties and seventies they elegantly slope in the rhythm of swirly, floaty, swinging, free, hippie-dippie design. The unstructured parabola breast. The racks of the nineties were buffed and pumped. And now they're puffed up, symmetrical, and design is all puffed up, engorged. And there it is, America's gift to international eroticism: breast implants. It's salutary to go from looking at forty years of centerfolds to the before-and-after shots for plastic surgeons on the hundreds and hundreds of websites for cosmetic empowerment. The photographs that the surgeons advertise themselves with are as shocking and as ghoulishly enticing as zombie movies. Cartoonishly globular, caricature breasts, made out of the tired and worn-out dugs of motherhood, breasts that have done their best, have been up in the middle of the night, have seen in exhausted dawns, done their thing creating. Breasts that you would have imagined would have earned a rest are due some manners. But here they are, made like the drawings from lavatory walls, the scars livid and jagged, puce and purple wounds. "After a year, the scars should be much decreased. Discomfort is generally negligible after two months." The manufactured breast is such a familiar, common thing that they no longer have to look natural. They are "good jobs"—the job itself is a matter of aesthetic pride.

Breast enlargement changes and dictates fashion. A woman who's suffered the surgical pain, the scars like open-heart surgery, is always going to boast a cleavage: those banging, bim-bam bazookas are going to be out and proud. The mannequins in the kids' clothes shops in South Beach, Miami, are all made with impossibly augmented breasts. You look in the windows and you're staring at plastic models of women who themselves have plastic tits, and the girls are going, "That halter neck would look great on me."

Whatever the morality, the aesthetics, the politics of erotic imagery, what is also amazing is that American thing: the commitment. When all's said and done, a secondary sexual characteristic is not the arena, it's not the VIP area. Breasts are the advertisement, the flyer. And it's the willingness to believe that you need to go to any lengths: "Yo, girl, you get those 34FFs, you deserve them. You've earned them." There is an odd egalitarianism about cosmetic surgery. Don't be cheated of the dream by genetics, or diets, or age. You can have the bam-bam-bing-boings of an eighteen-year-old *Playboy* centerfold, because that's America. If you work for it, if you really, really wish for it with all your might and your eyes tight shut, then you'll get it.

But it won't do what it promised on the box. A nation that is as breast-conscious as America does something else to its women. This obsession means that men are always, always, always staring at your cleavage, your nipples. And it means that women who meet men face-to-face are always made aware with the handshake and the name exchange that they are, if not sexually available, sexually accountable. They are being assessed. Men can't help it. Heaven knows they try not to stare, they maintain fierce eye contact, but they grow up programmed to follow a ball with centerfolds and these boom-bam-bubbubs. It's in the culture, what can I say? "Nice top bollocks."

Women can do one of three things. They can ignore it, which is easier some days than others, or they can confront it: "Hey, soldier, eyes up and front." But that's not always practical or helpful. Or you can dress for breast, like going out on a mission, like wrapping up for the cold. A woman says, "There's going to be men out there," and she can either go offense or defense. In America you see women wrapped up with their shoulders hunched forward and bowed backs, in bras that are too small for them, and you know these are the mammary martyrs: self-conscious, exposed, resentful. Or you go proactive, DEFCON ballistic, and get them out for the boys. Make it their problem: "Deal with it, guys. You are never, repeat never, going to get a soapy tit wank from these bad babies."

If you visit the vacationing, flirty, balmy bits of America, you'll see men and women being pulled around by breasts, like magnets, both defined by this strange and original cultural obsession. And just while we're here, whatever happened to the areola? Most girls under thirty didn't even know they'd got a couple, or that they had a name (not to be confused with the aureola, the golden corona that surrounds a saint's head). Areola is that pink or tan ring around the nipple. In the fifties they were huge: they stood out like the ends of ice cream cones, but now they're shrinking.

They grow paler, nipples get smaller and longer, they go digital, changed from being the big switches and dials of old stand-alone radiograms and appliances. Now they're touch-sensitive on and off buttons. Like touch-screen technology, you just scroll them up and down.

And the last thing you notice about the *Playboy* girls is their pubic hair. The sexual alopecia. I feel nostalgic for bushes; it's where I came in. But they've shrunk down to nothing. Past the American wax, the French wax, the landing strip, the Hitler moustache, the arrow, then the Brazilian or the Hollywood. Sometimes, I'm told, called the Sphinx, after a bald cat discovered in Canada (pussy, geddit? Of all the places to be a bald cat, Canada must be the worst). So it isn't named for the female-chested, lion-eagle-snake creature who met men on mountain passes, asked them three questions, then tossed them off.

You have to consider the immense commitment to aesthetic satisfaction, to arrange the mise-en-scène just so, to arrange the decoration, the walk-through ambience, to be that minimal. To put up with the pain, the regular, awful pain and intimate humiliation of having your legs hoiked in the air and having hot wax applied to your arsehole and then ripped off by an uncaring immigrant woman who has to do this to maintain a toehold job that perpetuates the legend of America. "What did you do when you got here, Mommy?" "I ripped the stubble off strangers' cunts." Bring me the huddled masses yearning to be hair free.

I can't choose a favorite *Playboy* centerfold: they are all of them marvelous. As we used to say as lads, you wouldn't say no to any of them for eating crisps in bed. They are the caryatids of freedom and good, hygienic fun. But there is one that sticks in my mind: January 2007, Jayde Nicole. Jayde has apparently just come for a visit. She stands in my doorway with this "Hiya, it's only me, fancy nailing me to the sofa?" face. Outside it's snowing—one of those lovely, crisp, northern days, fir trees heavy. Jayde is wearing boots, white socks and a woolly scarf with Canadian maple leaves. Silly girl. So gagging for it she's arrived without pants or anything else. She's not even got goose bumps, but she stands in the doorway, one knee cocked, her big winter breasts keeping her warm. With a snowy grin and one hand on the door handle, she's completely Sphinxed. Her vagina looks tight, like a little, neat, hairless, minimal Wendy-house noo noo. And there, just above where her pubic hair would have once grown, is a tattoo. They haven't airbrushed it out or put concealer on it because it's telling, it's cute. It's part of who Jayde is. She's standing there naked, shaved, available in a centerfold in the noughties, smiling at strangers, and above her prepubescent pudenda is one indelible word. *Respect.* Who says this is a nation without irony?

My favorite comment on American sex is this unlikely quote: "The scent of these armpits aroma finer than prayer." It seems to encapsulate the contradiction: the fervor, the sweat and the piety of America's relationship with sex. You'd never have guessed it was Walt Whitman: "Song of Myself" in *Leaves of Grass*.

11

Loneliness

In 1897, someone in the family cut out and kept newspaper articles about the might of American production. There was a small cluster of them, a passing interest. "Here is the potential of the National Forest: 25% of our entire territory is forested, apparently, and wheat production in 1895 was 467,102,947 bushels." I imagine they were kept as comforting reminders that freshly American relatives, the newly departed, were sharing in this bounty. That the national and the personal would be synonymous: they were in the right place, had done the right thing. Here is a cutting from the *Ladies' Home Journal of Philadelphia*:

> Uncle Sam set apart a royal pleasure ground in North Western Wyoming and called it Yellowstone National Park. To give an idea of what its size—3,312 square miles—really means, let us clear the floor of the park and tenderly place some of the great cities of the world there, close together as children do their blocks. First put in London, then Greater New York, Chicago, Philadelphia, Paris, Boston, Berlin, St. Louis, Hong Kong, San Francisco and Washington. The floor of the park should be about half covered, then lift up Rhode Island. Carefully, so as not to spill any of its people, set it down and press in the West Indies. And even then there are 200 square miles left.

There's a map showing how it would all work. I like this, because it's jauntily written and must have taken an absurd amount of research, but also because it's an early example of what in Europe is seen as America's obsession with size, the bigness of stuff, the constant rapture of girth, weight, length and heft, the race to build taller, longer, heavier. But what's so conspicuously telling in this description of Yellowstone Park is that the lady has chosen to fill it. Not to compare its size with other wildernesses or lumps of nature, with how many Saharas you could fit into it or how many Niles could swim round it, but to pack it with cities. All that brick and cement, the steel and stone, the smoke and filth and fetid air, the people. It would be an international stew of masses. Such a contradictory image. The best way to imagine how big the empti-ness of nature is, is to jam it with humanity.

There is, in this picture of the wilderness full of cities, a pre-science of what America was becoming. Almost as soon as the West was broached, there were calls for tranches and ranges of its pristine horizon to be protected; reminders of that great, God-given otherness; that for every hectare that was built and tilled, a hectare of wilderness was buried and lost. And there is something else that is a whispered leitmotif that sighs through American life. It is the keening of loneliness, the ghosts in the wild. The first stories of Europeans moving west are of the emptiness of the land. Whenever I read the memoirs of the trappers, who worked from Louisiana to the Hudson Bay and sometimes spent years explor-ing the tributaries and streams of the unmapped High Country, I can never overcome the terror of being alone in that vastness. And there are desperate letters and diaries from the first families who farmed the Great Plains of Nebraska and the Dakotas, Min-nesota and Wisconsin, particularly from the women. The creaking wind, the whispering emptiness, the unending toil, punctured by setbacks and occasional small triumphs. Many of them were Ger-man or Scandinavian, people who had come from tight, support-ive little communities; the sadness of missing, the warm pity of homesickness, the truth of being tiny and alone, was actually often maddening. Suicides were not rare, and to answer the emptiness America created a vernacular to celebrate it, a lonely character and a form that was the embodiment of the triumph of the solitary: the cowboy.

Cowboy films are built out of loneliness. The overcoming of

it, the acceptance, the single, defining riff of a man of few words. One of the most despairing images in all cinema must be the final shot of *Shane*, when a small boy, whose father is dead, shouts after the only man who is left in his life, the only man he loves: "Shane! Shane! Come back!" The man is condemned to be a wandering hero. His attempt to graft onto a family, to be part of it, is thwarted by his inability to overcome his own nature and calling. He rides away into the infinite, disinterested land. The jaunty, whistled sadness of riding into the sunset, the lonely-ever-after ending of classic Westerns, haunted my childhood. *High Plains Drifter*, Gary Cooper on the empty streets at *High Noon*, John Wayne riding to his brother's farm in *The Searchers*. What's particularly and peculiarly American about the genre is that its preordained ending is loneliness. It is a celebration of solitary men and bereft and widowed women left desperate for affection. So much of the Western tradition deals with the most despairing and angst-ridden emotions, but they're movies made for kids. It's as if America was trying to pass on an unpleasant but necessary lesson of life: that you were alone, and you needed to toughen up and shut up.

Not only were cowboy films solitary, they also extolled the virtue of people who are particularly bad company; who can't or won't make conversation. Cowboy films are always authentically, explicitly moral, and rigorous in the accounting of actions and consequences. French intellectuals may take the solitary cowboy as an existential parable, but there's nothing philosophical about them at home in America. Here, the cowboy is a practical role model, a man who copes with the vast alone.

The New World constantly refers back to and touches its loneliness. It's the back beat of country music, in Edward Hopper's pictures, Ansel Adams's photographs, the constant silence and reflections of American fiction, all in a way that is quite alien to European—and in particular, English—writing, which always seems so crowded, replete with character. European novels are about people; American ones so often about their absence and fragility.

To drive from coast to coast is one of those road trips that Europeans like to do. Kids think it will be back-to-back movie scenes, a Groundhog Day of ironic theme parks. They're surprised and rather shocked at how very blank-faced the middle of America is. To traverse the great heartland is not something you should undertake if you're feeling insecure or unloved. The small towns rise out of the road, a single street of convenience stores, unskilled restaurants, a couple of motels, a church, a school, the final gas station, and you're through them and away. Sometimes you see someone on the street—an old man and woman jogging, a face in the window of a shop, a dog barking behind a link fence—and you're made suddenly to consider what a life must be like here, the hollow needle of empathy, the insight too intense, like a bone in the throat. Compared with Europe it's the plainness (not ugliness), the utility, the blandness of it, that wears us down.

These places are still within hailing distance of their hard birth. They still crave comfort and convenience above aesthetics. It's what I like about them: they're created from an ambition that life should be softer and easier for your kids than it was for your parents, not as confections of civic vanity or the toy-town fantasies of patrician landlords. These little ribbons of community, laid out along tarmac, that bleed one into another like roadkill, they grow repetitive. You catch the flash of a red barn in a stand of trees, cast like a meteorite into the land, and you try to imagine the life that sprouted here, the first person to break the sod, who, exhausted or satisfied with the journey, set down his belongings in this place that was to be the end of a long trek. I once went through a town on the flat plain of Ohio, it was called Xeniya. It had been hit by a hurricane. I've looked it up, it must have been 1974. Thirty-four people killed, 10,000 homeless. Nixon visited, briefly. The elements that had turned Xeniya over had cut a great furrow through the town. One side of the street was kindling and rubble, the other side frozen with shock. You could follow the mad trench of the hurricane, see where it had changed direction, bucked on some invisible instruction, plowed through careful lives, pulled by a racing, gray-maned storm. And in the middle of the motorway of destruction, there was a single clapboard house, white, pristine, unviolated, surrounded by nothing but the crunchy floorplans of its neighbors. It was a startlingly prescient image, and all the papers ran pictures of it against the darkling sky. Everyone said, "What a lucky house," but it didn't look lucky. It looked lonely, all on its own. Everyone else blown to Michigan. Who would it borrow a cup of sugar from? Whose lights would reflect in its empty windows?

Xeniya means "welcome" in Greek. The handful of speculators who planted it in 1803 voted for the name as an advertisement. Its motto is "city of hospitality." It also likes to be known as the bicycle capital of the Midwest. Lincoln passed through here, made a speech from the caboose of his train to pretty much everyone in town, but nobody wrote it down. It was once the home of the Shawnee Indians. Tecumseh was born hereabouts. The Shawnee called it "the place of crazy winds." The city's website says that the seasonal curbside leaf collection is canceled, and gives a number to ring to report a broken streetlight.

The great interior of America still feels like it's on probation. It has not conquered the wilderness, rather come to an uneasy truce. Dotted in the great midland are the occasional, sprawling herds of trailer homes with their sagging pickups that mock and mimic the old covered-wagon trains, surrounded by wonky barbecues, plastic garden furniture, kids' bikes and bits of picket fence and fairy lights (there's always a string of fairy lights implying some desperate festivity). Communities are auditioning for the land that they gingerly squat on. It may not work out—it's not unusual to come across the wreckage of these failed trysts: ghost towns, the remnants of communities that gave up, separated from the land they stood in, leaving behind the husks of life. The first time I saw one of these abandoned places I thought it was spookily thrilling, like finding a corpse or some piece of archaeology. My American friends for a moment thought I was being ironic. What could be memorable about an ex-place? This un-burg? I assumed they were precious and rare. I come from a continent where towns, even the meanest hamlets, are immutable, everlasting. They live on for hundreds or thousands of years, through wars and pestilence, through flood and storm and famine, through industry and agriculture. Only in the north of Scotland or parts of rural Ireland will you find abandoned communities, and they probably went to America. In Europe, communities grow fat and slump to become embalmed by history. Nobody gives up on a historic place. They either stop caring or they care too much. The old and pointless become demented slums or obsessive museums, but in America, if it doesn't work, it gets binned. There is a civic ruthlessness that had to be learned by immigrants. They didn't bring it with them, and they learned it at some personal cost. Americans still up and off more than any other people I've come across. They travel to new cities, to new states, and set down tentative taproots, make new friends, energetically join new churches and communities and just as suddenly unearth it all again, tug up the roots and move. There'll be a yard sale, a promise to stay in touch, and they're off, pulling the U-Haul trailer, as if the ability to migrate was inherited, or a condition that you were never really cured of: the fever to be elsewhere.

On the long, slow-motion, flatlined highways at the heart of America, along with the pleading billboards for last-chancers to get a bed with a pool or pray for forgiveness, an astonishing number of storage facilities are dropped at the side of the road, painted luminous colors, the evidence and the accomplishment of serial lives boxed up and bagged then dumped in small, dark, fireproof containers. Storage is the embodiment of procrastination, a thin purgatory between life and extinction, because you can't make the decision for inanimate euthanasia, so things live on in these out-of-town hangars. I wonder what it's like there in the dark in those little cupboards, with the kitchen utensils that served breakfast for years to children late for yellow buses. The teenage rooms packed into boxes, the rock posters and stacks of magazines, the mille-feuilles of vinyl records, the muscle-building springs and lumps of iron, the scrapbooks and greening photographs of lives and loves that became obsolete, the cuckolded sheets and the headboards, dark with the ghostly impression of bored heads, gardening equipment dusty from old harvests and summers.

There is, in storage units, the echo of something much older. They are the tumulus of goods to be taken into the afterlife, where in heaven you will once more be reunited with your scatter cushions and gas station glasses with all the state maps, with your sweetcorn forks and Christmas decorations all waiting for you on the other side, with the roof rack for a car that was junked a decade ago, a single ski and a broken gold plastic bowling trophy. They are the mausoleums and the propitiation to the kitchen gods of our lives, the sadness of the past that is too precious to leave and too awkward to take. So you pay a standing order for their upkeep until finally it drifts far enough over the mind's horizon and the monthly payments dry up and the reminder letter is forgotten and misplaced, and then the padlocks are undone, the vaults are raided like Egyptian tombs and the evidence taken out and burned, sold and stolen. Forsaken at the edge of every American town, these are the reliquaries to the great American loneliness, where, appropriately, no one ever goes to pray.

The cowboys' silent, sunset loneliness has its assumption of reflective character building and self-reliance, but there is another belief that came out of New England in the 1840s, and takes the great emptiness of America's nature and sees in it not something to be overcome, not as the inanimate stone that you hone your life against, but as a metaphysical hymn, a great mystical enigma, within which there is the transcendent secret of the Godhead, and life, and the truth that loneliness is the soul of nature and the prayer of enlightenment, the heart of happiness. Something to be searched out and embraced.

Ralph Waldo Emerson wrote the book on nature. He is one of the most opaque and least likable of great Americans, the most resistant to a fond empathy, though in his lifetime he was adored and respected around Boston and Concord. Throughout the nation and across the ocean in Europe, he was highly thought of. He began as a minister whose lectures and sermons spellbound hundreds, whose ideas were said to be a new vision of a truly American philosophy. He resigned his living as a pastor because he came to believe that the ways of practicing religion in church were ancient and redundant and unbefitting to a New World. He believed that America must free itself from Europe and invent a new style of writing and understanding, a new way of communing with itself. After the consumptive death of his wife at twenty, he sued her family for her inheritance and took off for Europe, where John Stuart Mill gave him a letter of introduction to Carlyle, the irascibly bad-tempered Scot who also believed that modern times were in need of new intellectual and spiritual heroes and revolutions, while at the same time failing heroically to personally consummate his own marriage, about which it was famously said that it was very good of God to let Carlyle and Mrs. Carlyle marry each other, and so make only two people miserable and not four. Carlyle and Emerson were much taken with each other. Emerson also met Wordsworth and Coleridge, and took a chunk of their sublime romanticism to his new American philosophy.

Back home he read Kant, who said that all knowledge was transcendental, and he dabbled in the Vedas and the *Bhagavad Gita* of Indian mysticism. He became a figurehead for a group of new thinkers who called themselves transcendentalists. Emerson lectured and wrote treaties and essays, and masses of clotted, cabbagey poetry. Reading him is like trying to hack your way through a swamp of creeping verbiage. Even at the time, people said he was incoherent and unintelligible. There is in his streams of visionary consciousness an Old Testament, hallucinatory quality, that is never quite illuminating. He said that nature is a language that you have to learn, that the universe is made of nature and the soul, and the word and the will of God can be intuited from communing with nature. He met the young Thoreau, whom he encouraged to keep a journal, a piece of mundane advice that the young man said changed his life. He immediately went and spent a year on his own in a hut, by a pond, and wrote *Walden*, which is a diary that oscillates between eye-rolling minute tedium and laughable hyperbole, with sections of profound whimsy and social condescension.

Walt Whitman sent Emerson a first edition of *Leaves of Grass*.

Emerson wrote back four pages of criticism that contained the famous phrase "I greet you at the beginning of a great career." For all his verbal gardening, there is something marvelous in Emerson recognizing this astonishing poem that is unrelated to and unlike anything written in the New World or the Old, by an unknown author, and yet understanding its brilliance when everyone else who read it thought it disgusting or mad. Emerson's praise was the stake up which Whitman's reputation grew, but transcendentalism itself launched some heroically loopy attempts at rural utopianism. There was Fruitlands, which sounds like a theme park but was actually a transcendental farm that wouldn't use beasts for work nor eat them, nor for leather; and Brook Farm—a more serious concern—a collective based on "industry without drudgery, and true equality without its vulgarity" where everyone, men and women, was supposed to work equally at what they felt suited them best, thereby leaving time for intellectual and literary pursuits. Nathaniel Hawthorne was an early investor in this enterprise that was half soviet collective, half writers' retreat. It collapsed in a mire of debt and accusations that it undermined marriage and family. Emerson himself, while making encouraging noises, declined to join in, mentioning drily that at Brook Farm one man plowed all day and one man looked out of the window all day, and both received the same wages. Brook Farm sounds like the plot for a comic film: the great intellectual seriousness and literary queeniness set beside the need to muck out stables and dig ditches. The transcendentalists despised cities and the metropolitan, seeing them as populated by stunted drones, unheroically cut off from the mysticism and vision of nature, and the elevating simplicity of rural work.

Emerson and his transcendentalists did manage to plant and grow a remarkably robust strand of American thought and belief that has been woven into its counterculture throughout the 1950s and 1960s protest movement and the civil rights movement, and the unquenchable optimism of Americans to set up new and improving societies and communes and New Age utopias. Both Emerson and Carlyle are figures who led to socialism and the cooperative movement, but also they have a chilling connection to the mysticism and heroic agrarianism of fascism and those separatist survivalists hoarding assault rifles and tins of baked beans in the wilderness.

Emerson called for a new way of seeing and writing, and recording a new world. It was serendipitous in the decade that led to the Civil War. It birthed a series of books that were a literary nascence, that invented a distinctive and assertive American voice; Whitman's "Song of Myself," Hawthorne's *Scarlet Letter*, Melville's *Moby-Dick*, Longfellow's *Hiawatha*, all connected by the land. All refer back to the wild, and particularly to the spiritual healing of natural places. Longfellow said, "We want a national literature commensurate with our mountains and rivers. We want a national epic that shall correspond to the size of the country . . . We want a national literature altogether shaggy and unshorn, that shall shake the earth like a herd of buffaloes thundering over the prairies." At precisely this moment, John Ruskin, the art critic, who incidentally also failed to consummate his marriage, was writing his great work *Modern Painters,* in which he invented the pathetic fallacy: that is, pathetic in the Victorian empathetic sense. It is: "To signify any description of inanimate natural objects that ascribes to them human capabilities, sensations and emotions." American literature and the national imagination were being molded into a wild transubstantiation, a supernatural, animistic, pathetic fallacy. The wilderness is no longer bewildering, it is a testament. It is not the background or the scenery, it is a constant, omnipresent, deific character, a messenger and a prayer, a metaphor and a refuge. And finally, the earth is a moral arbiter. The loneliness of the wilderness has been turned into the blue-domed, log-pewed, sunrise-altared American church of national greening.

Hawthorne mocked Emerson and transcendentalism. Melville was not a fan. He said, "Emerson had a defect in the region of the heart, a self-conceit so intensely intellectual that at first one hesitates to call it by its right name." It is possible to understand that people did hang on his every word and that he was read in schools as one of the fireside poets. But ironically he is not part of the new literature, the shaggy and unshorn literature that would shake the earth. Unlike Melville or Whitman, he sounds too European, still looks to England for the grace note and applause. In some of his quotes you can hear the echo of what made him such a compelling speaker, the lightning rod for an authentically American thunderclap. He was a clever if repetitive phrasemaker: "man is a god in ruins"; "A man is what he thinks about"; "children are all foreigners"; "common sense is genius dressed up in working clothes"; "nature always wears the colors of the spirit." It was also he who pointed out that if you built a better mousetrap, the world would beat a path to your door. Emerson's house burned down and was rebuilt from public conscription. He began to lose his memory and probably suffered from dementia. But nature, in its great wisdom, intervened and, possibly with gratitude and a pathetic kindness, offered him a passing shower which gave him pneumonia.

The great gape of loneliness was a defining, solitary character of America, and must have been the one that European immigrants found the most pitiless and profound: as hard as the land itself was its emptiness. This would have been the most alien property of the New World. Overcoming it, taming and finally imbuing the emptiness of the New World with Godliness was a philosophical triumph. Emerson said that heroes are no braver than ordinary men, they are braver five minutes longer. It is possible to suppose that one of the consequences of the solitary aloneness of this place, and the coming to terms with that loneliness, led directly to another defining characteristic of America and Americans: the equal and opposite bookend of neighborliness.

12

Philanthropy

When Clifford, my grandmother's brother, returned, legless, to America it was as a war hero: if not exactly dashing, then charming, an elegant catch. He married Harriet Pearson, an heiress whose family fortune came from coaches, which was lucky because Clifford didn't seem to have much interest or skill in stockbroking. His granddaughter remembers him as remaining very English. He kept his blue passport and citizenship in a bedroom that smelled of England, pomade and a pair of monogrammed hairbrushes. The Depression took the cream off Clifford and Harriet's money, and they moved from a grand house to a small one, ending up in the comfortable gentility of a service department. They had a daughter, my father's cousin Caroline: beautiful, polished, popular and always smiling. This very American girl married Ted Ewald, a German-American whose grandparents had come from Hanover. His father had been one of the first to make a business in advertising, notably in using pictures to sell cars.

Detroit was motoring into Motown. Printing was evolving, magazines and papers putting on bright, chromaline pages. Billboards grew along the verges of the newly planned, multilane roads. In Europe, motorways are autobahns, but in America they're the freeway, an American name that has an intrinsic beauty, a perfect piece of copywriting, a two-syllable slogan, a poem to the New World. The road that bore humming freedom, that gave you freedom. The Freeway should be America's motto.

Old Man Ewald, Henry, laid down a new industry and made a fortune. He rode the freeway, understanding the aspiration of consumers who are avid to consume and eager to be seduced.

America was a sure thing, and the advertising business was the right business in the right place at the copyright time. His company, Campbell Ewald, began in 1911. Campbell bowed out early; he'd been brought in because Henry was too young to legally start his own company. It is still based just outside Detroit, still sells the dream of Chevrolets and General Motors, and is still one of the biggest advertising agencies in America. Along the way Henry acquired a Chevrolet dealership, which he used as a laboratory to try out ideas. And Ted, his son, cousin Caroline's new husband, liked the look of it, and ran it, and administered the foundation of all the money he'd been left.

The Ewalds lived in Grosse Pointe and brought up six children. My first visit to the States was for my cousin Wendy's wedding. I remember the freeway over Detroit, looking down on the acres of new cars parked in rows, like a primary-colored harvest, and the forest of pylons that grew around the power station that galvanized the city: a futurist vision of nature, metal agriculture. I remember the illuminated freeway billboard that shone out the number of cars manufactured that year, the digits rolling over as you passed. I remember being called over by the private security guards on a quiet, lawn-margined street, and asked what I was doing. Walking. (The only people who walked in Grosse Pointe were domestic servants, and they were all black.) And the country club, where we went for brunch—the first time I ever ate brunch—served by waiters whose simmering hostility was apparently palpable only to me. It's difficult not to sneer at Grosse Pointe, to revert to the European smirk of Old World good taste, and list the landmark houses here which are noted by style. They make a sort of poem that goes: Tudor, Tudor, Italian Renaissance, Colonial, Neo-Renaissance, Tudor. Tudor-Jacobean, French-Colonial, Colonial, Neo-Gothic, Georgian, Georgian, Mediterranean, Tuscan, Tudor, Cotswold, Georgian, Neo-Gothic. Venetian, Tudor, Tudor, French-Gothic, Neo-Renaissance, Tudor, Tudor, Colonial. Altogether, they look unmistakably Neo–Grosse Point. The Old World front can't hide the rich suburban truth. The assumption of historical façades isn't cultural insecurity or even snobbery. These are trophies, the plunder of success: the taking of the arms and flags of the defeated and hanging them on your wall with the pride of victory.

I was surprised and a little shocked at the open, pitying hostility to Europe. Men in plaid golf slacks and button-down collars, with severe hair and enormous carbuncle rings that had something to do with being a student once, would chug martinis on their patios and slip into an easy, barbershop mockery of Europe. The teensy-weensiness of the cars, the vastness of the bureaucracy, the awful-ness of the food, the unhygienic bathrooms, the confusion of the roads, the weedy money, the absurd ritual and pointless tradition, the inconceivable evil of our politics, the pathetic cowardice of the military, the supine deference of the people. But most of all, the cruel and inhuman discomfort. How could we boast 3,000 years of civilization and still not come up with a shower that worked or a towel that was bigger than a napkin? Europe's beds were too small, its rooms too cold, and where was the air-conditioning?

They told me all this not with malice or bad manners, or even as historic revenge, but with a sort of rough, honest kindness, allow-ing, encouraging me to make a full confession, to receive absolu-tion from this, the one true faith of the freeway. It was plain as the fins on a Chevy convertible that America, and the life that America and Americans made for Americans, was patently and comprehensively better than any other life that had ever been made or lived anywhere in the world, ever. And for me to see it for the first time, to be among it, to touch it, smell it, pick it up and pop it in my mouth, must be a revelation, a damascene, Michigan conversion. The Old World scales should fall from my eyes and I would see in color and breathe deep and, like a sudden Baptist tent service, might rise up and admit the error of my collective past. Having arrived with the smug and ancient wisdom of my own culture—a belief that there was nothing in the world that could touch the ancient grandeur and subtle intellect of Europe, and that by comparison America was obviously and incontrovertibly a naive supermarket of popular "stuff" where all art and beauty were decided by the democracy of money, and the muses came mob-handed, and could be bought like everything else—I had no less assumed that I would be arriving with the gifts of sophistication, élan and taste, like a missionary bearing beads and mirrors.

The kindly and hospitable wives sometimes worried that I might be taking their husbands' home truths personally and would pause to commend some bit of European accomplishment to make me feel better. The china of Meissen, the silk of Milan, the paintings of Monet. And as quickly, the men would tell me how many of these things were in the museums of Chicago, Los Angeles and New York, as if the objects themselves were migrating. Given half a chance and a fair wind, the Sistine Chapel ceiling and the Brandenburg Concertos would travel steerage to get to America, where they could start again, possibly as cartoons and music for the movies.

The final haymaker argument was the truth that everyone wanted to be an American. The rest of the world was really a disorderly queue waiting to get vitamin-enriched milk and easyflo honey. The bottom line was, wherever you were, whoever you were, you'd rather be in Brooklyn. And, as sweeping generalizations go, it wasn't far off the mark.

The center of Detroit was devastated in an act of self-mutilation worse than almost any Third World squalor or despair. Cousin Wendy drove me through the civic acres of abandoned houses left out for the drug addicts and the hopelessly homeless, the schizophrenics and the damned. From pundits I heard suggestions that the heart of the city should be fired like a grouse moor, to encourage fresh growth, or bombed like a seeping, brokeback wreck at sea. That the city should be humanely put down, with the duality of a dystopian sci-fi movie. The distinction between Grosse Pointe, where the owners of the means of production and their descendants lived, and the city where the laborers in production lived, was stark, and across Europe would have been seen as a social and political cautionary tale, a gross recrimination. But here, I was astounded: no one saw that. No one thought the cheek-by-jowl inequality was an embarrassment or a reprimand, or even unfair. Grosse Pointe was the beacon of encouragement, the prize. It was the proof that America worked, and that work was rewarded. Far from shame, these men with their tartan slacks felt pride in their achievement and the achievements of their grandparents. What could look from Europe like the heartless eugenics of capitalism, here in the heart of America was proof that the deal worked, that the opportunity model was sound. Wealth was guiltless because poor people were the rich-in-waiting.

Ted Ewald would have been incensed if I'd suggested there was anything unjust in Grosse Pointe. In fact, I think he rather regarded me as a long-haired Brit art student with a deep-pink suspicion. His great passion was sport. He backed boxers, owned a slice of the Detroit Pistons, the basketball team, for a time, and he didn't just enjoy sport, he believed in it as a symbol and an instructor for life. And practically, as a civic force for good. Sport straightened out the wayward, taught the underprivileged self-belief and dignity, and it made black people rich. And there plainly weren't enough rich black people. The richer the black people got, the better it would be for white people. Ted spent a great deal of his time handing out grants and scholarships to kids who wouldn't have got much of an education without them. And when the city of Detroit came close to calling in the receivers and couldn't fund sports in the school system, Ted stepped in and picked up the tab, paying for it all himself.

There were those in Grosse Pointe who thought this wasn't quite the thing at all. This wasn't playing the game. If you wanted to do good works, well, there were plenty of opportunities in this suburb. Handing out money in the dark city was to cheat the nascent entrepreneurs and go-getters in the slums of their chance. But Ted was proud of Detroit. He wouldn't hear it mocked. After he died, Caroline built the Caroline and Ted Ewald Library in what might yet be called Post-Neo-Renaissance Venetian. It sits on the site of the Chevrolet dealership, and there is something memorable about that. Not just the memory of Ted, a man who inherited a lot and did good things, supported his community, but building a library out of a car lot is like turning swords into plowshares. Pickups into can't-put-downs. It isn't just replacing an old model with a new one, it's replacing an old idea with an ancient one.

Philanthropy was rediscovered in America. There is a particular relationship with charity that is unlike the stealthy, apologetic palming of donations from the Old World, like tipping the postman with a Christmas box. The European motivations of piety and pity, of metaphysical self-interest and self-saving to assuage the past, of charity as a means of perpetuating your name, leaving something more than the detritus of your labor, are all here, are all present in American charity. But there is something else: the sense that it's not just a personal act but a civic obligation. There is a duty to improve the lot of others. Charity isn't personal, it's public. It's owed not just to God and salvation but to the nation: the idea that America itself deserves its citizens' charity, not because it is poor but because it could always be richer.

America is layered with the given graffiti, names of its generous dead. There isn't a museum or hospital, a theater or municipal amenity, however humble, that can't be blessed with the remembrance of the comfortably-off and defunct. The money left to Ivy League universities in America isn't about the needs of learning. Harvard's endowment is $26 billion. The cost of being an undergraduate is still $47,215 per annum. This money isn't about need or any conceivable projected pessimism.

Charity is a pastime, an occupation for rich Americans. There is so much charity money that it's coined its own name: philanthrocapitalism. It makes its own weather. The Bill and Melinda Gates Foundation attracts the wealth of Warren Buffett with a takeover of goodness, charitable acquisition and amalgamation. The amounts of money involved are so large they have their own gravity, pulling in other bequests. The legacies and endowments themselves become hedge funds and corporations. Instead of paying tax, they donate the things that their taxes might have paid for. American charity is big and brash and free enterprise.

The philanthropic model was created by the son of weavers, a child from Dunfermline who said, after amassing one of the largest fortunes in the modern world, that he would sooner leave his son a curse than the almighty dollar. Andrew Carnegie's parents came from the pitiful insecurity of piecework in Scotland to conditions that weren't much better in America. Andrew was a formidable child, not just driven by his poverty but pulled by the desire for knowledge, power and achievement. He read at a local mill owner's library, which was philanthropically open on weekends for the poor. In America, he got himself a clerk's job on the railway, was promoted for being a fast and accurate telegraph operator.

F. Scott Fitzgerald pointed out that at the heart of all great fortunes there is a crime, and Carnegie's was his big break. He profiteered from insider dealing in railways stock. To raise a tiny scrap of capital, he asked his mother to remortgage their $700 house. She did, and he made a fortune in steel. In 1889, Carnegie's steel output was as large as Britain's at the height of its industrial power. When he finally cashed it all in for $230 million, he had a special vault built in New Jersey for the bearer bonds. Carnegie never touched them, nor visited the vault. Never saw the distillation, the reduction of his life to stacks of Gothic paper. It was said by his secretary and later biographers that Carnegie couldn't bear to visit his wealth because he thought it might vanish, might all be a ruse, a spell, a vast cosmic joke, which doesn't sound like the superstitions of a man who made steel, nor an East Coast Presbyterian Scot. What's more likely is that he flat-out despised it, the dead weight of cash. Not the expression of his luck and genius, but the dehydrated sweat of thousands and thousands of migrant workers. The one thing that the self-propelled very, very rich seem to have in common is a collective understanding that the money was never, ever the point. Carnegie believed that money would go off if you left it on the shelf. Cash was a plow, a pickaxe. Cash was the means of production and employment. It wasn't love of money that made the explosive, fecund, golden age of America. It was the brilliant, cavalier disregard for money, that wanton risk, the lack of respect for dollars and cents, that was the whip and the spur to the States' expansion.

By birth and experience, Carnegie was very liberal—possibly even socialist. He would have found more in common with the New Age Internet entrepreneur than today's flinty CEOs of mass production. He devoted his retirement to getting rid of the evidence. He spent money with a philanthropic frenzy. And although he left his wife and daughter comfortably off for the rest of their lives, there is no dynasty of Carnegies elegantly wallowing in the vast spoils of steelworks. He took to giving money away in a conspicuously different way than he had done when making it. He said the only way to make a fortune was to put all your eggs in one basket and watch the basket. In giving it away he spread the eggs over a great variety of personal niggles and concerns. They were the concerns and the niggles of his race and his childhood: education, instruction and religion. Though a born-again American, he separated the religion and the education. A great believer in spelling reform, he paid thousands for schools, but only if they severed all church affiliations. He bought organs for 7,000 churches, and would most famously be associated with libraries, donating 3,000, but only if local authorities would match his gift with land and running costs. He began with Dunfermline's. He gave money to forty-seven American states, to Canada, Britain, Ireland, Australia, New Zealand, the West Indies and Fiji. What he wanted to leave was learning and church music, the traditional hand-me-downs of the rich. Posterity has a short shelf life, and today organs and libraries are both archaic, bordering on obsolete. The great pipes fall silent and go for scrap, the books are cleared away for Internet cafés and community centers.

What Carnegie—along with a handful of other industrial Midases—really left behind was the expectation of charity. It is assumed that the rich will donate. There is a great social and fiscal machine to help them do it: thousands of dinners and balls and auctions, concerts, trips, lectures and expeditions to make the dispersal of wealth amusing and fun and sentimental. There are careers to be had in charity management. Museums and theaters employ specialists to cajole and smooth the parting of the wealthy from their wealth, explaining what they're donating to and exactly where their riches will go. In turn, they are offered a bespoke involvement, the satisfaction of being a contributor of more than money, but also an opinion, an expertise of a home-grown sort.

It is easy to laugh at all this, the drawing-room gavotte of cocktail parties and celebrity appearances, the frock and hairdos, the embarrassing sycophancy, but it has become an American cultural ritual, no less venerable than the ceremonies of praise-singing in Africa. This is an elaborate and expensive part of the fabric, of an egalitarian state where all men are born equal. At the end of your turn at the table, you leave your chips and donate them to the next player. It is expected. To die merely rich, without a hospital ward, gallery or civic water feature to your name, is to depart impover-ished of the thing that does matter, the one thing you can take with you: the good wishes and rosy encomiums of those you leave behind.

The mechanics and performance of charity are mockable. The purpose and product aren't. The good works that successful Amer-icans leave behind them may wither and collapse, be superseded and replaced, but their abiding legacy is a tribal but communal belief that the citizen has an obligation to the community that goes beyond what he gives to the state, and an individual has a responsibility that can't be mediated by the state. And although that can be found in many countries, it is never as universal or generous as it is in America.

One of the most singular bequests to the commonwealth of Amer-ica was the one that Special Agent Richard Rush came to London to collect in 1838. He picked up eleven padlocked boxes containing 104,960 gold sovereigns and accompanied them back to Philadel-phia, where they were melted down into gold dollars with a value of $508,318.46—something close to $50 million in today's money. The cash had been arrested from the English courts after a protracted legal wrangle. It was the bequest of James Smithson: if he had no legitimate or illegitimate heirs, then his fortune was to be left to the United States, to found an establishment for the increase and diffusion of knowledge. Britain and America had fought their last war barely twenty years previously, and Rush had been chosen to go and collect the winnings because he was popular in England, a civilized gent, handsome and patrician. He'd been an ambassa-dor and the secretary of the treasury in Washington. He had also been at the heart of planning the War of 1812. But then he'd also been involved in the peace treaty. If you look at his portrait you see a familiar American face: long, inquisitive, clever and humorous. He is a type that you can still meet in every small town across the country. Although Rush was exceptional—he had gone to the College of New Jersey, which would become Princeton, when he was fourteen, joined a law firm at twenty, become a diplomat, civil servant, an expert in the navy. He even managed to get one college vote when he stood as vice president for the Federalist Party, even though through some oversight they never got round to putting up a candidate for the presidency itself.

But it was Rush's father who was the real leavening of a brand-new country; a really astonishing man. At just thirty, Benjamin Rush was a signatory to the Declaration of Independence. On his mother's side, he was related to William Penn, who gave his name to the state. Benjamin studied medicine and chemistry, also at the College of New Jersey, and then at Edinburgh, where he also learned French, Italian and Spanish. He was a friend of Tom Paine, and encouraged him to compose *The Rights of Man*, and helped publish it. Indeed, he came up with the name. He was a medical orderly in the Continental army, and conspired vituperatively and lengthily against General Washington. He wrote the first medical chemistry book, taught Meriwether Lewis frontier medicine, prescribed Lewis and Clark's expedition "Dr. Rush's Bilious Pills," laxatives that were 50 percent mercury. I think they were reusable: you swallowed one, suffered the violent scatological consequences, reclaimed the pill, washed it and saved it for the next poor sucker.

He opposed both slavery and capital punishment, and alcohol. He believed that Negroes suffered from a medical condition, possibly a form of leprosy, that made them black with curly hair and broad features. He also believed he was close to discovering a cure that would allow them to be welcomed into white society unblemished. It is a very American literalism that the heart of the terrible injustice of color was actually color, a matter of decorative options.

Benjamin Rush was inquisitive, enthusiastic, opinionated, and almost always wrong in specifics and right in generalizations. He was a great believer in bloodletting and successfully sued the writer William Cobbett, who suggested in print that he killed more patients than he saved. Rush went on to become the most venerable, albeit fatal, medical practitioner of his age. He started the dispensary which offered the first free medical treatment in America. He was one of the first to uncover the chemical nature of addiction, and he did one of the great services to medicine. He invented psychotherapy. His eldest son, also a doctor, was challenged to a duel and shot dead his challenger. The boy was consumed by remorse and guilt, which tipped the balance of his mind. His father committed him to a mental hospital, where he remained for thirty years. Benjamin Rush discovered that the mentally ill were kept in the most pitifully hopeless state: locked rooms in the forgotten attics and cellars and hospitals, without treatment or much care. So he instigated separate asylums and wrote one of the first-ever papers on the treatment of mental illness: *Medical Inquiries and Observations Upon the Diseases of the Mind* (1812). In it, he noted that patients did better when they had a job, that it wasn't just the devil that found work for idle hands, but depression and despair. So he arranged for them to do gardening and carpentry, animal husbandry, sewing and weaving, thereby inventing occupational therapy.

Look at the lives and the achievements of these two men, father and son, and you see a root and branch that is repeated over and over in America—perhaps not quite so augustly, but just as staunchly. There was, in the formative years of the nation, something in the freedom and the opportunity that allowed ordinary men to become exceptional, and for the exceptional to flourish. Compare them with the life of the father and son whose philanthropic gift Richard Rush carried back to America. James Smithson was born in Paris and named at birth Jacques Louis Macie, taking the surname of his mother's deceased husband, who was not his father. That was Sir Hugh Smithson, the fourth Baron Stanwick, a Yorkshire deminoble who was friendly to his son, perhaps even fond, but never recognized him. His illegitimacy was an embarrassment and a shame. His father had other dynastic problems to solve. The earls of Northumberland had run out of male heirs, and as this was one of the great aristocratic houses of the nation, immortalized by Shakespeare if not by conception, the elder Smithson was brought in as a sort of sleight of hand, a hereditary understudy. Changing his name to Hugh Percy, he married the female heir, bringing with him a great deal of money and gaining another title, the dukedom of Northumberland— abracadabra!—revitalizing the moribund ancient genes of the lords of the Marches. His real son James went up to Oxford. He was clever, and became inventive: a chemist and a mineralogist. He was elected to the Royal Society and published many papers in his lifetime. He was respected, and invented the word "silicate," having discovered the need for it. At the end of the eighteenth century, science was one of the few areas in old Europe where illegitimacy could not overshadow accomplishment.

His enormous bequest to America was immediately plundered by senators in pork-barrel deals to grease their own states, a great portion of it going to build roads in Arizona. But eventually, Congress stepped up to this postmortem obligation and replaced the money, finally agreeing to stump up matching funds to build a suitable museum. The Smithsonian is one of the most liberal, wide-ranging and exhausting museums in the world, containing everything from the space shuttle to Julia Child's kitchen. The breadth of its interest and acceptance of what makes culture and deserves to be in a national museum is the most forgiving and amusing in the world. The collection runs from the most aesthetically rarefied to the homespun and popular; more egalitarian than any national collection. Whether Smithson would have approved, no one can say, but it's certainly kin to his life and experience and the Enlightenment. The highest ideals for the most mundane purpose—an educated meritocracy. It is an inescapable irony that Smithson, the man unacknowledged by his father, who in turn pretended to a grander name that wasn't his to legitimize, sent his own good name to the New World of new starts and new ideas and second chances. He never set foot in America. He didn't leave his legacy to a place but to an idea. Or perhaps the culmination and the fruition of many shining, humane ideas.

It will take you a week to thoroughly explore the Smithsonian, but over a weekend you can get a feeling for the generosity of his vision and its position as an ornament in the life of the nation he never saw. Or you could visit Alnwick Castle, ancestral home of the dukes of Northumberland, set on the blasted northeastern coast of England. You can pick your way through the tours of pensioners to wonder at the world's largest tree house and a poison garden. The parable is as fresh today as it was at the turn of the nineteenth century.

In my own family, Ted and Caroline's daughter, my cousin Wendy, became a photographer, who was herself the recipient of a MacArthur award, the philanthropic jackpot that has no published shortlist and a secret panel of judges. One day, the recipient receives a phone call that tells them they've been awarded a great deal of money without strings or rules; just the best wishes and some expectations. They invariably think, "This is a practical joke." Those gifted fit the span and gamut of applied culture; and of course it is a joke, a practical jape on the Old World. It is the smile of enlightenment, of pluralism, of philanthropy and the promise of America.

13

Germans

At the end of my first journey to America I traveled to New York. I'd been invited by a friend of my father's to come and spend the weekend with him and his wife at their free-world dacha on the less fashionable, further shore of Long Island. He was an Englishman, born in Lancashire, who'd come to America as a young reporter and gone to Hollywood, where Charlie Chaplin suggested he'd make a great light comedian. He'd interviewed every president since Roosevelt and knew a national biography of Americans. He'd reported the country through the Depression, the war, the civil rights movement and Vietnam. He'd reported Nixon's impeachment, the tune-in-and-drop-out hippies, and over the years he'd gained an American family and a mild American accent that was inaudible to Americans, who heard only a mild English one. He was the great sympathetic explainer of Britain to America, and America to Britain, and he was also, if all that were not enough, the most urbane, witty and readable journalist of his century. Alistair Cooke was a past master at just this form of teasing, elliptical, dropped introduction. He had witnessed the last march of Civil War veterans and reported the end of the Cold War. More than anything, he was America's raconteur. An elegant and surprisingly dainty man with elegant hands with which he would mime illustrations, play jazz piano and obsessive golf.

The first time I met Alistair had been in our flat in London. He was about to embark on a series of television programs with my father. He spoke almost, it seems, without break or interruption, for four hours, and he never said a dull word, never missed the beat of a story or fluffed a punch line. It was a bravura performance of pancontinental anecdotalism. At the end of the evening, our little living room was crowded with the shades of the New World: Sherman and Stonewall Jackson, Patton and Eisenhower, Duke Ellington and Bing Crosby, Babe Ruth and Eleanor Roosevelt, Frick and Rockefeller. The great, the gaudy, the good and the gimcrack. But alongside them were the massed chorus of immigrant Americans: not there as a supporting cast as they would have been in a European story, but together the collective star. The famous and the memorable merely bobbed for their moment in this great, spinning, churning stew of people. They were the point, the energy and the engine of this narrative.

The English press thought that Alistair Cooke *was* the special relationship, that mystical bond that is supposed to traverse the Atlantic like fairy gossamer but with the strength of a mother's love, a connection that reaches beyond the necessity of diplomacy and admiration, a deep and abiding, filial friendship. Alistair was too good a journalist and knew too much to be gulled by this easy cliché. He was cynically steely about the arrangement. Over the years this "special relationship" has been trotted out, but its frequent tiffs and slights are a deep embarrassment for many Britons and a shuddering annoyance for Americans. Every new president is richly backed into a corner at a press conference by a gang of eager British reporters pleading that he reiterate the vows of specialness, and with a thin smile of practiced public relations, the president will inevitably deliver an anodyne and bland statement of best wishes, a desire for peace and democracy, and shared history, and the British will heave a sigh of relief that they're still the favorites. This cringing need to be especially loved, the constant sensitivity, is a particularly British neediness. It led to the instigation of the Commonwealth, where countries that had been invaded, abused and plundered were begged to come and say that, all in all, it was worth it, because we gave them a bloody good post office and a railway.

The special relationship with America is even more craven. The phrase was coined by Ramsay MacDonald, but without much weight or emotional meaning. It was really blown up to be a sort of engagement by Churchill, who was half-American himself, and liked to dress the necessity of loans and aid in an Anglo-Saxon romance of blood and belief. But it was Dean Acheson, the great American secretary of state, adviser and manipulator of presidents from Eisenhower to Nixon, who most clearly and honestly summed up the truth of the special relationship. "Of course," he said, "there is a unique relationship between Britain and America. But unique doesn't mean affectionate." He went on to point out the truth: that America had fought England as an enemy as often as it had fought with it as an ally, and most famously and crisply he pointed out that Britain had lost an empire but failed to find a role, which stung Harold Macmillan into a pibroch of bitter hurt, like a girl who's been asked for the ring back.

This relationship has always been the larger cog turning the smaller. America sold armaments to Britain in the First World War and lent the money to buy them. In 1914, Britain and its empire had the richest and deepest reserves in the world. In 1919 it had the largest debt in the world. The gold had simply been passed across the Atlantic. America had fought in the same war for half the time and had come out of it the winner, and considerably richer. The war bonds issued by the Bank of England to pay off the Great War debt have only recently been finally redeemed. The Treaty of Versailles that was the final contract of America's victory was negotiated by Woodrow Wilson, the great internationalist and meddler, the man with a plan which included the steely desire to break up or curtail empires, particularly the British one. He set up the League of Nations in the image of America, and Congress refused to ratify it. After the Second World War, the Marshall Plan was the single largest gift of aid ever made. It cost America billions of dollars and it still stands as one of the most far-sighted, humane and worthwhile pieces of philanthropy—though it was sold to the Americans and Congress by the mercurial Dean Acheson as being an invaluable investment against Communism.

Throughout the Cold War, Britain's relationship with America mimicked East Germany's with Russia. Eisenhower refused to condone the tawdry mugging of Egypt over Suez, drawing a definitive line under the era of empire entitlement. In his turn, Harold Wilson refused to be drawn into Vietnam, and then there was the murderous Cambridge spy ring, and the death of trust.

The special relationship is noticed mostly in its breaches, its rows, its insincerity, and the stickily nostalgic memoirs of power-struck diplomats. But the cold, historic truth is that Britain was never the most eligible or nubile candidate to slip between the star-spangled sheets. It should have been France. France had far more in common with the New World. It was the French who finally turned the tide of the War of Independence, it was France that sent ships and soldiers from Lafayette to help this new coun try. It was France that followed the example of revolution with one of its own, copying the high-minded declarations of freedom and equality and the rights of man. They came and gave America the keys to the Bastille in gratitude. France sold Louisiana to America in the most favorable real estate deal in history. And then there was the biggest birthday present ever donated from one lovelorn nation to another: the Statue of Liberty. I like to imagine the mayor of New York signing for it and a UPS guy saying, "We've got this parcel out in the harbor," and the French ambassador standing there with a thousand-cheese-eating grin, saying, "Go on, open it!" And the mayor says, "Oh gosh, I can't guess what it is," and pulls the ribbon. "Well, isn't that dandy? I don't know what to say. We certainly don't have one of those."

But very quickly after independence the Americans came to mistrust the French; not least because the French aren't to be trusted and simply can't help themselves mocking and patronizing Americans. They may have been brought together by a common enemy and some highfalutin ideas, but the nations are as far apart in sensibility and temperament as it's possible to find. America should have had a special relationship with its neighbors in Latin America, but its history and its involvement in the southern continent is special only in its necessity. Propinquity piles on the resentment. Even its friendship with its northern neighbors is marked by the rote teasing of a bored uninterest. The Americans are naturally friendly individually, one at a time. America itself has always stood aloof. Unlike almost every other country in the world, America has no favorite nation mates. It is the nation that was founded to be the "other place," the alternative to a hopelessly compromised, worn-out world. America is still an experiment into the better way. Even the most modestly accoutred or educated American considers himself more blessed than any other citizen of any other place, simply by being put in the United States by God and Providence.

Personal prejudice is reflected in public policy. Tellingly, the department that deals with relations with the rest of the world doesn't have the word "foreign" in it: it is the State Department. It looks after the interests of one state alone. It might be called the Bargepole Department. Congress is truculently reluctant to ratify any agreement signed off by an administration while presidents look dawnward to becoming diplomats and statesmen and see golden horizons and themselves as peaceful Alexanders. Congressmen are far more parochial, mistrusting all foreign promises and adventures. So Woodrow Wilson's parsimonious and desiccated worldview was killed by home-grown politics. Many nations have found that treaties they imagined to be neutral aren't. America is alternately timid and truculent about "out there." They won't join the International Court or ban landmines unilaterally, not because they don't believe in justice or not blowing the legs off children, but because they don't want to be implicated or entwined with the old ways and the old folk.

The one nation America has seemed to gain something of a special relationship with is Israel, the sliver of the Middle East that has no oil and little strategic importance. America's affinity with it has brought little benefit and much opprobrium. It isn't down to a clever or vociferous Jewish lobby in New York, Washington and Hollywood, as is so regularly claimed by Arabs and European liberals. It is the recognition that the two places have very similar origins. Born out of religious intolerance, each sees itself as the ark of the chosen people, a holy place set apart by a higher calling that accepts immigrants from all over the world if they share a belief and a vision. Both are countries built on morality and hard work. Israel's rhetoric bears a striking similarity to that of America's Presbyterian settlers.

The irony of America's 300 years as a nation is that its special relationships, the affairs that have defined it, are not with its friends but its enemies. The long pose of the Cold War hugged America closer, defined and realized the nation far more than any mere crush of friendship. America has always understood that it is defined by what it stands against more than what it stands for. It's a nation for whom implacable enmities are more carefully and assiduously tended than friendships. This aloofness, this stiffness on social occasions, didn't arrive in the American psyche by osmosis, it wasn't inherited from the Indians or left behind by the Brits. In Europe we recognize this demeanor, it's familiar to us, because it's German. America may talk English but it thinks Krautish.

The largest self-identified national group in America are Germans. Fifty-eight million of them hold their hands up. That's 18 percent of the country, one in four of the white population. The 36 million of African descent—their Africa is a country, not a continent—count themselves as 11 percent of the population. Eleven percent are wholly or partly Irish, and wholly or partly drunk. Twenty-five million claim to be English by descent—8 percent of Americans. Someone pointed out that the Americans may speak English, but they don't ever think English. The only people who celebrate St. George's Day in America are the Boy Scouts, which is more than the Boy Scouts do in England. It's worth noting in passing one small but extraordinary statistic: sixteen presidents have Ulster parentage, what the American census politely and light-footedly calls Scots-Irish. That really is a fantastic overachievement for such a dour, humorless and unlovable little community.

It was Alistair Cooke who first told me that to understand America you must begin by understanding how much of it is German. We imagine that, because of the language and the inherited legal system, common law and Magna Carta, this would be at bottom an Anglo-Saxon sort of a place. One of the facts most Anglophobe people know about the Germans in America is that

Congress rejected German as the national language by only one vote. Actually, that's apocryphal. There never was a vote. There never was a national language. America has no official language: it's always been polyglot, with English being the default setting of official documents.

There were already half a million Germans in the thirteen colony states at the time of independence. The English royal family was also German. But 1848 was the beginning of the great migration of Germans to the New World, the year of revolutions in Europe. There was revolution in Paris and the abdication of the French king, there were revolts and demonstrations all over the district, German statelets calling for the creation of a greater Germany. While most revolutionaries want independence, the Germans contrarily managed to concoct a riot demanding more cohesion, order and a bigger nation. Individually, the princes, kings, dukes and electors promised the romantically incensed mobs and petitioners unity and democracy. And then, one at a time, reneged at their leisure with a Teutonic brutality, which in turn provoked a great exodus, a clearing out of radicals, dissidents and nationalists. They fled in their millions, west, to Brazil, Argentina, Canada, but mostly to the new United States.

Before '48, German immigrants to America had been overwhelmingly rural. Like the English, they were mostly religious dissenters; Protestants and evangelicals. They settled in Pennsylvania and the new territories of the West, and they farmed diligently. Early travelers said you could tell a German farm from a mile away: their fields were well kept and neat, the stock was fat and expertly bred, and German red barns were a model of the new improved, American peasant. But this second wave were urban, educated, political and romantic, and they arrived just in time for the Civil War; 176,000 joined up for the Union in the war to save a nation. There is a terrible symmetry here. Having just failed to create a unified state of Germans, German-Americans suffered the greatest number of casualties by nationality to keep a nation together. There is no doubting the German commitment to the republic, or their new patriotism. They may well have also had the highest military casualties in the

War of Independence, having been used as mercenaries by the English and also having fought for Washington.

The next great wave of German immigration didn't come from Germany at all. In 1874 the czar of Russia demanded that all people living in Russia should be obliged to do military service. There were German enclaves, mostly along the Volga and in the Crimea, who'd been encouraged to come by Catherine the Great, herself a German. Because of their superior farming abilities they were supposed to show the kulaks how modern Europe did things. German immigrants had been given tax breaks and land, their communities prospered Germanically and harvested the resentment of their Russian neighbors. There were constant demands for the privileges of these foreigners to be withdrawn. They kept their language and their own company, only integrating to undercut local businesses. Many of the dissenting German Protestants were pacifist, and the call to military service was a concession they couldn't make, so they embarked for America and the new states and territories, in particular Texas.

Germans in America were immensely successful, probably the most collectively successful of all immigrant groups. Throughout the nineteenth century 8 million of them arrived in America. Germans did what Germans do: they prospered. They farmed and manufactured, ran businesses and banks, wrote books and music, brewed beer and quickly learned to excel at basketball and athletics. They weren't just model Americans, they were the model for Americans. The federal states of America with its commitment to innovation and hard work, personal conservatism and public freedom, looked very like an idealized Germany. Germans were radical: they were at the forefront of organized labor. Being brewers, they voted overwhelmingly against Prohibition. And then came their Wagnerian reckoning. American intervention in the First World War was vociferously opposed by German-Americans—and a great many other Americans. It was also opposed by President Woodrow Wilson, who spoke of armed neutrality and offered to intercede between the warring forces. In 1916 he stood for election under the campaign slogan "He Kept Us Out of War." His

Republican opponent, Charles Evans Hughes, was also against the European war. You couldn't have voted for anyone to get you into any war. There was, it was said, "only a haircut between them." It was the election where Wilson ignored his opponent, saying that you didn't murder a man who was committing suicide, and he won by a whisker. He took the oath of office in February and had declared war on Germany by the first week of April, "to make the world safe for democracy."

But it wasn't the war that did it for German-Americans, it was the peace. Wilson's manhandling of the Treaty of Versailles left Germany a pitiful, bankrupt and pillaged place. The French had insisted that the old enemy be reduced to a sixteenth-century agricultural nation of miserably cowed peasants. The next grim decade of weak government, unemployment and inflation appeared deeply unfair and vindictive from the distance of the New World. German-Americans who had kept their hyphenated heritage that way round heard the distant howl of fascism as a clarion that would blow away the humiliation, right the wrongs. Seen from America, its echo chimed with many of the concerns of white workers and the middle class in the Depression. Twenty-five thousand German-Americans joined an openly Nazi German Bund that opened an Aryan camp in a place called Yaphank, Long Island, not far from where I stayed with the Cookes. This has always been a very German part of New York. They named the camp Siegfried. Yaphank was no stranger to camps: they trained volunteers here for the doughboy army of the Great War. That famous German Irving Berlin had been stationed here and wrote a revue called *Yip Yip Yaphank*.

The Bund bought a local farm and were initially welcomed by the community, but almost immediately were invaded by thousands of Brownshirts who marched from the local railway station every weekend carrying swastika banners and flicking Hitler salutes, the blonde girls in dirndls and plaits, the boys in leather shorts and red thighs. They did what Germans do outdoors: gymnastics, calisthenics, hiking, posing, tent-erecting and bellowing to oompah-pah bands. They drank beer and caroused with a romantic sentimentality. They quickly fell out with the local citizens: the local paper is full of municipal complaints about mess and noise and breakages and being intimidated by the hand-on-hip aggression of weekend hobby fascism. There was a local judge, Gustave Neuss, who was himself a German-American and a very rare Democrat in these parts, who'd been elected to the town council and became, cussedly, an implacable foe of the fascists, taking down car number plates to hand to the FBI at every opportunity. He went out of his way to confront the Bund. He is an American character out of small-town mythology. He would have been played by Jimmy Stewart. The fascists fought the local boys over access to the local swimming hole, and the yip-yip Yaphank youth retaliated by tipping over the Nazis' outdoor lavatories and digging up their swastika flower beds. Judge Neuss kept extensive records. There is in all this something comical, a suburban reenactment of what is beginning to happen in Europe. It was the anti-Semitism, the call to boycott Jewish businesses, to root out Jewish bankers in New York, that seems to have angered Judge Neuss most.

Having lost his seat on the city council, he continued the resistance against fascism by getting the camp's license to sell alcohol rescinded. After a beerless beer festival, the Nazis threatened the town that if their planning applications and licenses weren't allowed, they would sell the whole place to Negroes. Yaphank stood firm. As the war in Europe grew serious and the news darker, and America began supporting Britain with a lend-lease, so the position of the American-German Bund grew more extreme and powerless. Fritz Kahn, the first leader, traveled to Germany to visit the Führer, who kept him at a distance. He wanted to do nothing that would encourage American Germans. They were embarrassing, playing at the great crusade of blood and earth, already compromised by softness and the racial porridge of the New World.

When America came to war, the Bund evaporated. When shove came to push, German-Americans found they were more American than German, certainly more liberal than fascist, and they joined up in the thousands along with Italians and Austrians and Bulgarian-Americans. A few were interred as enemy aliens, but there was no

German Fifth Column in America, and during the whole war there was only one attempt to set up a German resistance.

At dawn on June 13, 1942, the German submarine U-202, the *Innsbruck,* surfaced off Amagansett, Long Island, and four German officers paddled ashore. They were wearing full naval uniform for the pragmatic reason that if they were caught in uniform, they would be prisoners of war and not shot as spies: a particularly wonderful piece of Teutonic rationalism. They were planning to set up as saboteurs and blow up selected military targets. While they were burying their uniforms along with stashes of guns and explosives, they were discovered by the coast guard John Cullen. He was grabbed by the collar and roughly offered a bribe of $260 to look the other way. He went straight to the police. Offering a bribe with a threat in Europe would have been familiar, and probably expedient. In America, though, it really wasn't. It's not that this was a nation above corruption, just not on that level or with that tone. There was a similar though possibly apocryphal story about a German spy landing off the coast of Norfolk, walking into a village and banging on a pub door to ask in perfectly accented English for a glass of hard cider. The publican gave him a drink, made an excuse and went out the back to fetch the local policeman. The only person in Britain who didn't know you couldn't get alcohol at nine in the morning would be a German spy.

The German spies in Amagansett took a train to New York City, where they made plans to blow up Pennsylvania Station. One of them, Herr Dusche, was having second thoughts. He went to Washington to hand himself in. A dozen FBI agents refused to take him seriously and he was continually being thrown out of offices for being a nuisance. Finally, with an exasperated fury, he tipped $84,000 onto the desk of agent D. M. Ladd and demanded to be taken as a spy, and seriously. If there's one thing Germans can't stand, it's not being taken seriously. And this time, the bribery with menaces worked. He was interrogated and gave up the rest of the cell. They were tried and, despite the naval uniforms, executed in the electric chair. Except for Dusche and another man called Berger, who had also cooperated. They were given long prison sentences that were commuted by Harry Truman at the end of the war. Dusche was sent back to Germany, and with a small, victorious act of clemency, was allowed to stay in the American zone.

The German operation to land saboteurs in America was codenamed Pastorius, after Francis Daniel Pastorius, a German Quaker and pacifist who was one of the founding Pennsylvania Dutch (a mispronunciation of Deutsch). He really was a remarkable man, not just for being the first to start an argument that would bisect American society and politics for 150 years, but because he composed the first protest, "A memorial against slavery," in 1688. "There is a saying that we shall do for all men like we will be done ourselves, making no difference of what generation, descent or color they are. Those who steal or rob men and those who buy or purchase them, are they not alike? . . . If this is done well, what shall we say is done evil?"

There is a lot in America's social and public demeanor that is undeniably German, a certain unbending righteousness and an unflinching belief in freedom of speech, particularly of the written word, but also a fear of nonconformity, the understanding that freedom should not be exploited at the expense of collective belief and taste. Germans and Americans have a singular liberality and a plural censoriousness. But mostly we can sense Teutonic iron in the way America sees the rest of the world: its innate sense of superiority, its unarguable assumption that other nations and people want what America has far more than America needs what the rest of the world has to offer. This doesn't come from Anglo-Saxons, with their insecure desire to be liked and appreciated. It doesn't come from Spain or from Africa, or the East. It is German. Not so much a belief but a knowledge that they are people blessed with achievements that are gained through intelligence, resolve and craftsmanship, and whose works are smiled on by Providence. The belief that America has a secret mission in the world is one that has been historically shared by Germans. Their relationship with the rest of us is never a meeting of equals. Every nation has a special relationship with America, but America has a special relationship with none but itself.

14

Evolution

When Alistair Cooke first came to America as a correspondent and student of linguistics, one of the men he sought out to explain English in the way of the New World was Henry Louis Mencken. "If I had been an American I would undoubtedly have worshipped H. L. Mencken in my college years, and gone round campus carrying the latest issue of *American Mercury*, as we are told the Chinese carry the thoughts of Chairman Mao."

H. L. Mencken was a German-American critic, essayist and journalist, born, raised and buried in Baltimore. He wrote for the *Baltimore Sun*. He was, and remains, one of the world's greatest polemicists, and an American literary stylist who helped create and nail down a distinctly American form not just of journalism but of language. He had a hot, unflinching gimlet eye. He wrote with the precision of a tattooist and the righteous directness of a guillotine operator. He became the most famous and widely read columnist in America during the 1920s and 1930s, and is the patron saint, or rather sprite—there was little saintly about him—of all columnists. We tend to fall into two schools, the Montaignists, classical, elegant, epigrammatic men of letters who raise their eyebrows rather than their voices, and the Menckenites, who roll up their sleeves and load words like grapeshot. Contrarians who write with spittle-flecked, bad-breathed grudges.

When Cooke met him, Mencken was at a low ebb. His bombast had left him marooned on the further shore of political and critical debate. Mencken's capacity for anger was inexhaustible. He stoked a wild ire that raged over a forest of subjects, from fundamentalism to idealism, collectivism, Democracy, Prohibition,

populism, anti-intellectualism, southerners, Anglophilia and Creationism, Christianity and chiropractors. And he managed to fit
in a puce loathing for Franklin Roosevelt and his New Deal. He
pointed out that if he had his way, any man guilty of golf would
be ineligible for any office under these United States. What he
was for was culture, and the language. The only thing bigger than
Mencken's irritation was his vocabulary, and he became the greatest living practitioner of American English. He plasticized it into
a vernacular that was direct and rhythmic, inventive and lethal
and witty. He was very funny. He took the freedom of speech at
street value, to shout, "A cynic is a man who, when he smells flowers, looks around for a coffin." His ghost still instructs blogs and
the web.

As Walter Lippmann said, he denounced life, and made you
want to live. Mencken wrote, "All successful newspapers are
ceaselessly quarrelsome and bellicose, they never defend anyone
or anything if they can help it. If the job is forced on them they
tackle it by denouncing someone or something else." If he didn't
invent it, then he perfected first-person contrarianism. There was
barely a subject or cause he couldn't make an awkward stand on.
He was an extreme believer in freedom of speech, and a fearless
defender of civilization, but would forcefully point out that a poet
over thirty is simply an overgrown child, and that "an idealist is
one who, noticing a rose smells better than a cabbage, concludes it
will make better soup."

He had little sympathy or empathy for suffering, complaining
humanity. Crowds were moronic. The opinion of the masses was
stupid, wrong and venal. Most firebrand libertarians love the idea
of humankind, just find humans awkward. Mencken couldn't suffer them by the gross or one at a time. He said he never lectured,
not because he wasn't a good speaker, but because he loathed the
sort of people who go to lectures and didn't want to meet them.
There was a fundamental, skeptical suspicion of the goodness of
humanity. An atheist's understanding of original sin: "It is hard
to believe a man when you know that you would lie if you were
in his place." And most famously he wrote that "democracy is the

theory that the common people know what they want and deserve it, good and hard." And that "giving every man a vote has no more made men wise and free than Christianity has made them good."

Mencken may have been a monumental, ironclad, oceangoing cynic, but he matched this with a transcendent enthusiasm. He believed that man was, if not perfectible, then improvable. He was passionate not just for invective but for culture, particularly German culture. He liked German literature and the English language, though he couldn't find anything good to say about the English themselves. He mistrusted Anglo-Saxon perfidy, their silky manners, the assumption to rule, and closer to home, the Anglophilia and snobbery that infected the ruling class in America. He liked the German virtues of romantic music and poetry, hard work, direct speech and hard drinking. He spoke to the innate difference in races and people in a way that was reflected clearly and uncomfortably in the great stew of Americans. He got prosecuted for a libelously spiteful and very funny essay on southerners. Perhaps his finest moment, the coming together of his cultural and social prejudices and convictions, was at the Scopes trial.

In March 1925 Austin Peay, the governor of Tennessee, signed off on the Butler Act that prohibited the teaching of evolution in any of the state schools. Within two months the American Civil Liberties Union (ACLU) offered to support any teacher who would openly flout the law. A group of businessmen saw a chance to promote the tiny backwater of Dayton, and brought a young biology teacher to Robinson's drugstore to convince him to admit to teaching Darwinism. John Scopes was initially reluctant, but agreed, and set off what was instantly dubbed the trial of the century, and universally headlined as the Monkey Trial, a confrontation between God and modernity that galvanized America and amused the rest of the world. To argue over the science of natural selection and the absolute, unarguable correctness of a literal reading of the Bible seemed, in Europe, bizarre. This was the roaring Jazz Age. In this year, 1925, Fitzgerald published *The Great Gatsby*. The first surrealist exhibition was held in Paris, George Bernard Shaw won the Nobel Prize in Literature, and Mussolini came to power. John Logie Baird invented television. Paul Newman and Margaret Thatcher were born, and the American president Calvin Coolidge was elected. Called Silent Cal, for his mannered and sober demeanor, he also was the wooden star of the first talking newsreel.

He inherited the presidency on the death of Warren G. Harding, and was not the Republicans' preferred choice. During the election campaign, his son died from an infected blister after playing tennis at the White House. He said tersely that all the pleasure and the pomp of the presidency was extinguished, but he carried on campaigning with a stoic dignity. Coolidge was a small-government conservative, uncomfortable in company. When he was asked why he went to so many society dinners, as he so plainly loathed them, he replied, "You've got to eat somewhere." Much mocked by Dorothy Parker, who once sat next to him at one of the hated society beaufeasts, and began by saying she had a bet with a friend who'd said she wouldn't get more than two words out of him, Coolidge paused for a moment and drily replied, "You lose." By 1927, only the richest 2 percent of Americans paid any federal tax at all. Silent Cal succinctly pointed out that the chief business of the American people is business, and that aphorism is now more famous than he is.

Defending Scopes was the most famous trial lawyer in America, Clarence Darrow, a man with a face like a frost-damaged turnip and the huge hands of an arthritic seal. He defended over fifty murderers, of whom only one, the first, was ever executed. He often used insanity or diminished responsibility pleas, bringing the newfangled ideas of Freud to bemused American jurors and suspicious judges. He defended a black doctor and his family charged with murder, after their home in a white street was attacked by a lynch mob who feared for property prices. Darrow made a seven-hour summing-up, which is still considered one of the greatest pieces of courtroom oratory ever declaimed. The doctor was acquitted.

He also defended Leopold and Loeb, the privileged teenage boys who killed a thirteen-year-old child for the thrill of it. It was a case that salaciously entranced America. Darrow had their death sentences commuted to life, without divulging that they'd been lovers. Leopold was murdered in the showers in prison. Loeb had to identify him.

Darrow was born in the great agrarian Midwest and began practicing law in Ohio. He was a Democrat and an atheist, with a strong attachment to socialism and organized labor. He began his career defending union leaders, was a founding member of the ACLU and in his personal life was argumentative, complicated, depressed and political. He was charged and twice tried for attempting to bribe a juror, and though the cases finally collapsed, they were never satisfactorily refuted. In a plea bargain, Darrow agreed to never again practice law in California. In the film *Inherit the Wind,* about the Scopes trial, he's played by Spencer Tracy. His declamatory style, his left-wing politics, his defense of the lowest and the most vilified, and his willingness to bend rules and bully courtrooms on behalf of his clients have made him the model for dozens of lawyers in films and television.

The town of Dayton brought in a big star to help the prosecution. The Scopes trial would be the final, pyrotechnic, pyrrhic shot of William Jennings Bryan, America's most thin-skinned and long-suffering politician. Bryan was born in Salem, Illinois, raised as a Methodist. At a young age he started going to a Presbyterian church. He said later his baptism into this Calvinist Scottish kirk was the most important day of his life.

Bryan went into politics on behalf of the great square states, and their conservative agrarian population. All his life he was for the country and against the urban. He saw cities as places of sin and simony, filthy concrete and tar, mazes for tricksters and honeyed liars, conurbations that turned the honest hard work of the farmer into lust and debt. Anything that was good and honest and decent about America grew out of the earth, and was husbanded by those who guided a plow or herded a flock.

His constituents had a simple but profound faith in God and the word of the Bible that grew from the second Great Awakening, a raw movement that began in the 1800s and saw a vast increase in the congregations of low churches—Baptists and

Methodists—as well as the revelations of new ones, like Advent-ists. Revival meetings were held in tents and in camps across rural America. Bible literalism and the belief in salvation through con-stant revival became a collective, unifying belief among the farm-ers, along with debt and a dislike of suits and cities. And while at the top of the national government, church and state might be politely and constitutionally separate, in the creeks and hollows of West Virginia, the red barns of Pennsylvania and the sod-roofed saddlebag cabins of the Dakotas, religion wasn't separate from anything. Everything started with God.

Bryan stood for people who felt cut off from the great engine of the modern age. They believed that the country was the true nation and the nation belonged to them. They held the essence, the soul, of America, but it was being stolen by Babylon. Bryan's crusade was always nostalgic, harking back to a sentimental time of an imagined America, the founding fathers and their invention of a loose federation of self-governing states made up of farming communities and gentleman scholars.

Like so many great failures, Bryan's career was marked at the start by an astonishing success. It was a single speech. He already had a reputation as a churchy orator, and in 1896, his crusade was against the gold standard. The price of gold would make the inter-est on the loans the farmers had taken out ruinous. They'd been encouraged by banks to improve their agricultural output, to buy more land and invest in modern equipment and machinery. The consequent and all-too-predictable world glut in produce, and European protectionism, forced prices down. The farmers couldn't meet their repayments, their farms were repossessed, and land prices collapsed. With a biblical eye, Bryan saw the devil in the gold and in the men who manipulated it. He called for the gold standard to be augmented with silver. Immediately this would increase the amount of money, and because America already had rather a lot of silver, it would place a lot more in the hands of ordinary folk. This idea is immortalized in film: the story of *The Wizard of Oz* is an allegory about the gold standard. Dorothy's family are poor farmers, the yellow brick road is gold. Dorothy's ruby slippers were originally silver, and Bryan is rendered as the cowardly lion, all bluster and boasting, but terrified to strike.

It was a rather bizarre idea that held great sway among poor Democrats. Bryan addressed the Democratic convention with his pulpit oratory voice that boomed with biblical authority and quivered with welling emotion. He threw out his great bellows of a chest and proclaimed that "the humblest citizen in all the land, when clad in the armor of a righteous cause, is stronger than all the hosts of error." And like the payoff of some romantic novel, this tore the veils from the eyes of the delegates. It was a sensation: out of nearly nowhere, or at least the back of beyond, Bryan carried the nomination with the clarion exclamation, "You shall not press down upon the brow of labor this crown of thorns. You shall not crucify mankind upon a cross of gold." Well, that fair did it.

It's often said about fairy stories that happy endings all depend on when you stop the telling. Bryan's biopic should have rolled the credits over the ecstatic tears of boater-hatted, flag-waving Democrats. But it didn't. It went on to Dayton, Tennessee, three decades later. He lost the election. All in all he lost three presidential elections, something of a record.

Woodrow Wilson finally made him secretary of state. When Wilson reneged on his election promise and declared war on Germany, Bryan, a lifelong pacifist, resigned. He continued in politics, endlessly crossing the country through rural communities and one-street railway stops, railing against the evils of the godless city. And like an Old Testament prophet, whose prophecies are all in the past, he remained in the wilderness, his constituency dwindling, his rhetoric ever more shrill. He relentlessly banged his tambourine and waved his fingers at heaven, speaking on behalf of the mocked and passed-over God-fearing poor folk who prayed before their meager dinners and put the fatted calf on the tables of the rich and godless. The Scopes trial, with its mass press interest, was right in the middle of Bryan's sweet spot. The newfangled idea of natural selection came from atheists and abroad. It was doing battle with God's holy writ, and conflicted with the rights of states, particularly poor, rural Low Church states like Tennessee, to decide their own morals and laws without interference from perfidious Washington.

Darrow and Bryan weren't strangers. Darrow had also stood unsuccessfully for office as a congressman. He had been an early admirer of Bryan's, supporting his stand against the gold standard because, he said, he always had an affinity with the debtor rather than the creditor. But soon they fell out. Too similar to get on, too different to make up.

As the trial began, Dayton filled with every itinerant hedge-row preacher and spiritualist evangelist. The Holy Spirit mingled with the world's press, who arrived by the busload along with the cynical Mencken, who reported on the impromptu prayer meetings on every street corner, the drugstores full of argument and incantation, and every soapbox Pharisee bawling damnation. Mencken went out into the woods and found a pile of born-again Shakers overcome with the spirit, lying in a great heap, jabbering in tongues. The town's businessmen smiled with their thumbs in their waistcoats and winked. Business boomed. Dayton was momentarily a red dot on the world's map.

The opening discussion in court was on whether or not the floor could stand the weight of the crowd. It was hot. Dangerously, maddeningly, violently, all too hellishly hot. Every so often proceedings were taken out onto the lawn, where the mass of God's witnesses sat under sunshades and ate picnics, and Darrow complained of the number of religious banners that might sway the jury. It became obvious very early on that he needn't have worried. None of the courtroom, the town or the state was remotely impartial. There was little doubt of the outcome, and a great deal of the case was put without the jury present. Darrow and the prosecution argued over points of law and points of order, and just points. Darrow wanted to call expert scientific witnesses. The judge was not just intimidated by Darrow, he was awestruck by Bryan, and more than aware of the beliefs of his constituents and state. Bryan sat in his chair accepting the constant well-wishes and fanning himself. Darrow stormed around the court, never taking off his double-breasted jacket. Scopes sat nervously in the dock.

The man who'd generated all this heat was merely a very young relief teacher, and although he was a man unquestionably made in the image of God, he was also completely beside anyone's point: the weather vane, not the wind. Originally the ACLU hadn't wanted Darrow to defend the case. They thought he was a publicity seeker and too histrionic. His past was tainted. He would turn the whole show into a legal argument and a vaudeville. It was Scopes who had insisted, "If it's going to be a gutter fight, I'd rather have a good gutter fighter." With a stroke of theatrical frustration and stand-up genius, Darrow called Bryan as a witness for the defense. The judge pointed out that he couldn't call the prosecution counsel on behalf of the accused, but Darrow knew his man, knew that he wouldn't be able to resist turning the stand into one final pulpit, and he was right.

Darrow began by saying that Bryan didn't have to swear to tell the truth. There followed a cross-examination that could only have happened in America. Darrow asked if Bryan believed everything the Bible said was literally true. Bryan said he did, except where passages were obviously figurative, like "you are the salt of the earth." "I would not insist that a man was actually salty." But Darrow continued, "Do you believe Jonah was swallowed by a whale?" Bryan protested that he thought it was a big fish, and that he'd stayed in the fish for three days. "Do you think the fish was made for Jonah?" Bryan replied that the Bible didn't specify. "Was the big fish made to swallow Jonah?" Bryan felt he was getting the better of this and said, "Let me add that one miracle is just as easy to believe as another." "Or just as hard," riposted Darrow.

They went on like this for a bit, for the amusement of the press and the edification of the sweating Christians. Where did Cain get his wife if the only woman on earth was Eve? If God cursed the snake to crawl on his belly, what had it walked on before? And what was the biblical age of the world? When pressed, Bryan admitted that it might have been created in 4004 BC. How do you think that estimate was arrived at, asked Darrow. "I couldn't say," said Bryan.

"What do you think?"

"I do not think about things I do not think about," replied Bryan.

"Do you think of things you do think about?"

"Well, sometimes."

"Do you think the earth was made in six days?"

"Not six days of twenty-four hours, I do not think they were twenty-four-hour days. My impression is that they were periods."

"Creation might have gone on for a very long time," said Darrow. And Bryan agreed it might have continued for millions of years.

"But I think it would be easier for the kind of God we believe in to make the earth in six days or in six million years, or in six hundred million years. I do not think it's important whether we believe one or the other."

Which, while not being a complete collapse of literal biblical argument, is certainly more than a nod in the direction of evolution. The judge reached for his gavel and adjourned. The jury never got to hear this exchange. The examination was purely for the wider jury of press and public, and the next day he ruled that it was all inadmissible, and was to be struck from the record.

"The three-times candidate for presidency came in a hero, and sat down at the end as one of the most tragic asses in American history," wrote Mencken, after the judgment was delivered, to no one's surprise, in favor of the Almighty. Scopes was fined $100, which was later overturned on appeal, on a technicality—the jury should have decided the amount, not the judge. The state of Tennessee, embarrassed by the ridicule the case had brought on it, quietly fudged the law into oblivion. The condemnation and the mockery of Bryan rang from coast to coast. He called for a rematch, demanding more time, more arguments, but he didn't have either.

William Jennings Bryan died five days later, a day short of the time it had taken his God to create the world. They said he died of a broken heart. Scopes admitted that there were some who thought Darrow's cross-examination had killed him. Darrow privately joked that it wasn't a broken heart that killed Bryan but a burst belly. He was an assiduous glutton.

Mencken said that God had aimed at Darrow but hit Bryan instead. Darrow was never one to avoid a bit of a gloat, and he reveled in the pyrrhic national victory, pointing out that he'd made up his mind to show the country what an ignoramus Bryan was. "And I succeeded."

He had one more major case to defend. The black doctor, Ossian Sweet, and his family in Detroit. But after that he declined into a sad and debilitated shadow of his old power, suffering from pulmonary heart disease. The energy with which he'd held courtrooms left him, and he died in 1938 a hermit, locked away with his long-suffering but devoted wife. Mencken too outlived his fame. His fairy story should have ended in the thirties. He was hoist with his own bellicosity, his war of words dumbfounded by the real thing. The Second World War did for him.

Having believed that the Great War was an imperial argument manufactured by kings, in which America should never have become involved, he assumed that the second round would be more of the same. That, combined with his hereditary sympathy for German culture, meant that he found himself an ever more lone and ranting voice. He said in retrospect that his wishful thinking and cynicism led him to write some pathetically callous things about the morality of war. That Hitler wasn't all bad. And he unforgivably discarded the first evidence of the Holocaust as mere Anglo propaganda. As the smoke rose from Europe's chimneys, so did his denials. Finally, to the relief of the *Baltimore Sun,* he resigned his column and took gardening leave to organize his cuttings.

These three loud and large men, Mencken, Darrow and Bryan, are each readily identifiable as American types. Looking back, they seem far more similar than they are different. Although their philosophies all originated in the Old World, their characters, and in particular their voices, are all completely rung out on the anvil of the New.

It was Mencken who first coined the term Monkey Trial, harking back to the original insults pinned to Darwin. But it also referred to Scopes, who found himself, by his own admission, a spectator in a cage at his own trial. Scopes retreated back to a private obscurity. He was the only protagonist who had never craved the manna of publicity. He never taught again, but went to work as a chemist for an oil company in Texas, oil of course being made from Jurassic plankton and algae, 180 million years ago, give or take a biblical day or two. Under Creationism, it is an impossible substance. Scopes became a Catholic and died in 1970, having privately admitted that he never actually taught evolution in his class. He lived to see Darwin get to the Supreme Court, for a final judgment in his favor. That didn't happen until 1968.

The retrospective judgment on the Scopes Monkey Trial is unanimous. Whatever the official verdict had been, it was the triumph of reason over belief, one of the liberal milestones of the twentieth century, along with universal suffrage, freedom of speech, civil and gay rights. And Darrow and Mencken were right. Bryan, as he always had been, was caught on the wrong side of the argument by ignorance and bigotry. At the end of the trial Darrow made one of the most quoted and rousing speeches heard in a court. You can still see Spencer Tracy do it pretty much verbatim. It finishes:

> Ignorance and fanaticism is ever-busy and needs feeding. Always it is feeding and gloating for more. After a while it is the setting of man against man, and creed against creed, until with flying banners and beating drums we are marching backward to the glorious ages of the sixteenth century when bigots lighted faggots to burn the men who dared to bring any intelligence and enlightenment and culture to the human mind.

You can hear in this speech the rumble that grates along the stress line that has crept from America since the first European settlers arrived. The colliding beliefs of the Enlightenment and nonconformists. Most of the time the friction has produced the heat and the energy that galvanized the nation. Enlightenment never hoed a row, toted a bale nor hammered a rivet. It was the ethic of the Reformation that actually built America, but the light of reason that directed it. These two have never sat happily together. Their specific freedoms and obligations collide. Darrow's use of the word "faggot" instead of kindling, or plain logs, is resonant. The faggots don't just burn witches in Salem, they are also the symbols of the reasoned empirical republic, taken from Rome. The embodiment of strength in unity: it's that old Washingtonian log basket again. They can also be the fuel that the pious use to punish the heretic, or the dry rationalist, the believer.

But there is one other telling event that occurred in 1925. Three days before the judgment in the Scopes trial, *Mein Kampf* was published. It augurs another uncomfortable way of looking at the struggle in Dayton. It has been said by his apologists that in the last days what most worried Bryan was not whether Cain was incestuous, or how big the fish that swallowed Jonah was, it was the growing intellectual popularity of the science of eugenics. In the 1920s the belief that Darwin's theories of survival of the fittest and natural selection pointed to the improvability of man through selective breeding and neutering was widely hailed by clever, fashionable folk. It was argued by H. G. Wells and George Bernard Shaw, and proselytized by Leonard Darwin, the inheritor of Charles's genius genes. And I would guess it was almost certainly believed by Mencken, with his constant allusion to national traits, and the lumpen stupidity of the lower orders. Darrow may also have thought genetics and breeding had culpability in crime.

The belief that degeneracy could be bred out of humanity was implied by rational science, and although this is only conjecture, Bryan would have seen this as an obvious godless threat to his great rural constituency, the simple and the unlettered, the family of honest and trusting faith who worked with their hands, rose early and went to bed early. Eugenics was a city idea, a soft-handed, smiling theory to degrade the awkward and the unsophisticated. It was a direct contradiction of the biblical injunction that all men were brothers and that we were all made in the image of God. Eugenics tore up the Sermon on the Mount and replaced it with a brutal, reductive competition. The winner was always right and always destined to win. It was a belief that was bereft of empathy, sympathy or charity, because it was scientific. The argument at Dayton might have been won by the Enlightenment, but Mencken had its postscript. "I set out laughing and returned shivering. The fundamentalists are on us, they will sweep the south and middle west, Bryan or no Bryan." And so they have.

The Creationist Museum is in Kentucky. A safe haven, a reserve, its natural habitat. They say they put it here because of the large population that lives within five hours' drive. Though why someone would drive five hours to look at a museum that proves there's nothing to see is just another of those good old God-fearing mysteries. It is an impressive modern building. You expect to see something churchy, wooden. What you don't expect this museum to look like is a museum: secular and rational. It is surrounded by a landscaped garden with playful topiary clipped into mythic animals and dinosaurs. There are armed and uniformed security guards, polite and vigilant, as if there might be a preemptive strike by suicide atheists or the devil.

You walk into a mise-en-scène of dinosaurs, and you realize there is a singular, omnipresent problem with the place. Everything they can exhibit belongs to the enemy. All the proof a believer needs is in the bedside drawer of his motel. They can make jokes about archaeologists, geologists and paleontologists. They can claim there were brontosauruses in the ark (baby ones). They can show in considerable detail how the antediluvian cruise liner was built. They can delicately explain how Cain wasn't really committing incest, and anyway God condoned it so it doesn't count. And anyway this is Kentucky. But when you see a rudimentary Bible-made Christian chap in a denim onesie with a pudding-bowl hairdo, looking like he's come from an audition for *Seven Brides for One Brother*, staring into the jaws of a plastic *T. rex*, you realize that even with his Old Testament nostalgia he's not making the connection. It's easier to imagine sharing the earth with familiar thunder lizards than with this spiritual separatist.

The big set piece in the museum is the diorama of Adam and Eve in the garden, a kitsch, hyperrealist hallucination that looks part Jeff Koons, part born-again manga. The innocent, nearly knowledgeable couple seem to be Mexican. Her long hair covers her modesty, foliage his penis, and presumably the lack of a belly button. This prurient prudery is presumably for us, as these two still have no concept of nakedness. The couple stand in a gaudy forest with an awkward collection of attendant animals: deer and wolves, panthers and penguins. It's a taxidermist convention, the trophy room of some utterly indiscriminate hunter. These animals, so perfectly honed for their particular niches in the scheme of things, are lost in this idealized playpen. The penguin, with his insulating feathers and flippers for Antarctic acrobatics, the beak unused to apples and bananas, is a willful piece of silliness.

There is, along one corridor, a dense section devoted to the Scopes trial. Most of the visitors walk past it. It's not as interesting as the destruction of Sodom and Gomorrah, or the gift shop. Here, like punchy boxers reliving a long-gone fight, they explain again that actually Bryan won the case, that it was a godless, biased urban media that distorted the facts and censored the arguments. This wall of yellowing clippings and grainy photographs explains more about today than it does about 1925. This world of Creationism is girded against the future. Anything new will be, by the very nature of nature, bad. All discovery, any proof, will stretch the absolute belief a little thinner. The less we know the better. This museum is God's bunker. Far from being omnipresent and omnipotent, God is cooped up here, storing the Kool-Aid and the ammunition. God lurks in the doubt, in the maybe of things, in the unprovable, in the moments of scientific darkness which become Creationist certainties. If only, at the end, Bryan could have puffed out his chest, spread his hands and said that the Bible wasn't the facts, but it was a great truth. Just as science is a world full of facts, but is rarely the whole truth, and as metaphor, simile and parable are as vital and inspiring and enlightening as experiments, hypotheses and proof. But he was never going to do that, because it wasn't his role, it wasn't his time, it wasn't in his blood or his breeding.

The long arm-wrestle between religion and reason in America is both productive and destructive. It is as much whom you believe as what you believe, or more precisely, who shares your belief. To use the useful biblical analogy, both sides have shibboleths of belonging. Religious literalism comes with a lot of other secular assumptions. It is provincial, conservative and community. Rationalism and doubt are urban, liberal, intellectual. The number of Americans who believe in Creationism and the literal truth of the Bible, with the caveat that they don't all see it the same way, stands at 30 percent. The number of atheists who believe that the Bible is wishful folklore is about 20 percent. The other 50 percent think this Bible is inspired by God, but not the factory manual. In Europe the headline in those statistics would be that a third of Americans don't believe in evolution, but I think the surprise figure is that only 20 percent are atheists, and that one way or another eight out of ten Americans still trust in God.

There is an odd, tangential postscript to the Monkey Trial. In 1922 a Robert Yerkes suggested that chimpanzees might be taught sign language. The suggestion wasn't taken up for forty years. Chimpanzees didn't seem terribly interested. But a chimp called Viki was bribed to be an informer, and learned a handful of words. And, more famously, Washoe, a chimp who'd been captured in the wild as an infant, was brought up with a human family and learned hundreds of signed words, combining something like thirty of them into simple two-word phrases. For a long time this was thought to represent an understanding of the rudiments of grammar. Washoe was encouraged to adopt an orphaned chimp, Loulis, to whom she passed on signing, and a rudimentary understanding of homework. More recently, in the seventies, there was Nim Chimpsky, who also learned hundreds of signs. You notice the names here, the last being a nerd lab pun on Noam Chomsky, the radical students' favorite. But somehow Viki is more demeaning. You know Viki. We all know Viki, Viki makes sandwiches at school football games. Viki writes round-robin e-mails about footpaths. Viki is a game, plain girl who drinks gin. The anthropomorphic naming of scientific experiments casts some doubt on their detachedness.

As far as I know, attempts to make chimpanzees speak have only ever been undertaken in the United States, managing to bring together the fundamentalist and rational dichotomy of their society. They also fulfill a childhood myth of American films: talking animals. The science here is so plainly a fig leaf to make a real live Disney character. And there is a more disturbing and darker reverse eugenics, a missionary zeal to bring words to the speechless, enlightenment to the savage beast. The scientific justification for wanting to know what a chimp thinks is unclear, except that it would be cool. Researchers hung out with their chimps, went to the bottom of the garden to smoke dope and drink beer. They had a sign for "pass the joint." None of this would have helped the chimp be any better as a chimpanzee. Indeed, the subjects became so habituated they considered themselves human, and other chimpanzees as animals. There was an implicit morality to what was taught, with manners and politeness insisted on. The more like humans apes behaved the better. Nim Chimpsky referred to going to the toilet as dirty, and started prefacing the names of people he didn't like with the sign for dirty. The sign that taking a shit is dirty at all is entirely human, reminding us and the apes that cleanliness is, if not next to godliness, next to the next-best thing: humanness. The chimp wranglers always mention regretfully that the apes never grow out of nappies or learn to use a litterbox, these being the most rudimentary signs of human civilization. Kanzi the bonobo "was an ape on the brink of the human mind," as if that were a good thing for a bonobo. Humans tend to favor bonobos over chimps because their group behavior in the wild seems less raucous, less bawdy, more Edenish.

Critics of the program pointed out that all the chimps ever did was ask for things and invent strategies for getting them, as if this were a base and selfish objective, "no better than pigeons pecking colored paper for corn," said one researcher, sniffily. For the humans there was a much greater reward. You had a really cool pet. You were able, in a sentimental, quasiromantic, religious way, to get closer to nature, to gain a selective, unscientific understanding of the anthropomorphic. There is also the molding and manipulation of a needy, endlessly grateful friend. When the chimps got big and stopped being grateful, and were behaving like brain-damaged humans, they were rejected and sent away to research labs and unwanted animal sanctuaries, where they taught other chimps how to sign "tickle me, and don't bogart that joint, my friend."

Ultimately, what the researchers wanted was to make the chimps replicate human emotion and sensibility, to show some sign of an aesthetic or spiritual life so that they might be awarded human rights and protectionism, because to be more human had to be an unconscious aspiration and an improvement. Or to show that nature's right to exist is a sliding scale, dependent on how closely you resemble or can mimic us, and therefore God. As it turned out from closely observed video footage, what the chimps were very, very good at—far better than their human handlers—was observation. They'd imitate signed words that their handlers were mentally forming to encourage them. Researchers who study chimpanzees in laboratories tend to stress the differences between apes and humans. Those who take them home concentrate on the similarities. Both these positions are self-serving—for the humans—and mean nothing to the chimpanzees or their ability to be a chimpanzee. It is here that the rational and religious planes of America collide, in the idea that a monkey would be more precious if it could wipe its bottom and wish you Happy Christmas. That is far closer to Bryan's view of the world than to Darwin's.

15

Moonshine

"You from over the water?" asked the wiry boy with a quid of Red Man tobacco, like a juicy goiter, under his lip. He had a look that was unmistakably Celt: bony, pale face, amused gimlet eyes shining out from under his filthy, high-crowned trucker's cap. We were in a bit of a field up a hollow. His cousins and I had been playing splits with a bowie knife. The boys liked to throw the knife as close to my feet as possible to make me jump. I seemed exotic to them, or perhaps just odd. I jumped a lot. I'd watched them torture a kitten to tease a toddler. They weren't overly concerned with consequences. I wasn't going to play chicken. And we were all pretty drunk.

"Yes," I said, imagining that over the water was the Atlantic. His father had been looking over the land with the idea of perhaps growing something, and was the only man in these parts who'd ever been abroad, serving as a sharpshooter in the Korean War. A lot of boys from hereabouts went into the service. A lot of them found a familiar home as snipers. "He don't mean the ocean, he means the Ohio River." "Yes," I said, "I'm from over the ocean. A long way over the water." "Huh," said the boy. "You got cars where you're from?"

I came to be in the southern Appalachian corner of east Kentucky because my cousin Wendy from Detroit had moved down here to teach photography in a one-room school up Kingdom Come Creek, and to take pictures with her large-format camera on a tripod with a black cloth over her head. The pictures gave everybody a direct and intense look, like they were already dead. I was still in the middle of my lingering pose as an art student at the Slade in Bloomsbury.

Wendy bought a parcel of land out here and built a cabin with a couple of bedrooms and a porch, and a darkroom. Flat land is at a premium in the mountains, and while she'd probably have left it to the squirrels, the locals thought it a waste not to plant something, so Errol from up the creek limped across the ground sucking his teeth. One of his calves had been sliced off in a coal mine. "It would be good to grow sorghum here; make molasses. No one's done that in these parts for a spell." So they planted sorghum, which grows tall like cane, and is crowned with a foxtail of seeds. Folk would stop by and look at the rows of plants and say how they hadn't had a stir-off in these parts for they didn't know how long. "But then in the old days, well, there was a story. And did I have a good recipe for biscuits. Because you needed biscuits for molasses. And then there'd be monkey balls. Bet you never had monkey balls. Kids couldn't get enough of monkey balls."

It was in this field in Letcher County, Kentucky, that I really, irrevocably, lost my heart to America. Or to the idea of America. The steepling, holy, admirable concept of it. Which was contrary, because this steep corner of the nation had probably seen less of the dream of America than almost any place in the country. Most of the folk who lived here were born here, their kin were from hereabouts for as many generations as they could tell. Generation and kin were about the only things they had a glut of; that and stories, and hindsight and religion.

The original stock of inhabitants had sailed over from Virginia, most of them exiled Jacobites deported after the Battle of Culloden in 1746. The English, with their customary subtlety, named everything that was big, fat or long "Cumberland." The Cumberland Plateau, the Cumberland Mountains, Cumberland Gap. All for the Duke of Cumberland, or Butcher Cumberland, as he was called by the people who had to live under his name. The crowing victor who dashed their bloody romantic dreams and gave them their last view of home, glen and brae.

Letcher County, on the far eastern edge of the state, is coal country. Next door to Harlan County, Bloody Harlan. This pocket has some of the worst labor practices, the most corrupt and violent industrial relations in America, not to mention the desperate and grievous bodily battering of the land, the poisoning of the rivers and the salting of lungs.

It was the midseventies. I arrived from London and its punk rock and inflation, an angry, fractious country, to come to these mountains of Kentucky. It seemed as far and as different as I could get in the English-speaking world. Even other Americans knew little about this place, and what they did know wasn't good. Hillbillies and incest, tent religion, violence, poverty and vendetta. Down here in the dark, secret valleys and hollows they turned their faces away from the misunderstanding and shrugged, asking to be left alone. The prejudice was mutual. Kentucky's slogan, painted on all the state highway signs, is "Unbridled Spirit," which doesn't tell you much. There's a graphic of a horse, in case you miss the "unbridled" pun, which goes with the Kentucky Derby and the big business of breeding over in bluegrass country. But actually, you might think as you drive by, wouldn't an unbridled spirit be a bit of a bore, rather annoying? But it's better than the slogan it replaced. The one I remember. That was "It's That Friendly." Kentucky: It's That Friendly. What does that mean? Sounds like the catchphrase from a 1950s sitcom. Of course the mountains of Kentucky were themselves the punchline of a sitcom, *The Beverly Hillbillies.*

What I found was what I was looking for, without ever knowing I was seeking it. It was a solid eyeful. The mountains rose with the simple beauty of children's drawings, stacked one behind the other. The mist clung to piney slopes and the creeks ran through their dark cleavages. Up the dirt tracks and in the secret folds there were hidden cabins and immobilized caravans, but mostly stuff was handmade, much repaired. There were yards full of spavined motorcars, chicken runs and the rutty implements of agricultural thuggery, and there were the dead white goods that would lie shrouded with bits of old carpet at the side of the road and drown, doors akimbo, in the rilling beds of rivers. It was a place unflattered by wealth, never petrified by investment, never self-conscious with vanity; a hard, resourceful, taciturn landscape that kept itself to itself with a monosyllabic, handsome functionality that didn't look for compliments or favors.

The folk who lived up here lived half on credit and half on hind-sight. Their nostalgia was the Scottish kind. English nostalgia is all for riches and sophistication, for cleverness and prettiness and wit. It is for a better past, of country houses, the nostalgia of pressing your nose against a cold window. Scottish nostalgia is all down-ward looking; it's about hardship and sustained disappointment, not overcoming troubles but wrestling them to a standstill. It's nostalgia as a cautionary tale, the thankless lessons, the flinty mor-als. I like it better than the swooning and tinkling-laughter type. The people here in Appalachia were constantly obliged to their ancestors, to the bony land they'd inherited, to their community, a belonging that was like predestination: it couldn't be joined half-way through, and could never be shrugged off. The generations locked together like the teeth of a great mill that ground out the corn of small, brave lives.

I don't know how long I stayed in Kentucky. In memory it seems longer than it probably was. But the memories remain, as clear and pristine as Wendy's big portraits. There is a magic real-ism about my bespoke retrospection for this place. I am an unreli-able raconteur. The images have become sharper, and word-perfect with the retelling. There is clarity in distance, the polish of a better, improved story. The mountain people could tell stories, they were born with a metronome of narrative in their heads. Every one of them had the need and the ability to make nostalgia Homeric. There is a theory that the English spoken down here is closer to Shakespeare than the verbiage at Oxford. Their vocabularies are peppered with arcane tones and rhythms that are biblical and rus-tic. You'd go into a shop and the girl behind the counter would say, "You'd like a poke?" She'd mean a bag, or what the rest of America calls a sack. Poke is Old English, and Old Lallans Scots—as in buying a pig in a poke. My grandmother in Edinburgh would go out for a poke of tea. The storytelling was Celtic. The mountain accent is distinctively singsongy. It has plenty of twang and lots of elbow room for the emotion. It has a vibrato of irony, a glissando of humor, it can be menacing and sentimental in the same breath. It goes very well with fiddles and banjos. It makes kids sound older than their years and old men sound like breathless swains. It is one of the most beguiling and evocative voices that English has ever made its own.

Mountain people were the most thin-skinned I'd ever come across, the quickest to take offense, except perhaps the Scots. We're pretty thin-skinned. The folk in Letcher County would hate me for starting the chapter with the over-the-water story. "Why did you just write down that silliness from some ignorant drunk hillbilly, make us all look dumb?" It wasn't that the folk were unfriendly to strangers. They were invariably cordial and hospitable to me: polite with an easy grace. What they minded like the devil was the merest implication, a single consonant, of judgment. Particularly from outsiders. Apart from wanting to know if there were cars in London, most folk were remarkably unconcerned and uninquisitive about where I came from, as if in turn they didn't wish to be seen to be making impolite assumptions. They did want to know what I did. "Student artist" rarely sparked further inquiries. And they were interested in what sort of cousins Wendy and I were. Second cousins. Genealogy and heredity are abiding interests. Families are close, and they crisscross over the years. So knowing exactly how people are related is a constant reaffirmation of belonging and place. They would use kinship as a sort of honorific. So a man who recommended a mechanic would tell you his name and then say, "He married my wife's second cousin, they're from over Black Mountain."

It was poor. Really poor. I'd never seen white poverty like this. A third of our neighbors lived below America's poverty line, which is kept pretty conservative. There were kids who only got fed at school, and there were those who barely got to school. There were more skinny, illiterate teenagers than you'd expect to find in the richest country on earth. Indeed, their existence had come as a surprise to America. In his 1964 inaugural address, Lyndon Johnson promised a War on Poverty: the most wide-ranging program of social improvement to get people fed, housed, educated, in better health, and to put them in work.

Kentucky is a middling state. Whenever you look at lists of

roads, universities, rainfall, size, it sits somewhere comfortably in the medium. Except that it has twice as many millionaires as Hawaii and its average income is half of Hawaii's. The bluegrass, picket-fence, horse-breeding bit of the state is exceedingly comfortably off. The mountain bit digs dirt and lives in penury. Kentucky bobs along in the bottom three impoverished states along with its next-door neighbors West Virginia and Mississippi, and Kentucky is very white. Over 90 percent white—one of the least diverse states. They're English, Scots, Irish; and most of Johnson's war against poverty was focused on cities. On black and Hispanic ghettos. The realization that some of the poorest people in America were Anglo-white and still living in the Depression was shocking, but it was also compelling, and a lot of northeastern liberals, students, volunteers, do-gooders, and lots of documentary makers and features writers came to the mountains to make a difference or make a record.

And the folk here, well, they were deeply offended. They were hurt, and then they got angry. They were insulted by metropolitan America. They didn't read its books or its papers, they didn't listen to its music or watch its films. They didn't hold with its fashion, they didn't want to eat its dinner or walk its dog. They really hadn't noticed how everyone else had got on, how poor they were, until these nasal-voiced, soft-handed, smart-arsed carpetbaggers arrived to pity them and talk down to them, and ask them impertinent questions. Oh, there were folk who were richer, and there were probably fellows who were better off than Balthazar. There were people with more money than sense over in Lexington, but the mountain folk didn't feel destitute. They didn't have much, but then they didn't hanker over much. How many shorts can you wear at once? How many pickups can you drive, how many hogs can you eat? So they took the news hard, and they took the do-gooders harder. It was the disrespect, the kicking of their dignity, and it came to a head in 1967 in Whitesburg, the capital of Letcher County.

A Canadian documentary maker, Hugh O'Connor, was filming a miner in his rented house, with his permission. The landlord, Hobart Ison, stormed up in a mighty temper and told the filmmakers to stop, to get off his property. He pulled out a gun, shot the camera and then the director. Mostly, when they told this story, it was just one shot that went down the lens and killed the director. O'Connor died at Ison's feet. His last words were: "Why did you do that?"

The community closed up and folded in on itself, called in the old allegiances and alliances against outsiders. Most people supported Ison. He was one of theirs. O'Connor wasn't. It was decided there couldn't be a fair trial in Letcher County so it was moved next door to Harlan. The jury was hung, apparently eleven for conviction, one for acquittal. At a second trial Ison pleaded guilty to manslaughter, and was sent to jail briefly and then paroled. This story was told a lot. It was the biggest thing that had happened in Whitesburg for some time, certainly the only thing that had got it into the *New York Times*. And it was always told with a degree of humorous pride and mountain justification. The truth was less easy than a local man pushed beyond endurance and paparazzi stalkers. O'Connor wasn't a tabloid news snapper, he was a highly regarded documentary maker, employed by the government to shoot a positive montage of American life. Ison, by accounts, was a singular and difficult man with a bad temper and a lot of money troubles. But then that could have been said about almost anybody. He had a lot to be bad-tempered about. The postscript to the story was that the old revolver he'd used turned up again years later, as the murder weapon in a convenience store robbery.

The tale of Hugh O'Connor and Hobart Ison was particularly close to Wendy, who'd joined a local community arts project called Appalshop that was set up by Johnson's War on Poverty to make documentaries about mountain people and their lives. They even made one about the shooting, with an acknowledged, gingerish irony.

The Appalshop was rather a success. A lot of the filmmakers were local, and people quite liked telling stories to keen and respectful youngsters while whittling a spoon. They wanted the world to know about the sins of mining and the hardship of life that made them valuable and memorable. Mind you, it was a joke everyone told. Jokes were more for familiar comfort than surprising humor. They'd ask, how many mountain folk does it take to change a lightbulb? One to change the bulb and half a dozen to tell you how it used to be done. I always thought they ought to add another half dozen to ask what a lightbulb was, and another twelve to point out that lightbulbs were the work of the devil, as there were none mentioned in the Bible.

The sorghum grew tall, and Errol came and rubbed a seed between his hard palms and sucked a stalk with his thin mouth, and quizzed the sky with his pale eyes, and declared that it was time for the stir-off. There was quite a lot to be done: wood to be gathered, a pit to be dug. There was a tin bath to be found, and the portable mill in the back of somebody's barn. Most communities shared a mill: three grooved gears turned by an axle that you fed the stalks through and squeezed out the sap. In the old days it would have been driven by a donkey or a mule, but we attached a lawn mower to it with the wheel tied down.

The weekend was gray, or maybe it was sunny. I remember being hot. Boys came from way up the creek with machetes and we cut cane all day. It was hard and dusty, stripping the leaves, saving the seed heads, stacking the cane. We joshed and bantered, because humor makes work go faster, and I felt for the first time the unexpected pleasure of collective physical work. Women came with trestle tables and foil-wrapped ovenware, with picnic boxes and cool boxes full of drink; there were frankfurters and grits and chicken and corn and potato salad and Russian salad, and macaroni and cheese, and pies and cakes. All sorts and fashion of cakes. Europeans share a cozy derision of American food, for being ersatz and coarse, childish and unsophisticated, but there is nowhere in the world that bakes like rural America. Breakfast cakes, morning cakes, coffee cakes and pancakes, bundt cakes, car-rot, pumpkin, chocolate, cheesecakes, upside-down cakes, marble, chiffon, velvet and angel food cakes. And each came with a recipe that some grand ancestor swore by: a spoonful of vinegar, an extra pinch of bicarbonate, never to be made in a full moon, or, "When my pa came back from the war, the first thing he asked for was a slice of this cake." The recipes were offered and exchanged like love letters, they bound this community with eggs and sugar, jam and chocolate, covered it with fancy icing and preserved fruit. Lives measured out by the cupful, the pinch, marked with the familiar shared seasonal smells of vanilla and cinnamon, caraway and nutmeg, marking the years. Recipes arrived as memories of Europe and stayed to become slices of friendliness, welcoming neighbors, thanking teachers, meeting in-laws, spoiling the sick. Cakes and pies and cookies were the commitment that built the heartland of America as surely as tractors and plows. Around the feet of these women, kids rolled in the grass and mucked about with knives.

The stir-off was a moment, a thing, a peg in time. People smiled broadly, said they couldn't remember when they last did this. Their grandmothers had always said that they couldn't wait for the pancakes, and wouldn't the kids just love monkey balls. "I suppose this isn't something you've seen before back East? Or in Europe?" No, no, it isn't.

One of the boys, about my age, I can't remember his name— Caleb, Ethan—let's say Caleb, asked if I'd like to see his hog. It was big, worth a visit. I said sure. I liked Caleb, and I think he liked me, but he was wild and a bit mad and a bit funny. He had an edge to him, a hint of something strobing behind the lids. There was someone else in the cab of his pickup, must have been a couple of boys he was giving a lift to, so I sat in the back with the tools and the tarps and the mess that everybody carried around. Caleb drove like all the boys drove: with a gut-clenching bravado. The dirt road climbed a mountain as directly as possible, not dawdling for the views. There was a drop through pine trees to a river on one side and a scree slope on the other. It was narrow with tight bends. He drove too fast and flipped the back wheels over the drop. The cab bucked and shuddered, and I was tossed about with the tools and barked my shin. It gave me a fright. I thought I could be bounced out into the ravine, so I grabbed the big jack and hit the top of the cab hard. It clanged like dinnertime and left a dent in the metal. The truck slid to a stop. Caleb's head poked through the window, saw me holding the iron, possibly registered the look on my face. "What the dang you do that fer?" His expression was taut and black. I said if he drove over twenty again I'd put the thing through the windshield. He paused and smiled. "You only gotta ask."

The pig was big: a huge, lop-eared, mud-colored sow. We stood and looked at it in the shit-thick pen. "That's a big hog," he said. "Must be near-on half a ton." I agreed that it was a big hog, so that he knew I'd understood the gravitas not just of the pig but of seeing the pig; that I'd get my story right. "Shall we go back?" This time I rode in the cab. We must have dropped off the other two. There was a girl walking down the hill in front of us with cutoff jeans and cowboy boots, a little yellow T-shirt. She had dark hair in a high ponytail that swung in time to her hips. She had hold of a child. We pulled up beside her and Caleb said, "Hi, you going to the stir-off?" She looked in, ignored me, and gave Caleb a thick, black look. She must have been about sixteen, a handsome, strong face with freckles and wide, pale lips. Her look was older than the rest of her. She said nothing, kept walking, and the truck idled along beside her while Caleb thought about what to say next. He settled on "Get in." She went on walking, looking ahead. "Come on, darlin', I'm going there anyway." Without looking round she replied, "I'm not putting her in a truck with you."

"I'd never do anything to hurt her. I want to talk to you."

"I ain't gettin' in no truck with you, and I ain't got nothin' good to say to you. You go about your business, Caleb."

Caleb crawled beside her, trying to think of something else to say. He swore, and left the girl and the child in a fog of dust and grit. "Who was that?" I asked. He told me—I don't remember her name—"She's my girl. She thinks we've broken up, but we ain't. We're engaged. And that there is our child"—he said another name. "It ain't just hers, she's both of ours. They live with her folks over the other side. They don't like me."

We drove back to the sorghum in silence. Caleb was troubled, kept shifting in his seat, trying to get comfortable with himself, trying to look nonchalant. He drove to the edge of the field with the trestle tables and the kids and flattened his foot to the floor. The truck ran straight through the middle of them. People grabbed each other and dived out of the way. He ran over a little bicycle and turned the wheel hard, and reluctantly the truck lifted two wheels, tottered, and rolled onto its side. Caleb fell on me. I had just enough room to squeeze out of the passenger window. I remember I was laughing. I don't really know why; it wasn't funny. I suppose I was drunk.

Men ran over to the truck. The women watched and stood back in the way that women watch men fuck up. Caleb climbed out through the driver's window. The men heaved the cab back upright. No one said much. Someone asked if I was hurt. I wasn't. Caleb was told not to move. The truck rocked on its axles, and he took two fast boxer's steps forward and punched the wing mirror twice with his right hand: hard, flat jabs. First time he broke the glass, second he knocked it clean off the cab and broke his hand. The men were angry with him. They were angry because he could have killed a child, and they were angry that he'd brought his way-wardness to the stir-off, which was a nice day, a family day. And they were angry that he'd done it in front of me, a stranger, an out-sider, showing them all up, violent and stupid. But they didn't say anything because they didn't want to say it in front of me. Caleb stood there, jaw working, left fist balled tight, right limp, dripping blood. "You'd better come up to the house, I'll put something on that," I said.

"No, it'll be OK."

"It won't." I took his elbow, felt him resist, then relax. A couple of the boys came with us, stood in the bathroom and cracked beers. The hand was a mess. Two fingers were plainly broken, the knuckles wrecked. Blood dripped into the sink, the towels turned pink. I took the ridged bottle of surgical spirit and poured it neat into a wad of cotton wool. "This is going to hurt." He shrugged. "A lot." The boys smirked. I held the sock to his hand. He flinched like a man facing a bleak wind. "OK, OK," he said gently, with-drawing his hand, cradling it like you might a child. It was the only tender thing I ever saw him do. "You'll need to go to hospital, get someone to take care of that properly."

"No." He was angry. I've cared for worse.

When all the cane was cut and the juice extracted, it was poured into the great tin bath and a fire lit underneath. As the sun went down, the folk came and put up a circle of chairs, and the old ones were brought from up the hollers and out of the back rooms, and sat with their families to watch the pan smoke, making suggestions about the set of the fire. And Errol moved about with a strainer tied to a broomstick, skimming the liquor, and there was more food: baked taters, big bits of pork bacon. Someone had a guitar and they'd sing, the old folk taking the lead to start. Mountain music. They sang their sad and sentimental songs, their funny and nonsense songs with confident, open throats and broad chests, voices spinning off in a descant.

The music that came out of these mountains so perfectly reflected the place and the people, grown from Scottish folk through the hard, bare years, it became a brilliant cadence. The one-sided conversation of bluegrass. The songs that were the things they wished they'd said as they drove home in the car, the things they wanted to say but never managed. The stuff you want to say about yourself and the stuff you want to tell God. The difference between rock 'n' roll and country is that rock is sung to a stadium, a festival, the world, but country is sung to someone. It's like eavesdropping on a raw life; it is a music that grew beyond the singalongs and barn dances, weddings and wakes and picnics, and affected everyone in bedrooms and back rooms and barrooms. The songs that gave a fluency and a rhyming oratory to the thick-tongued.

In between the singing, everyone had suggestions for the molasses: faster, slower, hotter, cooler, and then what color it should be. Tan or chestnut, should it be sticky as tar or thin as a lawyer's handshake? The light flickered and dodged over their weathered faces, with their good bones and deep lines. The twisted hands clapped and waved, and just outside the ring of light the old boys and the young men passed preserved jars of moonshine back and forth. It wouldn't be polite to do it openly, there were lifetime abstainers here, Methodists and Baptists who'd signed pledges.

Religion was such a central and abiding echo in these hills: fundamental, certain, unflinching. The great word of the Reformation, shaved into ever more direct and literal stern sects of one truth. Churches that relied on hard work and hard justice, that preached palliative care for the human condition, rather than a cure. There were churches that met in front rooms and in fields, that had preachers who traveled with lungs like bellows and black books they'd slap and rock like colicky babies. There was the Pentecostal Church, the Church of Serpent Handlers, a particularly Appalachian belief that sprang from the gospel of Mark: "And these signs shall follow them that believe. In my name shall they cast out devils, they shall speak with new tongues, they shall take up serpents. And if they drink the deadly thing, it shall not hurt them. They shall lay hand on the sick and shall recover." The healing services, the speaking in tongues, glossolalia, were common, as were the handling of snakes and the occasional nipping of strychnine to prove God's power to overcome the symbols of temptation and the vile begetter of sin.

Snake handling was said to have been instigated, or at least propagated, by George Went Hensley, an itinerant Pentecostal preacher who started his own sect while on the run from jail for selling moonshine. He got through three wives and fathered a great many children. As a child he'd seen a woman in a charismatic service pick up a snake, and his religion spread through the coal-mining towns. As he was illiterate himself, his wives had to read the Bible to him. In 1955, preaching in a blacksmith's barn in Florida, he produced a five-foot rattlesnake from a lard can, wrapped it round his neck and rubbed his face with its head. He preached in tongues, and when replacing the snake in the can, it bit him on the wrist. The congregation implored him to get medical treatment. He refused, and he died. But not before blaming the congregation's lack of faith. The sheriff pronounced his death suicide. His last remaining wife, perhaps with some irony, said it was the will of God. Praying with snakes was illegal in many states. In Kentucky it was a misdemeanor that merited a $50 to $100 fine. Some places you got the death penalty, though juries were reluctant to convict. The ACLU supported the rights of churches to test faith with snakes. There was a local man who made whiskey money catching the rattlers and cottonmouths for the local Pentecostal church. He thought they were mad, but he was glad they were.

Glossolalia, the gift of the holy ghost, is given to mountain people more than most. The language they receive is holy gobbledygook. Gobbledygook could be a word invented by God to describe speaking in tongues. There are those who believe it was divinely instigated, the language of holiness, perhaps the language of angels. Xenoglossolalia is the mysterious ability to speak a language you can't possibly know or have learned. There have been a number of studies in Pentecostal churches to see if the trance-made sounds might have a grammar or repeated rhythms to indicate that they might be more than exclamatory whale song. There have been one or two examples. There was an American woman who spoke Swedish when hypnotized, an Englishwoman who was said to go into a trance and speak ancient Egyptian hieroglyph. Some Pentecostalists believed that the tongue of tongues was given to them for missionary work. They set out from their little mountain churches to travel the world, trying to find the heathens who would miraculously understand their jabbering and be converted.

The old-timers round the fire arrived at a rough consensus about the consistency of the molasses. It was ladled into plastic flagons and shared out. Extra was taken for the bedbound and the absent. People began to walk back to their pickups, the headlights swung round, casting long shadows. Figures looked like characters who had fallen out of picture postcards and Sears catalogues. The hatched mountains were pearled by the light and then returned to ink. The fire died and we crept closer, passing the fruit jar. And then, oiled to a thick-tongued bravado, piled into an old, souped-up, tightly sprung and patched muscle car and poured into the night to deliver moonshine. We would grunt around the back roads with the lights off, the jars chinking in the trunk, and drive by the light of the moon. You could see other cars twist and turn miles away—we were on the lookout for state troopers, who were on the lookout for moonshine runners. The expectations and the darkness and the drink made it exciting. Otherwise it was like delivering groceries.

Moonshine is corn liquor distilled in secret in the hills. It was the mountains' most famous craft industry. Letcher County was dry. You couldn't sell alcohol or consume it in public. Prohibition had never been repealed here. Europeans are always surprised by the idea that there are still abstinent places in America. In fact there are near-on 500 municipalities that are teetotal. Half of Kentucky was either dry or what they call moist: that is, you can't serve bagged alcohol or booze by the glass, so no off-licenses and no saloons. You can get a drink in a restaurant that has more than fifty people and gets more than 75 percent of its income from food. A lot of Alaska is dry, half of Mississippi, and for many years Kansas was completely abstinent. When Prohibition was repealed in 1933, it clung to its state autonomy to keep the pledge for another fifteen years.

In Letcher County there was a great deal of illicit drinking, which suited me. I was well on my way to becoming an alcoholic. Indeed, this was probably the last magical year when drink was truly my friend. We got on well together, and I had a phenomenal capacity and tolerance for it. I could drink the local boys into a vomiting, insensible heap. I found the one talent that was useful here. We would drive across the county line to bottle shops for slabs of beer and cases of Wild Turkey. Illicit moonshine was always more expensive but it had an old-time cachet, and tasted of lighter fluid and liniment, and burned like the sin that it was. The sheriff in Whitesburg, a round, bow-legged man who wore cowboy boots and a ten-gallon hat and had big, silver gunslinger pistols in a quick-draw holster, would stand in the main street and watch the cars tool past, measuring with a practiced eye how low they were on their back axles, intimating trafficked booze. His office was lined with cases of beer.

Dry counties have rather worse road accidents than wet ones.

They say it's because you have to drive further to get a drink. I think it's because you drink to get drunker. We all drank constantly, but the whiskey goes with these people—certainly went with me. The Celtic curse, they call it in American AA meetings. So many stories were not just lubricated by John Barleycorn, but motivated by him. Alcohol was the departure and the destination. Whiskey was the captain of the story, and the pilot at the wheel. We'd pass the bottles in wooden rooms, over fires of rubbish, and weave them into the lives that seemed to be made up mostly of tinkering. Everyone was mending something, or just about to mend something, waiting for the loan of the thing that would fix the other thing: the door, the pump or the tractor.

I remember these lives as being great lists of things to do, and things that ought to have been done. The queue of exhausted and decrepit machinery, the buildings that needed attending to, the men and women slowly getting around to patching up home-made lives, always in need of some piece of care that was always on the way, just round the corner, at the post office. The sliding days that were ripe for interruption by a bottle and a few boxes and an old door on a fire, a trip to a bar to ponder a jammed and gummed motorbike, a chair with a broken leg, a henhouse with holes. It was life as an alfresco museum of restored artifacts. It was the only place I'd been in where reverie was current events and everyone's job was hyphenated and transient: miner and farmer, lorry driver and carpenter. Careers were all seasonal, temporary or resting, all bound with stories.

Errol had been a sniper, a coal miner and a farmer. He used to go out onto the mountain to collect ginseng. He'd get a good price for it from a middleman, who would pass it on until it reached Korean herbalists. He wasn't entirely sure what they did with it—something foolish and Oriental. "Probably to get their peckers to stand up. Most of that medication is to get hard-ons." But the mountain women used to make tea from it, when health and medicine was all homegrown.

Errol's nephew would mow grass. There wasn't a lot of call for grass mowing, because there weren't a lot of lawns in the mountains, and if folk found themselves with a bit of grass they generally cut it themselves, or didn't bother. But the nephew persevered, because he had a new sit-upon motor mower, the one we'd attached to the mill at the stir-off. He'd got the motor mower because what he really wanted was a car, and the mower was the only thing with a gas engine he could get credit to buy. If he kept up the payments on the mower for a year, then he'd have a borrowing history, and that would let him buy a truck. He needed a truck so he could drive to do laboring work or move things. That was the plan. Wendy had a bit of grass. I left him a note to bring his mower. It was a pictogram—he'd never made it to school. He'd get the truck because he worked hard and was a good guy, and people wanted to help him out with his plan, but he'd never get a driving license or insurance.

Credit and debt were the unremitting drone of mountain life. Everyone owed, everyone was in arrears, and no one could see a time when they'd earn more than they owed. The old folk would say that it was the fault of modernity, everybody wanted everything instantly, no one saved, no one put off their pleasures, and anyway they wanted too much. But it had always been thus. It was a community that lived beyond its own means because the means were so fragile and faint. The net of obligation and debt, the knock from repossession men and moneylenders; putting off till tomorrow what you can't pay today was like the weather, it was constant. The lifetime of insecurity was the maker's setting of mountain people. Booms passed them by, and bust was what they lived with, the endless tinnitus of fear.

There was nothing immoral or unethical about their borrowing. When I think back on it, all I see is their immense bravery and strength, families living in the face of calamity. The simple, preachy religion of poor white America is intensely practical. It insists not only on the perfectibility of man but on the unending struggle against his own born nature. The original sin is a hard inheritance. To come into the world already in debt. Someone pointed out to me that Catholicism was trying to avoid hell, but Protestantism was trying to achieve heaven. Your life was a test. You were meant to make something practical and useful. Your God-given soul was his investment in you.

Prohibition is in retrospect seen as utterly foolish: intrusive, hypocritical, a crude attempt at social engineering and religious manipulation. The view that Prohibition was an absurd wrong turning in the American journey of self-determination and increased freedom is almost universal. History isn't just written by the victors, it's usually written by the drunks. Or at least the bibulous. The writers of amusing, brilliant and damning literature are on the side of beer and a chaser. The companionship of the saloon and the licentiousness that alcohol lubricates is always going to be a better story than abstinence. Rogues and roués are better characters than parsimonious milksops.

But there is another way of looking at the experience of Prohibition, a contrarian observation. It was the first campaign of the women's movement. The initial protests were overwhelmingly made by women in response to the endemic drunkenness and domestic violence, and the loneliness and neglect that had grown up in the dour, thankless new communities of the South and the West. Before Prohibition, Kansas had an ordinance that made it illegal to sell a drink to a man against the express wishes of his wife. The amount of drinking done in America grew like a flood with the thirst of the new immigrants from central Europe, and the instigation of an efficient German brewing industry. Every American beer you can think of is brewed by Germans, and there were technical improvements in the distilling industry that meant the price of drink tumbled. Saloons blossomed, and piecemeal women, in despair and fury, tried to force their men out of bars, which apart from selling drink also were the meeting places for business, politics, sex and that masculine freemasonry that explicitly excludes women. The temperance movement was indivisibly part of the suffrage movement. Women's groups, mothers, church congregations would picket bars, hold open-air abstinence meetings. They were met with a bellowing fury and indignation. Humiliation, ridicule, insult and violence. Mothers and children were manhandled, beer and filth were thrown over them: their protests were universally peaceful. The parlous state of many American women and their children was a national shame, and the Women's Christian Temperance League motto, "A sober and pure world," set about protecting families from drink: from the drunken fist and the wasted wages. Later, male ministers and then politicians took up the cause. In local elections they discovered there was a desperate desire to do something about the terrible waste at the heart of working-class communities. And the abstinence movement moved from the parlor to the street, to the pulpit and to the hustings.

In 1919, in a wave of postwar patriotism, it was easier for government to snub the lobbying of German breweries, and the bill against manufacturing, trafficking or selling alcohol was passed. It was followed by the Volstead Act, enforcing Prohibition. The next thirteen years saw a boom in organized crime, smuggling, corruption, hypocrisy; and finally, as the Depression hit, the countermovement to rescind Prohibition was moved and motivated by a Republican woman, and then widely backed by Democrat men including Roosevelt. Interestingly, the reason given for repealing the act wasn't libertarian. It was that the law was so obviously and pandemically flouted that it brought the courts into disrepute, and legalizing alcohol would weaken organized crime and strangle political corruption.

More important, but less often touted, it would open considerable new streams of taxes to fund the New Deal. And when it was all over, metropolitan America breathed a whiskey-laden sigh of relief and wondered what on earth all that had been about. How had they ever got themselves into such an absurdly embarrassing state? How humiliating to have to drink your gin out of a teacup. How very un-American. Abstinence was seen not in moral or religious terms, but in how contrary to the brash, free-and-easy enthusiastic culture of the New World it was. It's not easy selling self-restraint and seriousness and early bedtimes. Prohibition was undoubtedly a failure, but it was also undoubtedly a brave and human attempt to improve and protect the lives of millions. And it was in the other great tradition of the New World: if on one hand there is the belief in individual freedom and self-determination, minimum interference and maximum opportunity, so there is also a parallel belief, set up right at the beginning of America, a burning desire to create a better society, a decent moral community.

In the Old World, the desires of the rich and entitled had cast injustice over the lives of the many, so in the New World no one man's pleasure should be bought at the expense of another's aspiration or opportunity. And nothing blighted the lives of the blameless and the powerless like drunkenness. To profit from that was immoral, and though Prohibition may now be the stuff of period drama and noir films, America still struggles with the same moral dilemma, but this time over drugs. And now the prohibitionists have the upper hand. All the same arguments apply to heroin and crack cocaine as did to bootleg whiskey. To legalize it would undermine organized crime. Indeed, most personal crime, against person and property, can be traced directly to drugs. Drugs would raise taxes that could be used to treat addiction, and legalizing them would stop the law being flouted. The rules for marijuana have already been relaxed to the point where they barely exist in some states, not because the ethics have changed but because enforcing the law has become incompatible with society's view of the seriousness of smoking a joint. It's difficult not to draw the conclusion that what still makes drug prohibition acceptable is to do not with the drug but the section of society it affects most. The cost of keeping such a shaming proportion of black and Hispanic Americans in jail, and the disproportionate human cost of trafficking and dealing that falls on the ghettos and immigrant neighborhoods from central America, is more acceptable than the state having to take on a role as a drug dealer, or condoning commercial drug dealing.

So Letcher County in the seventies was the end of an evangelical ideal that still held out for the vain, righteous experiment to relieve man from the weight of his baser nature. To impose sobriety in body and spirit. I never enjoyed drinking in better company, with people who were so distinctly foreign and yet so surprisingly familiar, in a more memorable and imposing place.

I should leave a postscript to Al Capone: "This American system of ours, call it Americanism, call it capitalism, gives each and every one of us a great opportunity, if we only seize it with both hands and make the most of it . . . When I sell liquor it's called bootlegging. When my patrons serve it . . . it's called hospitality."

16

Movies

There are places that come to you as déjà vu, that you see with the warm familiarity of a previous life well traveled. Few tourists' pleasures are as subtly thrilling as the confirmation of seeing something you already intuitively know. There isn't a word for this odd but intensely cozy little emotion, like unexpectedly getting the answer to a question on a subject you know nothing about. It's as close as most of us get to second sight. And while the Taj Mahal, the Parthenon and the Eiffel Tower are spectacular tricks in the mind's eye's spy list, still nothing is as panoramically familiar as your first live sight of New York. Not a single exclamation of ruin or edifice, but an entire novel you know by heart. It is the eternal, expanding cityscape that man-hugs you as you cross the bridge from Queens on the way in from the airport.

You already know so much about the place: you know what the people sound like, you know what they think, you know about their theatrical anger and their dust-dry humor. You know how they walk, their gestures, how they order their coffee. You know what they eat, what's in their fridges and closets. You already know what the phones and the sirens sound like. New York is a club you've been a member of for a long time.

Someone once said that Paris was the world's second city. I expect it was an American. Extravagantly sycophantic quotes about Paris are generally American. Whoever it was, they were wrong. They were looking the wrong way. Undeniably the globe's other place, its virtual second home, is New York. It's not just because Manhattan looks so memorable, or that it was the gateway for so much immigration. It is the first city of the electric age. We know it because it's been in our living room, kitchen and bedroom all our lives. New York is the greatest, most enduring, leading-man, heartthrob location of the screen. New York is the stage of our collective dramas. It isn't the most filmed place—that would be California, the suburbs of Los Angeles. But even after countless repetitions, L.A. slips off the eye like spit down a windshield. California, for all its imploring braggadocio, refuses to register as a real place. There is a tourist commercial for California on European television at the moment. It usually interrupts cop shows and medical dramas made in L.A.; there is an irony there that would die alone on the pavement in Hollywood, which continues to be the disposable wrapping that stories come in. A half place, made of cellophane and cardboard. But not New York. New York is a star. And this is where films should grow from, and where they might have if it weren't for the weather.

The one thing you probably won't be expecting in New York is the climate. No one in their right mind would build a city here. Well, only the Dutch, and they built a whole country below sea level. New York bakes in a cess of gritty fug all summer, and congeals into gray slush all winter. There are a couple of days in the spring and autumn when the sky is madonna blue, the air crisp, and the light bright and sparkling, and that's when they take the pictures and make the romantic comedies. Once upon a time, all American films were made in New York. They were one-reel two-day shoots for Nickelodeons, until they decided to shoot a cowboy film, so the Hollywood story goes. The first cowboy film was *The Great Train Robbery*. The crew took the Pullman west to Arizona, getting off at Flagstaff. The weather was unbelievably New York–ish, so they got back on the train and ended up in an orange grove outside Los Angeles, and the rest, as they say, is fiction. California does have a relentlessly unimaginative and blandly friendly climate.

I want to leave New York for a bit and go back to Kentucky, where I taught film. With the American conviction that an expert is someone who knows more than you do, the staff at the local college asked me if I would talk to media students about British films. I wasn't much older than the students, and my qualifications for talking about British film were that I was British and had seen some films. I don't think filmmaking was their major subject; they were probably doing something more useful; ball bouncing, perhaps. Kentucky kids were manically enthralled, to the point of single-minded insanity, by basketball.

Before I went to my first class, cousin Wendy, who really did teach, asked if I knew what I was going to tell them. "Well, in a general sort of way I imagine it will more or less be a sort of seminar, you know, questions and discussion." She gave me a wary, on-your-head-be-it look. I was led to the classroom by a real teacher, who said this was a voluntary module, so the kids had all chosen to be here, and they got credits for turning up, but I wasn't to expect much in the way of background knowledge. "Just have fun," he said, without conviction. And I walked into a classroom that was instantly familiar from a hundred films. The children were huge; squashed and bent around those little, all-in-one chair-desk combination things that you only get in American films. They arranged themselves in the slumped curlicues of sullen rebellion. Boys sucked pens and leaned heavy heads on ball-bouncing hands. The girls searched for split ends and drew hearts on their folders. It was a tableau of mulish intimidation, and I was an intimidated mule. I paused, waited, half expecting them to leap into a dance number, but they ignored me.

I had decided not to take on all of British film, but a single aspect. That aspect would be Ealing comedies. There was plenty of cultural scope to examine, and I started by asking them simply what their favorite British films were. Silence. Could they name any British film? *Mary Poppins,* offered a girl at the back. Boys snorted. She blushed and gave me a furious look.

OK, any British stars you like? Charlie Chaplin? I offered. David Niven?

Who's David Niven? "Some faggot," offered a fat boy with a shaved head.

What about Elizabeth Taylor and Cary Grant?

"Hey, they're not British," called the furious girl. "They're American."

Well, they were born in England.

"Yeah, my grandmother was born in Minsk, she's not a Minski, she's American."

I retreated. Well, what's your favorite foreign film?

They started chatting to each other. The real teacher began to look desperate. "*Enter the Dragon*," said a boy in the front. The others made approving kung fu noises. The girls curled their sticky lips.

Any other un-American films?

"Who'd want to see an un-American film?" said the fat boy.

"Yeah, who'd make an un-American film?" someone said.

"Commies," replied the brainy lad in the front.

"Maybe the French," said a girl with a particularly strong southern accent, her blonde hair pulled up in a pert and perky ponytail. "Movies," she said slowly, as if talking to a foreigner, "are American."

The film I'd chosen as the first example of British filmmaking and the small-island charm of Ealing was *Kind Hearts and Coronets*. The lights flicked off, the projector began to click, and the screen in front of the blackboard fluttered into life. And we were, for this moment, all together in the dark of our age's defining craft.

If you haven't seen *Kind Hearts and Coronets*, it doesn't really matter. It's a worthy and brittle dark comedy about class and snobbery. Dennis Price has to kill eleven relatives to obtain a dukedom. Alec Guinness plays eight of them. The film is a flashback, with Price writing his memoir from the condemned cell the night before his execution for the one death he didn't commit. In the end he is rescued by a devious lover (a suicide note is conveniently discovered), on the understanding that he will kill his wife to marry her. The final scene of the film is Dennis leaving jail with the two women. He wonders to the audience which one he will do away with, and then realizes that he has left his incriminatingly confessional autobiography in the cell.

Now, I thought I knew this film well, if not intimately. It was a comfortable old cardigan for a Sunday afternoon. Alec Guinness does his admirably theatrical multitasking with the help of a lot of Old Vic prosthetics, uniforms and wigs. Dennis Price is lugubriously and venally Dennis Price. The women are the two versions of female that English audiences had grown accustomed to: a clipped, upper-class icon and a coquettish eighteenth-century-style trollop. It had, I was sure, in a patronizingly Old World way, everything an American audience would admire about English culture. There was wit, badinage, sophistication and class. The performances were of an assured and mannered staginess. Well, nothing is as straitening and as flattening as watching something homely you take for granted through the eyes of foreigners. There is a strange, subordinal companionship in the darkness of the cinema, even this makeshift one. Something of the anthill. You pick up the chemical messages, the invisible body language around you.

It began badly, in black and white. These kids had never watched a whole monochrome film. They knew they existed, they didn't know anyone looked at them for fun. Why would you? And it got worse. For the first time, I saw what a terribly smug, inverted meander of little, English, thoughtless tosh it all was. The lazy cleverness, the sonorous banter that relied on an audience already in on the joke. The pert performances not taking the medium too seriously, as if silently winking. "It's only the flicks, darling, say your lines and pick up the check, and back to the Bard on Monday." The plot didn't for a moment have to work as a plot, because we'd all agreed not to question it, to overlook its ineffable silliness in the way we wouldn't mention a chipped teacup or the stain on the landing carpet. But mostly it was the willful disregard for the contemporary, a period piece made not to illuminate the present but to snub it, cut it dead. English cinema as a chintzy, airless drawing room without windows.

Kind Hearts was made in 1949. The Best Picture at the Oscars that year was *All the King's Men,* a complicated story of political corruption. *The Third Man* took the Palm at Cannes. It was the year of *Manon* and, most damning of all, the year the sublime *Bicycle*

Thieves was shown. As the credits rolled and the lights flicked on, the kids resumed their positions of dumb insolence, but now with added resentment. I coughed: Are there any questions?

"Was this made in the war?"

No, why?

"Well, I wondered if that was why they couldn't afford to get more actors."

"Is it a fag film?" the fat boy interrupted.

No. No, not at all. Except that Dennis Price was actually gay, but in a private sort of English way. And Guinness was probably gay, but in a sort of noncombatant, only-on-the-weekends way.

"Oh, I thought that was why they dressed up as women."

Oh, heavens no, no. No. That's a great old tradition. Goes back to Garrick. It's like pantomime. The dame, you know.

And they looked back at me with blankness on their already studied blankness. They didn't know. Pantomime? Don't you have pantomime here? Oh, well, crikey. We all grow up with it, we take children at Christmas. They're fairy stories, there's only about half a dozen of them, and they're all the same. There's a dame, who's a man dressed as a woman, and a principal boy, who's played by a girl, then there's a princess, or Cinderella, who is a girl, and then there's an animal. A horse, or a cow, or a goose, who'll be a couple of men, and there are sweets, and slapstick, and very old jokes, and a lot of double entendres that only mean one thing. And the leading boy gets the princess, or Cinderella or whomever in the end, and that's pantomime.

The girl with the ponytail and the Tennessee Williams accent said, "Let me get this straight; you go to a show where you all know the story and there's an old woman who's a man, and a man who's a girl, who falls in love with a girl who's a girl, and there are animals with men in them. And you take kids to see this?"

Well, it's a lot more innocent than it sounds. And great fun, I added without conviction.

When *Kind Hearts and Coronets* was originally shown in America (not a huge hit), the Hays Commission, which oversaw the morality of movies, insisted on some changes. Some of the chat about infidelity and divorce had to be cut, and there was a scene added right at the end where we were shown the incriminating book actually being discovered, just so there'd be no misunderstanding that Price would be dangling from a rope. In the home version, with a sort of English cynicism about the ways of class, of course, we all assumed that, being a duke, he'd get away with it. And the children's rhyme "eeny meeny miney mo" had to have the "nigger" removed and replaced by "sailor," at a time when sailors could travel in the front of southern buses, but not if they were also black.

In retrospect the only true and observant remark in the whole lesson was from the girl who said that movies were American. Not since the Renaissance has one country so completely dominated the cultural form. Movies are American, and America is movies. Their language, stories and morals, their cast of characters, the layers of assumptions and conventions, are all American. Films may well be made all over the world, but they are cast in the American model. They dress up in other cultures, they can talk in other languages. But the beating heart of a film, its rhythm, always sounds American. And film has done more to sell America—its ideas, its romance, its self-belief—to the rest of the world than anything else. But more profoundly, and indelibly, film has sold the idea of how to be an American to Americans.

Oscar Wilde came to America and lectured down coal mines. Dressed in velvet breeches, he told them in his inverted, contrarian way that nature followed art. And they loved him. Nowhere has this trite after-dinner aphorism proved so true as in America. They look and emote like film without quotation marks. The vocabulary and expectations are linear and celluloid. Look at American politics and politicians, at American socializing, at dating, at their reactions to disaster, at their expectations of affection and retribution, at the pursuit of hard work and justice, at their sentimentality and conviction, and their addiction to happy endings, and the tying up of loose ends. They're all informed by film.

There is a belief that lives are set to music and are coherent, that our scenes flow one into the other. It's not only Americans who think this, it's now half the world.

The grandest purpose of culture is to teach us why and how we are the way we are, and the overwhelming culture of the last century has been the moving image. Its simple, repeated message has been "how to be a good American." The homely American gift to itself in the movies, the promise in its fortune cookie, made specifically for Americans as the chosen people of Hollywood, has been the promise of a dream. A dream is America's birthright. Everybody should—indeed, must—have a dream. Kids talk about their dreams with a votive reverence and an utter belief. The dream is the core motivation of film. The struggle to fulfill the dream, and the dream's invincibility.

On-screen, dreams come true; not as astonishing exceptions but as a rule and a right. The dreams also have rules, commandments: "Thou shalt not doubt your dream," "You must be constant and true to the dream," "You must work for your dream." This isn't seen as oxymoronic. And who wants to have a cancer surgeon whose dream is to play the double bass at Carnegie Hall? You mustn't use your dream to do evil, and only one dream per dreamer. And finally, if you don't achieve your dream, it's not the dream's fault. Terms and conditions apply.

Collectively, all dreams will be known as the Great American Dream. America is a dream bank, people come from all over the world for the American Dream, and they will be lent one, and if they work hard (see rules and regs) it will be given to them, and they can pass it on to their children. Children of course have the right to discard parental dreams in favor of their own dreams, because self-determination in dreaming is just all part of the broad American reverie.

It takes a particularly clear and optimistically hopeful mind not to see the trust and belief in the efficacy and justice of dreams as some huge, collective act of sentimental, childish naïveté. Dreams are at best a panacea, a philosophical placebo, a cynical marketing tool for salesmen and reality television producers. But they can also be seen as a unifying belief in Providence, a self-defining and biddable fate. Not the selfish wish list of teenage girls, but the coming together of the divine and the temporal. The dream may be heaven-sent but you need a shovel, or a college degree, to get it. The language of dreams may be gratingly whiney and annoying to European ears, but the theology of it would have been as perfectly sound to Wesley or Calvin as it was to Martin Luther King Jr.

Dreams can also be a synonym for film. The magic, flickering figures who can transcend time and physics, probability and death. Film makes anything happen, but it must also be wholly predictable. It can surprise, but rarely dumbfound. The most American of all the dictates of both dreams and movies is that they will end happily. Not all of them do, but they have to have a damn good moral imperative not to. The happy ending is the promise of America, not a dream but a covenant: it will be all right, we will prevail, we will overcome.

America's embrace of moving pictures is so patently universal that it's difficult to imagine a time when they weren't American. But at the turn of the twentieth century, when the Nickelodeons were growing popular, only 40 percent of the films shown were homemade. It was the French who commanded the most artistic respect. The effort in American movies was put not into content but technology. As ever in America, it was the mechanics, the means of production and distribution, that dictated the money. Edison, again, held dozens of patents on movie cameras, and was consumed with forcing a monopoly through licensing agreements. His main opposition was Biograph, who had a camera made by an ex-Edison employee, specifically to get round his patents. Films were eight or nine minutes long, and neither comedies nor romances. Directors made two a week and got paid a royalty by footage of film.

Biograph's chief director fell out with the money people, who were looking to do a deal with Edison. He left to set up his own company, to make a film that was unlike anything that had come before it. It has been called the first truly great work of art in this new medium. On lists of great movies, it still often comes in the top ten. It often has been called the single most important film of all time. It is the cinema's *Iliad*, a film that brought the movies home and made them an American dream.

But you won't see it in a cinema today. You'll have trouble seeing it at all. The last few times people tried to put on public performances they were banned or picketed. You can get it on the Internet, or you can buy it on DVD. In Britain it comes with a stern 600-word warning courtesy of the licensing board of censors, telling you that you are to view it from a distance, as a historical and social oddity. Don't get too close, don't feed it.

The Clansman opened on February 8, 1915, in Clune's Auditorium, Los Angeles. It was a big theater. The usherettes were dressed in Civil War uniforms. As the lights dimmed, the title was projected on the theater's curtain, which parted to reveal a screen glowing white. Out of the darkness thundered a full symphony orchestra, startling the audience out of their seats. The film was something over two and a half hours long, shown with an intermission. The story is of two families, set immediately after the American Civil War. The Republicans in the North are trying to force black majority rule on North Carolina. A Northern girl and a Southern boy fall in love. Freed slaves rise up and stuff ballot boxes, and set about lusting after white women. The Ku Klux Klan is formed to protect white folk. They are led by the love interest. The mulatto governor of the state tells his protector, a Northern senator, that he wishes to marry a white girl. The senator is delighted, until the half caste, astutely named Silas Lynch, tells him it's his daughter. The KKK ride to the rescue of beleaguered whites. A Southern family on the run are hidden by a pair of Union soldiers. The title board announces: "The former enemies of North and South are united again in common defense of their Aryan birthright." The film finishes with cowering blacks kept out of polling booths by the Klan's cavalry in their white robes, and a shot of a happy family under a crucifix. The blacks in the movie were all played by white actors in greasepaint, with rolling eyes, golliwog lips and woolly wigs. The star was a young Lillian Gish, who made her last film in 1987.

The director was D. W. Griffith, and he would change the name of the film to the portentous *The Birth of a Nation*. It was a stupendous success. An enormous hit. The first blockbuster. It was the first film to be shown in the White House, to the new president Woodrow Wilson, who was about to take America into the Great War. He said it was like writing history with lightning.

The Birth of a Nation made a fortune. It was cut and recut, and it was also immediately opposed by the newly formed National Association for the Advancement of Colored People, who tried—mostly unsuccessfully—to get it banned from theater to theater. There were those who wanted it censored not for its politics but because they didn't want to see black people on the screen. The film had two direct and lasting legacies. It reinvigorated the Ku Klux Klan, which had become virtually extinct. They showed it regularly in the South for recruitment, and it almost certainly contributed to lynchings and beatings. But on the bright side, film grew up with *The Birth of a Nation*. Griffith is credited with a large number of technical innovations: the use of a specially scored accompaniment, rather than a pianist making it up as the film went on. He invented the fade and the panorama. He instigated a more naturalistic, less histrionic form of acting, though it still looks pretty cartoonish today. He saw things in a particularly filmic way, rather than the static view of a theatrical event, and above all, he is credited with inventing the close-up. In truth he wasn't the first to use any of these things. His cameraman, the delightfully named Billy Bitzer, set up most of the shots. And though Griffith was called the father of cinema, the title should really go to the uncredited Bitzer, who taught Griffith, then an actor, how to make movies at Biograph. And anyway, all these techniques had already been used in continental films.

But what Bitzer and Griffith did that was new was to cut them for drama. The close-ups were of faces to underline emotion or details, to move plot. Bitzer and Griffith wove story lines together to give a sense of unfolding, complementary dramas, and that hadn't been done before. Audiences went to see it over and over, because the first half was enormous spectacle. There had been other historical epics, most famously Sarah Bernhardt as Elizabeth, but this was homegrown. This was about America, and recent history. The reconstruction of the South that is the background for *The Birth of a Nation* was as close to its audience as the Vietnam War is to us today—well within living memory. The self-pity and the wounded grievance of the South were still twitching. Film critics and historians have constantly tried to separate the artistic content of *The Birth of a Nation* from its politics, hoping that over time, like salad dressing, the clear oil of artistry will rise above the vinegar of history: that was then, it was a different time, attitudes were different. We have grown up, grown nuanced, are further from the making of *The Birth of a Nation* than *The Birth of a Nation* was from the death of Lincoln. But still the bald, racist intent of the thing is shocking. More shocking. Why make this film? Why choose a subject this contentious for the first grand epic of cinema? The answer lies between two men: Griffith and Thomas Dixon.

Dixon was a writer, entrepreneur, actor, playwright and a minister, born at the end of the Civil War in Shelby, North Carolina. His mother was a severely religious woman. They had inherited slaves. His uncle was Colonel Leroy McAfee, late of the Confederate army. Dixon's formative years were spent during Reconstruction. North Carolina was under a military governor, and the straggling Confederate soldiers would come by their farm begging for food. There were Northern carpetbaggers and bands of freed slaves, a great deal of grief and misery and resentment. Southern farms and plantations were heavily taxed, and many families, already bankrupt by the war, had to sell up. Dixon remembered one particular event. A war widow told him that her daughter had been raped by a freed slave. The local Klan came and caught the man, hauled him into the center of town, hanged him and shot his body full of righteous, vengeful holes. Uncle Leroy and Dixon's cousins led the local chapter of these chivalrous knights of the Old South.

But the event that really fired up Dixon was the night he went to see a performance of *Uncle Tom's Cabin*. Harriet Beecher Stowe's book was adapted into a play. It was the most successful play in

America's short theatrical history. At its height there were more than fifty traveling companies performing it. There were actors who played nothing else in their entire careers. A newspaper in Chicago begged that the city be spared any more "Tommers." *Uncle Tom's Cabin* had also been the most successful book of the nineteenth century, a worldwide phenomenon, read and wept over by millions. Just as teenage girls will say they couldn't love anyone who didn't love *The Bell Jar,* so it's difficult not to retrospectively think less of the great and the talented who swore that Beecher Stowe's sticky lament was unutterably moving. It is only readable as a historical odyssey, as the cause of an international outbreak of endemic tastelessness, like literary bird flu. You need Wellington boots to get through the sludge of the prose and goggles not to succumb to the sliced-onion lachrymosity. As a story, it falls apart. Characters arrive, declaim and get lost, plotlines taper away as the memory wanders. It's really a series of illustrative homilies on the wickedness of bondage, or rather, the wickedness of those who keep others in bondage. It leaves no sentimental artifice unfondled. It begs for tears like the rattle of an insistent charity tin. It owes most of its style to the pathos of Dickens, but with a stained-glass eye and a pulpit ear. No one gets out of Tom's Cabin looking good. Despite the desperate prose of the author, the cruel Southerners wresting babies from their sleeping mothers to sell them are not much more than moustache-twirling villains and the cretinous thugs of melodrama. The good whites are pompous Boy Scouts or ennui-ed intellectuals. Women are either vain, swooning, selfish belles or stern, sexless bluestockings. The object of all this syrupy pity, the Africans, emerge as worst of all. Patronized with an all-encompassing piety as universally childlike, naive, innocent, trustingly dim, unintelligent and gullible, yet also cunning, scheming, lazy, mendacious and sexually incontinent. Blacks are human, but they are a lower, lesser order of human. The best white folk can do for them is to care for them as you would simple creatures of nature.

Uncle Tom himself is one of the most impossibly perfect people that ever dripped off a pen, a paragon of slow Bible-reading, self-sacrificing saintliness. His unquestioning love and respect for his owners owes more to labradors than to humans. His white equivalent is a Little-Nell-style girl, who feels the pain of all slaves before succumbing to tuberculosis. There is a Northern liberal woman who may well represent the author. She takes a willful and feral black child under her personal tutelage as an experiment in husbandry to prove that the condition of slaves is down to their treatment. When the stern lessons fail she admits that blacks disgust her, and that she can barely touch the little girl. On meeting Beecher Stowe, Abraham Lincoln said, "This is the little woman who started this great war," an untypically catty observation that manages to be both patronizingly sexist and an accusation of war crimes. *Uncle Tom's Cabin* had a direct effect on the antislavery fervor that hardened the North's attitude to the South. It added righteousness to the Underground Railroad and spite to the provocateurs like John Brown. It was the most politically and socially inflammatory book in America since Tom Paine's *Common Sense*, which only goes to show that style has little to do with ideas whose time has come.

But most Americans didn't read it as a book, they saw it as a play, which often included minstrel music-making like "My Old Kentucky Home" and "Massa's in de Cold Cold Ground." A great many Americans being functionally illiterate, or illiterate in English, the theater was where they got their literature.

Dixon left the theater with a burning fury, determined to write a rebuttal. He was by no means the first Southerner to have this idea. There were shelves of anti-Tom literature, including *Aunt Phillis's Cabin*. Dixon wrote a trilogy of novels about the restoration and the Ku Klux Klan, the second of which is *The Clansman*. They too were best-sellers. They made Dixon famous, and like *Uncle Tom's Cabin* were turned into stage plays that traveled over America. It was this that Griffith first saw as a traveling actor. His childhood was similar to Dixon's. David Llewelyn Wark Griffith was born in LaGrange, Kentucky, ten years after the Civil War. He was from Welsh stock, with the addition of an unlikely sounding disgraced English lord to fortify his ancestors. His father had been a Confederate colonel, "Roaring" Jack Griffith. Kentucky was a border state that had some slave owners. Indeed, a lot of *Uncle Tom's Cabin* is set there. But it hovered between Union and secession. Lincoln said that he trusted God was on his side, but he had to have Kentucky, his home state.

It remained uneasily neutral until invaded by a Confederate army, when it reluctantly came out for the Union. It was a state that split families, and Roaring Jack became a bit of a local legend, a great orator who got himself elected a couple of times to the state legislature, but spent most of his time drinking, gambling and keeping out of the way of his long-suffering wife while her inherited farm slipped into ruin. He went off to join the gold rush, returning with $13,000 in his pocket. Or at least in his pocket until Louisville, where he lost the lot. He died when D.W. was ten, and this adventurous, garrulous, brave and attractive, funny and wholly useless man was the abiding influence of Griffith's life. His mother sold what was left of the farm and tried to run a series of boardinghouses, each of which failed. D.W. worked in a bookshop until they fired him for reading, and then he went on the road as an actor, crisscrossing the country until he washed up at Biograph and Billy Bitzer taught him to direct.

Griffith chose *The Birth of a Nation* because he believed it. He felt he'd lived it. Dixon insisted that his books weren't fiction or romance. They were a verifiable truth. He mixed historical characters with fictionalized ones. In his inverted-mirror version of the Civil War, Lincoln was the great friend of the South who sympathized with white society, but was thwarted and manipulated by liberal Republicans and abolitionist zealots who wished spitefully to beggar the South and force black rule on it. There was in general a great historical rewriting of the Civil War in the South, and out of it rose the comfort that somehow they had wrested their great lost cause from disaster.

Dixon wished to set the record straight for the South, with its mythic, sophisticated, genteel plantation society, where the slaves were contented and paternalistically well treated in their own best interests. There was a wave of revisionism among American old soldiers' associations, which were much more sentimental in the South than in the North. They rewrote the old battles and beatified Robert E. Lee along with Lincoln as equal saviors.

There was the nurtured myth that the South was protecting civilization from the clutches of savages, that they didn't lose the war but were overcome by the industrial might of the North, suffocated by immigrant conscripts and Michigan foundries. Dixon lamented that slavery was never the true cause of the conflict; that in fact it was the bane of the South. Slaves were the cross the South had to bear. How much better if the black man had never been brought to these Aryan shores. They were the lower and lesser race of humans whose natural home was darkest Africa. To attempt to raise them up to the level of white folk was a disgusting travesty. He saved the highest opprobrium and revulsion for the mulatto—the half-caste, the misbegotten Caliban. Beecher Stowe also loaded her hottest pity for the half-caste girls who were used as concubines by slave owners. The half-caste could pass as white, hide its true nature. They could ape and imitate the facile manners of their betters. In *The Clansman,* the mulatto who is first trusted tries to marry a white girl and is killed with righteous rage. A black man rapes a white child, who then commits suicide with her mother. The rapist's image is found on the dead retina of the woman. He is then caught and hypnotized into confessing, and is lynched in the town center, much as Dixon remembers from his youth.

When he'd finished with miscegenation, Dixon went on to write books castigating socialism. Griffith saw something more than the rehabilitation of the South in *The Birth of a Nation.* He believed that film would be the new way of showing history. He believed in an absolute historical truth, that if you went back to source materials and involved enough experts, you could accurately re-create history on-screen. That what you saw would be the revitalizing of the truth as it happened. Film, he said, would no longer be sentimental eyewash and slapstick. It had a higher calling. To be the repository of the past. Unarguable, immutable and complete. The accuracy of *The Birth of a Nation* was a vital part of its attraction. The costumes were designed by experts. The muskets used by the soldiers were from museums. The rooms that events occurred in were painstakingly re-created. When Lincoln is assassinated in Ford's Theatre the cast are delivering the exact line whose laugh covered the shot. It's a silent film. Who'd know? In fact all America knew, because the brand-new publicity department made a point of telling them that that's how accurate this story was. Old soldiers swore the battle scenes were uncanny, and audiences had never seen anything this grandiose before, edited with this rhythm and dramatic flair. This was the first film that traveled with a whole circus of promotional paraphernalia. It was a big deal; it was the real deal. It was looking into the past.

With a spooky perception, Griffith believed that ultimately all houses would have machines that could call up the past. That film would magically be shown to anyone who wanted to know what really, truly happened. A teacup premonition of both television and Internet. But you look at *The Birth of a Nation* today and you'll laugh out loud at the very idea that anyone a mere three generations ago could have believed this was remade newsreel, or that it was anything more than base, knuckle-dragging, racist propaganda. *The Birth of a Nation* holds the exceptional accolade, I think unique in all forms of art, as being possibly the greatest and the worst film ever made.

The controversy continued. Griffith wrote furious defenses and explanations, and made another film, *Intolerance*, weaving together four stories, from Babylon, Golgotha, the St. Bartholomew's Day Massacre and a contemporary love story. It is unwatchable. Two and a half hours of ponderous self-importance and weighty histrionics. Even watching the brand-new techniques doesn't lighten the load of its torpor. Griffith built Babylon in Hollywood. The monstrous set stood for years as a decaying memorial to hubris, and, for those who chose to notice, as a parable. The intolerance he was really illuminating was against himself and his vision. He was, in the end, very, very Welsh.

Intolerance lost money, and Griffith subsided into an unemployable fame, revered by directors, ignored by producers. He ended up shooting uncredited scenes on other people's movies. But *The Birth of a Nation* set America up as the home of film, and he set up United Artists with Mary Pickford, Douglas Fairbanks and Charlie Chaplin. The beginning of the studio system and the triumph of talent over technology. It would have galled Dixon, but the person who really learned the most from *The Birth of a Nation*, who carried on its belief in the veracity of filmed history, was Sergei Eisenstein, who made *Strike, Battleship Potemkin,* and *Alexander Nevsky,* all of which owed obvious homage to Griffith, not least in their manipulation of the past to serve a current political purpose. In America it seems that *The Birth of a Nation* may have informed a lot of directors about cutting and camera angles, but it also pointed the way less traveled: what not to do. History is treated by film with a louche liberality. It is a cloth that can be cut again and again to fit a star or a story, and America has trawled the world for history, and found without surprise that on film, all of it, gladiators and musketeers, samurai and country houses, outlaws and freedom fighters, submarines, men in kilts and turbans, become equally American. History illuminates the great Yankee inalienable truths of the pursuit of freedom, individualism, self-determination and sex with whomever you fall in love with, regardless of caste, creed or class.

The awkward controversy over *The Birth of a Nation* helped keep black people off the screen in meaningful roles for a generation. Racism was treated with tongs or ignored. The Hays Commission, the industry's self-appointed censor, in one terse sentence suggested to filmmakers that miscegenation was to be avoided, as it pretty much still is. Black and white can share the same cop car, the same hospital ward, and the same foxhole, but rarely the same bed. But them mixed-race children have grown up to be some of the most successful people in America: in music, on television, as models and actors, the faces of advertising and of the future. Dixon and Griffith's loathed and despised mud-colored mulatto ended up sitting in Lincoln's White House.

17

New York

I've never been unhappy in New York. I only discovered this recently. I've been to New York more often than any other city, except the one I live in. Then last year I woke in Manhattan, early, as travelers from the east do. The day was gray and chilly, and I got up and strode into the quiet streets of the West Village, bought a paper from an ancient deaf woman I've been buying the *Post* and the *Times* from for years, and went next door to a diner where, by habit, I have breakfast. It's not the best breakfast, it's not even the second- or fifth-best breakfast, but it's where I go. When you're a visitor to a city, you like to hurry up the habits, lay down a pattern, gain predictability in place of roots.

So I buy my paper from the same old lady, and I come and sit at the bar of this diner and order pancakes and bacon or a ranch omelette with hash browns. The omelette is particularly bad, presumably so as not to show up the hash browns, which are remedial. I read the first seven pages of the *Post,* and the op-ed page of the *Times.* I like it here because it's full of a familiar cast of New York extras: the Wall Street drones eating low-fat, bran-rich stuff and feeding their BlackBerries full-fat, sugary wishes and lies. There are old men in ancient caps and stubble, hugging canvas bags, writing purple marginalia in library books. An old woman with three crucifixes pulling the lily guts out of bagels, as if avenging some terrible baked injustice. Shopgirls in assertive tops and running shoes, dads taking their kids to school, prodding plates of oatmeal. There's an elementary school round the corner, and many of the kids have their breakfast here. I like eating with children. They've done drawings of themselves eating their oatmeal, and of the guy behind the counter, saying thank you for feeding them. He's taped them up on the greasy, streaked walls, along with the graying, framed photographs of old country people, and the health warnings that number the ways of café death, from coprophagous cholera from the chef's unwashed hands, via fire and electrocution, to inhaling a rope of gristle into your lung. All the paraphernalia of municipal, bureaucratic health that diners put on their walls instead of stuffing into a file marked "stuff," like the rest of us.

In the drawings, the counter guy is always smiling. He never smiles. I've never seen him smile; no one has ever seen him smile. Maybe he smiles at himself in the mirror secretly, humorlessly, just to show that he could if he wanted, but he chooses never to want. The kids draw him smiling not because he doesn't, but because they do. They lend him a bit of a grin. He's pale all over, with a white cap and colorless hair, a sallow, pulled-dough face, fading eyes and a mottled apron. He maintains, with, I sense, some pride, the long tradition of deadpan service that is the hallmark of human interaction in New York. He barely nodded at me and muttered something that might have been "Hey, how you doin'?" but could equally have been "I'm going to disembowel you with a spoon." He slopped some of his thin, pale, bitter paint water into a mug and pushed a plate of half-and-half nipples at me. I took a scalding sip and hoped against hope that this time it might not burn my tongue, and might taste of coffee, and I looked at the *Post*'s 72-point headline, which was a pun, two truncations and an exclamation mark, about someone I've never heard of.

And then I was instantly overwhelmed, poleaxed, transfigured by joy. A feeling of happiness that was so intense, so radical, so outside the spectrum that it felt like madness. And this is the city to go mad in—you're among friends. Inscribing the minutiae of alien proctology in the library's copy of *Wuthering Heights,* it's only two synaptic booths away.

Free-floating, radical joy is not me. I'm not naturally an easy-going, half-full, count-your-blessings man. You won't find me on the sunny side of the street. I worry, I fret. My factory setting is stoic glumness with panic on the side. So the moment of joy evaporated, like the high C of an aria. But it left behind it the small, bright echo of a revelation: that I had never been unhappy in New York. Over thirty-five years of coming back, I only had good memories, happy memories.

The revelation intimated that I might actually use New York as some sort of therapy: an unconscious homeopathic, geographic pick-me-up. "Ask why," said the revelation. Why, I asked. Not out loud, obviously. "You know why," giggled the revelation, and vanished in a waft of frying onion. And I did understand; I do know why I am always happy here. It's because I once was in love here. As a young man I came to New York to follow a girl I'd fallen in love with. We lived on the Upper West Side. You can fall in love with places, with cities. I love Rome, and Edinburgh, and Sydney, and I've got this on-and-off thing with Paris. But before I loved New York I was in love in New York, and that's a whole different thing. It invested such a gust of bright memory here that, all these years later, I can still feel warm and indelibly romantic with it. The city holds the memory of a young man's fancy: the siren call of youth, and a boundless ardor. So, like Humphrey and Ingrid, we will always have New York. That feeling of butterflies, the erotic suspense. Knowing you own the space you love in, these fathoms of glass and stone, the dark canyons of mammon, the glittering, steepling thrust of perpendicular arch, Gothic Manhattan, with all its crowded, crooning cast. All this bouncing, smoking, scalding, jazzed-up, kinetic city was once here just for me and for Amelia. It's not the same, of course. The love's still here: the red heart on the tourists' sweatshirts and caps—the cleverest piece of municipal marketing since the knickerless can-can. It isn't what it was. Ask any New Yorker and they'll tell you it's a different city now, and all for the worse. Change in New York is always for the worse. Always for the worse, as the city slowly gets better.

I have a journalist friend here, a mentor in New York. "Oh God," he said. "You're writing about America. You're going to write about New York in a book. Really, a book? Do you want me to look at it? No, really, someone should look at it first. Who's looking at it for you? You can't get just anyone to look at it. I should look at it. You've got to be careful, you could get it wrong. So wrong. And that would be the end. It could be really serious for you. I mean, if you don't get *it*. Don't laugh. What's to laugh at? I'm serious. This could hole your career. You laugh because you're English. You all laugh at what you don't know. New York isn't funny. We don't think it's a laughing matter."

How can there be a right way to see a city? You remember, the city is a thousand stories and this is just one of them.

"Oh my God, of course you can be wrong. Europeans always get it wrong. You wear shoes without socks, you drape coral-pink cashmere over your shoulders. The English are more wrong than anyone. Really, you never get it. New York is very complicated. It's nuanced, and it's not a goddamn joke."

No one would say this about any other city in the world. When you consider how cosmopolitan, how international the population of New York is, it does manage to be an immensely parochial place: self-reverential. There are celebrities in New York that no one's heard of in New Jersey. It is interested and influenced by itself. An English friend who dislikes America but loves this city says, "That's because it's not America. New York's not related to anywhere; it has no kith or kin on this continent. Everywhere else is like everywhere else. But New York is like a divorcée looking for a richer second country."

Or perhaps it's just cheating on the country it's with. Of course there are things that inhabitants of a city can't know. They can't "see ourselves as others see us." There are little things that only an outsider will notice, like that New York is the worst-dressed rich city in the world. There is an inexplicable lost connection between the countless clothes shops, sophisticated, expensive, modern, classic, amused, serious, postmodern, and vintage, and the stuff, the schmutter that people actually put on in the morning. It's a city where the rich dress worse than the poor. Generally poor people affect an élan that money can't buy. Style rises from the bottom. But not in New York. There's a one-class-fits-all, oversized blahness. They all shop in department stores and boutiques and fashionable chain stores. The assistants' hands are a frenetic blur of tissue paper and credit-card receipts. Everyone's humping vast bodybag carriers, but what do they do with the stuff? Do they just store it in their illuminated closets? Perhaps they wait a couple of days and take it back. Maybe no one's buying anything, just circulating credit cards. In the eternal struggle between beauty and comfort, comfort wins every time.

And then there's spontaneity. New Yorkers love spontaneity, love it to death. But they need advance warning. You want to give a New York friend a panic attack, turn up unannounced on a Wednesday and suggest going for a drink. It is easier to organize five guys to raise a flag on Iwo Jima than to get mates out for movie and dinner. Surprise parties are such fun, but require e-mail "save the date" warnings. And everyone needs to know how to dress. Being dressed appropriately is make-or-break important. Though why they need to be told when they all look so dreary, who knows.

And no one cooks in Manhattan. Every fitted and imported oven you find will almost certainly still have the instructions and guarantee inside it. Caterers count as home cooking. I was invited to a dinner party where we all watched our host, dressed in an apron and chef's hat, chide the Guatemalan maid while she grilled his speciality burgers. He added the final twist of pepper to the blue cheese dressing that came from an old family recipe brought by his great-grandmother from the old country. If we looked out the window we could almost see where she'd been dumped on the dock.

New Yorkers will tell you the height of their ceilings. They'll tell you unbidden, with a straight face. They'll tell you about other ceilings they've seen or heard about. They're serious about ceiling height. It matters. But only to New Yorkers and popes. The rules for going out with people you fancy, then getting off with them, then having sex on them, are so complicated and imbued with such runic angst and childish caveats that it is no wonder nobody's getting laid. That and the thought of having to get a child into any sort of school in Manhattan.

If you ask a New Yorker for an opinion on a restaurant, or a play or a film, they'll tell you what someone else says. They'll say, "The *Times* gave it five stars," or "The *New Yorker* recommended it."

"Some guy on TV gave it a thumbs-up," or that it's been slammed in three really vital and cool blogs. What other people say and think is very important to New Yorkers. An opinion is only valuable if it's an informed opinion, and an informed opinion is someone else's opinion. As a critic I find this very heartening. It's an open-mindedness that's to be encouraged.

New Yorkers know that theirs is the finest city in the world to eat in. There is better food in New York than anywhere else. Mostly because only here are there people who understand the right and correct way to make food. Take Italian food. I once had a discussion—not so much a discussion as a lecture—on Italian food, with a man who owned Italian restaurants in New York. He was very honest about my self-evident ignorance and lack of experience when it came to eating, because I'd spent most of my life in London and knew all about the food in London, and he'd been told by people who knew and had given him an informed opinion that food in London wasn't good. A dish was put in front of us. "Look at this," he said to the dish. "There is something fundamentally wrong here, and you should be able to tell me what it is." The suspects in this food crime were a sliced tomato, mozzarella and rocket. The mozzarella was made from a cow. It was rubbery and too cold. The tomato tasted like a potato that had been rubbing itself up against a tin of tomatoes. It was all assaulted with balsamic vinegar that tasted like acidic molasses and had never been any closer to Modena than Hoboken. Apart from that, he was right: I didn't know. The restaurateur rolled his eyes, his informed opinion vindicated. "It's the rocket. The rocket isn't authentic. If you knew about Italian food you'd know that it should be avocado." Yes, I understand that, but in Italy the idea of an authentic tricolor salad would be ridiculous. "Don't tell me about Italy," he sneered, as if I'd played a Jack to his ace. "I know all about Italy; I send my chefs there to get experience. And it's fine as far as it goes, but for really good Italian food you have to come to New York. Look at French food. Who'd eat in Paris now?" And there's no arguing with this. New

York is the mark against which all cities measure themselves. Because New Yorkers say so.

It's money that changed New York. City politicians might like you to think that it was policing and zero tolerance, and taking back Times Square and the night, and banning smoking. But really it was money and property prices. When I was here at the turn of the eighties, a few years after Gerald Ford had bailed out bankrupt New York, the public services were jammed with need and injustice, rubbish was piled on barges in the stinking river, the police were a righteous law unto themselves. Manhattan had a rough, dystopian excitement. The madman on the street shouted at the traffic with a particularly Old Testament vim. Where politer European cities might have had street mimes, New York has always had the Brechtian street theater of pavement psychodrama: the muttering, bellowing, gesticulating and teetering looney tunes for whom the drugs are no longer working, who look like characters from *Exodus,* prophets of urban collapse and carnal comeuppance. The city clanked and cracked with the stress of its own fear and anger. It lashed out at the unwary. The streets sagged and steamed with a subterranean fury. The fire escapes rattled like mad monkey cages. There was a metropolitan, decadent hysteria; it was all disco and glitter, big hair and Cuban heels, boys in makeup, eyelashes like nuked cockroaches, Armani suits with padded shoulders and sleeves pushed up to the elbow, hair that needed twenty minutes to get out of the house. There were Zapata moustaches and white socks. The film was *Raging Bull,* which famously got beaten to the Oscar by *Ordinary People.* It was the year of *Airplane!, American Gigolo* and *Friday the 13th.* Steve McQueen died of cancer with a coffee enema to go. Alfred Hitchcock died—but who could be certain? Peter Sellers and Mae West finally passed over, and the *New York Times* best-sellers were *Thy Neighbor's Wife* by Gay Talese, *Crisis Investing,* and Carl Sagan's *Cosmos.* Sagan passed as the cleverest man in a sports jacket and roll-neck jersey. It was the beginning of the decade when culture and intellect went on sabbatical. There was a lighthearted, smeary-lipped, mirror-licking pleasure in that; it was the coke and piña colada decade. And then there was crime. The big thing. Bigger even than disco. New York was the crime capital of the bits of the world that people actually wanted to visit. They might as well have put the weekly murder rate up on the illuminated news in Times Square, not that anyone in their right mind would have gone to Times Square.

The defining cultural contribution of the eighties to civilization is the apocryphal story. It was an art form everyone took part in, like folk art. Apocryphal stories went from mouth to mouth with a mewing pleasure. There were the alligators in the sewers, the hitchhiker with the axe, the heads found in subway tunnels, the heads stuck on the fender, the head in the laundry. And there got to be apocryphal stories about apocryphal stories: the visitor to New York who'd been warned by everyone to watch out for muggers. He leaves his hotel and strides down the street, a man bumps into him. Instinctively he feels for his wallet; it's not there. Give me that wallet, he bellows. The mugger hands it over and runs. The tourist returns to his hotel feeling like Dirty Harry. In his room, on the bedside table, there's his wallet.

My favorite one was about the visitor who needed a haircut. He asked a man if there's a barber nearby. Sure, says the man, and gives him directions. The visitor misses his turn and walks into Harlem, and finds the wrong barber. It's Friday evening, and everyone in the shop is black or Hispanic, meeting for a wash and brush-up before going out for a night's mayhem. The visitor stands in the door. A barber shouts at him in Spanish. He replies, "I'm sorry, I don't speak Spanish," and a very large, very frightening man in a leather coat says, "What do you want?" The visitor says, "A haircut," and the black man translates, and the barber gestures him to a chair. The barber talks in Spanish. The black man stands behind the chair, looking at the visitor in the mirror. He says, "What do you want?" "Well," says the visitor, "just a bit shorter all round really." The black man runs his ringed fingers through his own hair and says, "You mean like mine?" "Yes," says the visitor, "but not that curly." The world goes silent for a long moment, and then the black man looks into the mirror the way an eagle looks at a fish, and laughs, and translates, and the whole shop laughs. Actually, that isn't apocryphal. Idiotically, that was me. I helped out as an assistant janitor in an elementary school up by Harlem. The real janitor was a nice and friendly, very stoned Jamaican who was pleased to have someone to talk about cricket to. He told me where the barber was. Worst haircut of my life.

New Yorkers took a contrary, grim pride in their violence. They were proud of it, the muggings and the murders, the drugs and the rapes. You needed to be tough enough to hack it. New York asked, did you have the smarts? Were you street enough? It was like Stalingrad, but with all the besiegers on the inside. There were rules. You never looked rich, always wore flat shoes. Women wore their handbags like satchels. You learned to carry your keys like a knuckleduster, three quarters between your fingers with something hard, like a pen, pressed up against them. Women carried whistles and sprays, and occasionally a brick. Taxis were like riding in a Third World holding cell, except for the Checkers. Of all the things I miss most from the 1980s, it's the Checker cabs.

When you heard of someone who had been mugged or pushed in front of a bus, you asked technical questions. What was it they'd done wrong? Where was the mistake in the game plan? Because the point of living in New York was to avoid the bad stuff. People who got caught played badly, fluffed it. There was a spartan culture of victim blame. We all learned to understand what it must be like to be a wildebeest. "Look, kid, lions happen. Lions are a fact of life. If you get snagged by a lion you got no one to blame but yourself. And remember, when the lion gets the guy next to you, that's one more lion burger that's not got you in it."

It is safe now in New York, one of the safest cities in the world. It's not just safe, it minds how it goes. You can wear pearls in Times Square. You can wear nothing in Times Square. You can go and meditate in Washington Square. You're not even allowed to smoke in Central Park, let alone jump joggers. Now New York worries about its health instead of its safety.

When I finished emptying the bins at school, I'd go back down to the West Side and go for a drink at the Dublin House, a bar between Amsterdam and Broadway. I know a lot about bars. There's nothing any New Yorker could tell me about drinking. And what I wanted was a grown-up bar, a place to drink in. The Dublin House was one of the very best. Its job was the transfer of alcohol. Facilitating people who wanted it or needed it, and helping them drink efficiently without stress. It wasn't a scene, it wasn't a singles bar, it didn't encourage singing along or quizzes, or showing off, or overt behavior of any sort except the pursuit of the bottom of the glass. I spent hours and hours, days and weeks, at the bar of the Dublin House, drinking boilermakers: glasses of gassy, thin draft beer and a shot of Wild Turkey. I read with a one-eyed precision. The *National Enquirer,* then at the height of its sublime, looking-glass world: "Elvis Found on the Moon," "Are Your Teeth Talking to You?" "Voodoo Dentist's Rights," "Image of Christ Found in Puerto Rican Cellulite." And the *New York Review of Books,* which seemed to be no less than a catalogue of an alternative world. It was in the Dublin House late one night, comfortably numb, that I began my lifelong sadomasochistic affair with the *New York Review of Books.* First it was the cartoons, the caricatures. There had been a moment in my life when I'd wanted to be a cartoonist, but these saved me the trouble. And then I'd study the advertisements from university publishers, and wonder at the extreme academic potholing and the arcane pursuit of foot-note tenure and research grants that would lead someone to want to (a) write and (b) publish *Images of the Phallus in Central American Graffiti*: "essential reading for those seeking deeper insights"; or *Wordsworth: War Poet*: "a striking and exhaustively researched polemic," "an important addition to the rich literature of bellicose rhyme"; *Floral Tributes and the Holocaust*: "a milestone in Shoah studies." I rarely read the actual articles. I understood they weren't for the likes of me. They were soft missives from a gated community of errata. What I loved, what I grew hopelessly addicted to, were the personal ads: the lonely hearts, each little plea so carefully contrived and painfully, awkwardly dispatched into print.

They opened tiny glory holes into the damp and yearning lives of folk with such elevated and rigorous personal standards that stepping into the arena of advertising for sex must have been a hideous humiliation. I would spend hours constructing lives from these little anonymous messages. The archaeology of intellectual lovelessness. The neediness, the vanity, the telling clues of cultural snobbery. The tone of the personal columns in the *New York Review of Books* and the *London Review of Books* is culturally very telling. London's correspondents are no less desperate for love, but the columns here are a repository of self-reverential comedy, so arch and ironically knowing they have been anthologized. So a couple of typical New York offerings, taken at random, read:

Too good to resist. Striking natural beauty, sexy sophisticated and completely real, at the same time slender, lean, really cute, adventurous, curious, artistic, low-key humanitarian, trailblazer, fun-loving, athletic, not a false note. Light of heart, open, with unassuming, playful smile. Nature, outdoors-lover, appreciator of beauty, creativity, spontaneous, delights in exploration, discovery, hiking, sailing, New England, photography, architecture, great cook, great conversationalist (but not both at once). Crazy about making a difference, giving back, youth at risk, local agriculture. Seeking adventurous, verbal, secure man, 45–58. Values generosity, authenticity.

And this:

Fifties, Jewish, bisexual mensch. I'm intellectual, kind, funny, world-traveled, Ivy-educated. I've been married monogamously for many years. I'm now looking for a gay male friend, preferably with benefits, to help me explore my dormant gay self, Manhattan or Brooklyn.

Their English equivalent, also chosen almost at random, would be:

I have 39 years of magical experience behind me. Gay, epicurean land registrar and flamenco dancer.

Or:

Sorry is not the hardest word, auscultatory is. And bazouki. Lexicographal gymnast, retired male, 40, WLTM woman willing to easily concede defeat at Scrabble.

And my current favorite:

Animal in bed. Probably a gnu.

The New York approach is invariably an embarrassed gushing of way too much information, the hung-out confession without insight. The London effort is typically English, an inability to treat serious personal problems seriously or personally. Everything has to be made a joke, so that when it doesn't work you were only being ironic. The effort put into both is wearying, and the moral is perhaps that intellect and being well-read have no innate value to a contented or useful life. The number of hardbacks on your bedside table is in inverse proportion to the number of arched backs in your bed.

Once in a while, the big Irishman behind the bar, who was a strict practitioner of the credulous school of bartending, would tap the wood and stand me a beer. The place opened for breakfast and closed long after anyone sensible or sober was still out. I grew to love this place. If I ever have a memorial bar to commemorate the final few happy memories of my alcoholism, it would be the Dublin House. I drank my own wake here. It had been a bar since before Prohibition, and had come to an arrangement with the authorities to sell beer from the first floor. It was generations of Irish. The barman still had a brogue you could have carved a hurley stick with. Nineteen eighty was the height of what we call the Troubles. I was plainly English, and there was no point in explaining that I was actually Scots, that would have been just as bad. I'm the wrong sort of Scots. This was a Republican bar, full of the old grievances and the romance that are an immigrant's heirloom. We had a don't ask, don't tell agreement. I was a regular, and we were joined by the higher calling of drinking before eleven. At least I understood that being Irish wasn't all green wigs, bagpipers and leprechauns. I was harangued by a girl once who grabbed my arms and said I was part of a colonial, baby-killing, fascist state, and that the Brits should get their troops out of Dublin. I told her she'd convinced me. She burst into tears. Once in a while, a man would pass round the tin for the widows and orphans, and they'd raise their glasses to the boys. If I was asked I'd shake my head and turn a shoulder. It was one thing not taking an old bitterness to a new country. It was another to actually pay to send back Libyan Semtex to blow up my home. And one afternoon I couldn't resist saying as much to a particularly unpleasant Noraid hustler. He started with the jabby finger and the did-I-knows. The big barman leaned over, picked up his drink and poured it into the sink. "You're barred," he said. "You'd rather serve an English fecker than one of your own?" "He may be an English fecker, but he's no trouble, and that's rare for a fecking Englishman, and to be encouraged. You're a gobshite, and we've more than enough of them."

One evening I walked into the Dublin House to wait for Amelia, who worked as a waitress in one of the big restaurants on the park. When she'd finished her shift we'd go to the Mudd Club, or CBGB, or eat sushi downtown. It was cold. I was wearing a navy pea coat. I blew in with the freezing wind. The barman looked up and shouted, "Yo, Adrian, they just shot John Lennon." We were round the corner from the Dakota, where Mark Chapman had waited, first for an autograph and then for the whole life. "He's wounded, they've taken him to hospital." I thought it was a joke, another apocryphal story. An hour later, someone came in with the old news that Lennon was dead. Amelia arrived in tears. There were a lot of tears in New York. In the bar, where lachrymosity tended to be manly: a distant stare, a nose-blowing, they played "Imagine" and old Beatles records on the asthmatic, tinny jukebox. And as the night grew glabrous in its cups, someone put in a handful of coins; and "Auld Lang Syne," with its terrible, jolly accordion opening, swung over us again and again.

The mourning for Lennon was utterly unexpected. His death was sad and tragic, but this was New York: people died all the time. Eviscerated drug mules lay in piles in the projects, the heads of late commuters were igloos for rats down the subway tunnels. But this was different. The next day, outside the Dakota, there was a vigil. Hundreds of people with candles. It was bitter. They stayed all day, and the next day, and the next. The candles guttered in the sleet. The policemen in their furry hats slapped their huge, gloved hands on their dark blue bulk, dragging on cupped cigarettes. You could spin the radio dial and hear a medley of Beatles songs from one end to the other. As the weeks went on, the newsstands blossomed like early camellias with covers of Yoko and John. The shops and cafés on the West Side had handwritten notes in the windows: sometimes the simply funereal "John Lennon RIP" with a photograph, sometimes great emotional exclamations of hippie sorrow and alternative loss. And if I spoke out loud in a supermarket queue or was overheard in a restaurant, strangers would grab my hand and tell me how sorry they were, and particularly how terrible and shaming that the death had happened in their city. My accent made me a remembrance book so that I could take their condolences back home with me. I was both embarrassed and moved, more affected by them than I had been by the shooting. It was out of character. I'd never expected pathos.

Over thirty years later, across Central Park opposite the Dakota, in the acre they've named Strawberry Fields, there's a memorial to Lennon, and still on a clear autumn Saturday it is surrounded by tourists taking photographs. There is something that people have said over and over: "You know, he chose to come here." Lennon had fought a protracted and bitter public battle to be allowed to stay in New York. For all those for whom he was the voice of their generation, and was a profound genius, there were just as many who thought he was a drug-using, anti-American communist, an immoral exhibitionist who proselytized all the things that were undermining American youth. His story was a musical version of so many New York lives. This was always the immigrant city. This is where the big lady stands by the golden door. This is the once-upon-a-time place, the start of countless stories. New York is still somewhere you have to achieve.

The immigrants come from all over America. This is a city of choice and aspiration. If you can make it here, you'll make it any-where. If you're reading this in New York, feel free to disregard it, to laugh humorlessly at another Euro who really doesn't get it.

I was in a midtown bar, sitting in a booth with my girlfriend. We were drinking cocktails. Around about midnight, a well-dressed and distinguished middle-aged man stopped at the table. His date, a New York–discreet, handsome woman, hung back. "Excuse me," he said, "I'm sorry to interrupt, but we've been sitting behind you and I've got to say"—he looked at me—"you are without doubt the most pretentious, pompous, phony loudmouth I've ever had the misfortune to listen to for three hours. You ruined our eve-ning. And, miss"—he looked at Amelia—"you need to make some changes." Amelia smiled sweetly, and she did.

18

Pie in the Sky

St. Bride's is the journalist's church on Fleet Street. There have been seven churches on this spot. It's named for the Irish saint Brigit of Kildare, the virginal head of the old, equal-opportunity Celtic Church. She has, over the years, become the patron of babies, blacksmiths, chickens, bastards, children of abusive fathers, and printing presses. It must have been the combination of bastards and ink that brought her to hacks.

St. Bride's was the parish church of Milton, Dryden and Pepys, and it must have memorialized more godless reprobates, more unshriven sinners and bearers of false witness, than any other religious institution in the city. It is, by tradition, where journalists depart. More correctly it is the paddock before long and maudlin wakes. I don't exactly look forward to my final deadline here, but it's fitting. There is a chapel dedicated to journalists killed on assignment, an altar full of byline photos, like birthday cards. A reminder that, proportionately, being a journalist in a war is more dangerous than being in the Special Forces, and more important.

Above the font, on a little wooden bracket, there is the bust of a child with her eyes closed. She is an imagined image of a real girl whose parents were married here: Eleanor and Ananias Dare. He was a bricklayer who'd done well for himself, she was the daughter of a businessman. Virginia, their daughter, was baptized in the late summer of 1587. Not here, but in Roanoke Island in North Carolina. This face isn't the original one. That was lost, as was little Virginia Dare. We know nothing about her, except that she was born, baptized, and vanished. She was the first immigrant child born in America: the first American. With respect to the Indians, because the very idea of America belongs to immigrants.

The Roanoke community was set up under the auspices of the serial adventurer, poet, flatterer, flirt and squanderer of other people's fortunes, Sir Walter Raleigh. It was led by Virginia's grandfather, John White. And from the beginning it was a tenuous and chancy enterprise. The pioneers landed in the wrong place: they were meant to be in Chesapeake Bay. They didn't have enough supplies, they arrived too late in the year. They didn't have much that would grow. They got on the wrong side of the local tribe and it was the middle of the worst drought in a millennium. Eventually, as they slipped into failure, White was sent back to England with the only seagoing ship, to get more supplies. The round-trip should have taken six months, maybe a year. But he got back to England at about the same time as the Spanish Armada. There was no end to Roanoke's misfortune. He didn't return for three years.

What he found when he did was a ghost town. Carved into a tree was the name "Croatoan," the local Indian tribe. There had been an agreement that if things got too bad the pioneers would throw themselves on the mercy of the Indians. If they were in trouble, they would carve a cross. There was no cross. White sailed on to seek out the Croatoan camp, but the weather broke. The captain of the ship insisted on putting out to sea. John White was perhaps days, even hours from his dependent colonists, his daughter and grandchild, but the ship turned its face back to Plymouth, and he never saw America again.

Little was heard of the colonists. Powhatan, the king who caught John Smith, who was in turn saved by Pocahontas, told of a battle where he'd killed a lot of white people with the Croatoans. Some others said that the settlers had been sold as slaves to beat copper. There were, for a few years, reports of gray-eyed Indians. A Welsh missionary claimed to have been rescued by a Welsh-speaking savage, but nothing really. In the early days of these fragile colonies, people disappeared into the great vastness like scattered corn, or they succumbed to fevers and famine, accidents and malevolence, the natives and depression.

The life expectancy of sixteenth-century immigrants was not bright, but they were stubborn and believed in their power to overcome the hardships. These weren't the religious zealots who'd come later. They were a mix of the adventurous and the inquisitive, the desperate, the awkward, and the fantastically optimistic, no different from the people you see in the queue at passport control today. But the odds against success were very different, and the chance that any of them would ever see their English homes again, minimal.

Two hundred years from Virginia Dare's birth, America had fought and won its War of Independence, and 100 years after that it was the most successful industrial country in the world. Virginia Dare continued to hang in the colony's imagination. She grew to become America's lost Marianne, its Gavroche, the lost child of innocence. The firstborn of the New World. And then in 1937 a traveling salesman discovered a roughly incised gravestone that said it marked the last resting place of Virginia and her father, killed by savages. It stoked a romantic interest and speculation about her life; there were plays and books, and the discovery of more "Dare stones," apparently written to her grandfather, like postcards, about her life. She'd joined a band of Indians, married a chief's son, given birth to a daughter called Agnes. Agnes, in Greek, is also a virgin. The Dare stones were a wishful part-work, something like those prayers hung up in Orthodox churches. They were obvious fakes. But still, that doesn't deny that there was enough of an appetite and a need to invent them. Virginia got a stamp: her imagined parents with an imagined infant—an American nativity that never made the flight to Egypt. She was also the sacrifice of the firstborn to propitiate the earth. Virginia blesses and becomes the land, a little pagan goddess for all who follow.

This is the point where I have to begin wrapping things up. Lean back in the chair, lace my fingers behind my head, stare into the embers and draw some wise conclusions. Produce some suckable aperçus.

I did imagine that as I got to the end of this book, something would come to me out of the red, white and blue. But predictions are either trite extrapolations of the present or high-interest loans from the bank of guess what? It is journalistically seductive to view America from above, as a constant, binary combination of competing opposites, balanced on a seesaw: practicality versus ideology, Republican versus Democrat, conservative and liberal, church and state, North and South, black and white, coastal and middle, silent and vocal, disengagement and intervention, state and federal, cowboys and Indians, pro-choice and pro-life. Or, where we started off, with Clemenceau's barbarian and decadent.

It has often been said that America is a constant competition, a race between its hedonism and its vitality. But I think for most Americans it's simpler even than that. It comes down to Decatur's toast: "My country, right or wrong."

The founding fathers set up a constitution that was supposed to lock stability into the political system by matching the competing demands with checks and balances. But so often, stability ends up looking very like inertia. The tiny, incremental changes that are ground out through compromises may work for the smooth transition of the ship of state, but they can be at the expense of the individual.

I covered the 2008 presidential election and was, as ever, overwhelmed by the circus of American plebiscites, the horse-choking sums of money, the immense amount of time that has to be mobilized in a barely controlled arms race of spending and manipulation that stifles the clear and simple democracy of one man and one vote. There is only a sparse handful of exceedingly rich countries that could begin to afford to maintain the bulimically wasteful expense of an American democracy. It isn't the best on offer, or the most fair, or even the most democratic. It is just the most expensive.

Predictions about politics are inevitably pessimistic. What is inspiring about American elections is not the politicians or the platforms. Not the speeches that all sound like a cross between Baptist prayer meetings and the captain's homily at the end of an episode of *Star Trek*. It is the thousands of volunteers who turn up to help. Who man doors for hours on end, who answer phones and collate information, who carry trays and supply a million doughnuts. The volunteers congregate in every city and every state, work in empty shops, camp on sleeping bags, travel at their own expense, moved purely by the idea of politics. Not just its theory but its process. If you spend any time in maligned and patronized small-town America, you will see how much of the day-to-day administration of life is actually run by volunteers: people who help out with schools and clinics, mothers' groups and coffee mornings, who organize environmental projects and yoga classes, rubbish collection and traffic management. They drive buses and do odd jobs for the old. They collect in committees and in pressure groups. They keep records, write letters, and they bake cakes. Civic Americans feel responsible for the places they live in, and they reckon they have not just an obligation but a right to improve them. Citizenship here is more loaded and weighty with responsibility than anywhere else I know. The politics at the top is as depressingly confounded by special interests and single-issue dogma as everywhere else.

Amelia, the girl I lived with in New York, gave all her pocket money to the doomed Hubert Humphrey campaign in 1968. Now, as a married mother, she continues to work as a volunteer for the Democrats in elections. She believes that the defining motivation for Americans is justice. "Have you noticed," she said, "how many American heroes are lawyers?" From Atticus Finch to every other TV drama, masses of lawyers have become presidents. Americans like lawyers. They want to be lawyers. They want to marry lawyers, vote for lawyers, watch lawyers as entertainment. Lawyers, lawyering, is the go-to profession for second-generation immigrants. It's what your parents work eighteen-hour days in the convenience store for.

Lawyers are the new three-button, white-collar, cuff-shooting cowboys. They fulfill all the cowboy criteria. Workingmen with arcane skills. They can be both good and bad, sheriffs and gun-slingers. They have a strict code and they ride the range of litigation. If you get intimidated by a bad one, you need to go and hire yourself a better one. "See you in court" could be America's motto.

Both national and local politics beg one of the great unanswered questions of American politics: Where is the socialism? Whatever happened to a socialist America? "Socialism" is a political swearword of the deepest content, an accusation that needs no explanation or expansion. While "liberal" still hems and haws in the big room of politics, "socialist" is out the door, unconscionable, inexplicable and indecipherable: a political thought crime. Of all the free First World democracies in the world, and all the not-so-free undeveloped ones, America is alone in not owning an effective socialist movement. It is telling to look at what America has chosen to do without when it could have everything, but then perhaps if you do have everything, the one thing you don't want is socialists making you share.

America's CV, its rap sheet, would lead you to believe that here of all places would be the great social democratic nation. It says "all men are created equal" on the tin. It was built out of the classical age of reason, and the nonconformist religions that were the fire and anvil for most of Europe's socialist movements. Its immigrants were working people escaping pogroms and the misery of old hierarchies. America was forged in collective endeavor. It grew out of mass labor, fought a civil war for the brotherhood of mankind. Everything about its genesis and aspiration points to collectivism, but the check and balance on market capitalism of organized labor was beaten into a malleable subservience. America once did have a politically idealistic and formidably organized socialist movement, but in the heat of the economic and industrial boom, commerce, industry and the utilities clubbed and shot and intimidated the unions, and the courts supported them. Something happened. Socialism stumbled and lost its nerve.

In *The Grapes of Wrath* John Steinbeck, the outstanding witness of the American working class, wrote about "the little screaming fact that sounds through all history: repression works only to strengthen and knit the repressed." Except it didn't. Not in America. And perhaps it didn't because the repression was of a new sort never tried before: the repression that comes with freedom. Freedom that allowed titanic success and unimaginable wealth was also the freedom to fail without let or hindrance. The freedom to be born into failure. The freedom to be cheated, conned and plowed into failure, to be sucked down and fed with failure, to fail by color and history. The freedom that allowed one man to build a life that shone also—and perhaps necessarily—allowed another to hang in a shadow, parallel America, in a crepuscular dullness of coupons and jail, bailiffs, obesity and daytime TV. Now all that's left of the left are some gray, ponytailed ruminators in Vermont, Bob Dylan and Pete Seeger collections of some sad, echoing, brave music.

But how many Americans today could tell you who Joe Hill was? Once world-famous, Joe Hill was born in Sweden: Joe Hägglund. He immigrated to America and joined the Wobblies—the Industrial Workers of the World. He traveled the country organizing and writing songs—mostly alternative verses to popular tunes, like "Casey Jones, Union Scab"—then was fitted up for the murder of a butcher he didn't know, and executed. A great modern ballad was written about him: "I dreamt I saw Joe Hill last night." It's been sung by every protest singer for 100 years. It is one of the great, eye-pricking, throat-swelling songs of the workers' movement.

When Joe Hill's appeals had all failed and he was waiting for the firing squad, already a martyr for the labor movement (his last word was "fire"), he wrote to a friend asking him to "drag my body over the state line, as I don't want to be found dead in Utah." He was cremated in Chicago and his ashes were sent all over the world to be scattered on May Day. He was the man who came up with the phrase "pie in the sky," the most perfect evocation of the American Dream and the freedom to wish for an impossible success while living a life of real failure: to see it and to smell it, but never taste it. "Pie in the sky" was the mantra and the chorus of millions and millions of immigrants whose lives drained into the earth, whose bones were ground for the railways, the motorways, the skyscrapers and the shopping malls.

But there was a moment when a socially more equitable nation might have been realized. The last of this book's American heroes is Eugene Debs. He was born in Indiana to French immigrant parents. He left school at fourteen and went to work on the railways and joined the union. He had the intelligent, intense face of a small-town lawyer. In 1894 the Pullman Company, who made railcars, cut their workforce's pay by nearly 30 percent, because they said profits were down. The union called a strike. Pullman cars were boycotted. The *New York Times* called Debs "a law-breaker at large, an enemy of the human race." The government sided with the employers and called the strike illegal on the pretext that it interfered with the delivery of mail. The army was called in and killed thirteen strikers. Debs was arrested and defended by Clarence Darrow.

Debs spoke constantly against the Great War. Those who heard him said he was one of the most powerful orators who ever stood on a soapbox. He said the conflict wasn't for freedom or liberty, but for industry and banking and power, who were using labor to make new markets and war profits, which is what socialists all over Europe were saying. But Woodrow Wilson, having lied to get America into the war, came up with an espionage act which said that anyone who tried to stop men enlisting could be tried as a traitor. Debs was careful about what he said, but got arrested anyway. The Supreme Court decided that he might not actually have instigated desertion or hindered the call-up, but his intent was clear. He refused to defend himself, making just two speeches to the jury. He was sentenced to ten years in jail in 1919, a year after the war was already won. Woodrow Wilson vindictively refused to commute the sentence. Debs ran for president from his jail cell and won just under a million postal votes. The winner, Grover Cleveland, did let him out, and a crowd of 50,000 welcomed him home. Debs was nominated for a Nobel Peace Prize. He's not often remembered today. Here are some quotes from the speeches he made at his trial:

I am thinking this morning of the men in the mills and factories.
I am thinking of the women who, for a paltry wage, are com-

pelled to work out their lives. Of the little children who, in this
system, are robbed of their childhood, and in their early tender
years are seized in the remorseless grasp of Mammon and forced
into the industrial dungeons, there to feed the machines while
they themselves are being starved body and soul . . .

When the mariner sailing over tropic seas looks for relief from
his weary watch, he turns his eyes towards the Southern Cross,
burning luridly above the tempest-vexed ocean. As the midnight
approaches, the Southern Cross begins to bend, and the whirl-
ing worlds change their places, and with starry finger points, the
Almighty marks the passage of time upon the dial of the universe.
And though no bell may beat the glad tidings, the lookout knows
that the midnight is passing, that relief and rest are close at hand.
Let the people take heart and hope everywhere, for the Cross is
bending, midnight is passing, and joy cometh with the morning.

And:

While there is a lower class, I am in it. While there is a criminal
element, I am of it. While there is a soul in prison, I am not free.

I will risk one prediction as a parting shot. We are coming to
the end of Europe's tenure as the arbiter and mentor of America
and the American way. I expect my American cousin Wendy, and
our kith and kinship, will be the last of my family's transatlantic
connections. There will be no more entries in the cuttings book, no
more carefully collated photographs to search for family likenesses,
no more entries in the Bible. I don't expect our children will maintain our bond. For five generations we've remained close, which
is longer than most Americans of European origin, who though
they can generally point to a country, a region, perhaps a town, can
rarely still pick up the phone to a relative. The expectations that
drove the millions of immigrants west is no longer here. The Old
World has grown more like the New, much to the pursed fury of

the French. And the New World itself isn't that new anymore. The strident market and the innovation that America instigated has ironed out the differences between here and there.

We watch the same flickering images, share our music and pictures, suffer from the universal fears and tempers of fiscal gout. We dress the same, eat the same, and we grow fat. It may be a familiarity of contempt rather than fraternity, but the great historic difference in opportunity and belief that generated the building of America, that culminated in the Marshall Plan and the Cold War, is not so great now. Moving to the States is a career choice, not an irrevocable new start.

Seen from Berlin or Copenhagen, Palermo or Glasgow, America doesn't look like the city on the hill, or Europe's Camelot. The lessons back and forth have been learned, or at least taught, and the next century will, I guess, belong to the new immigrants of Asia and Latin America. They will have different dreams and new imperatives, and the checks will have to adjust their balance.

The European immigrants didn't inherit America, and they weren't given it. They took it, and they built it out of next to nothing. It was, in the ten thousand years of our civilization, the last experiment in creating a brand-new nation. Idealist, reasonable, ordered, from scratch. And that will never happen again. There are no more empty lots in this world to grow countries in. There will never, ever be another America.

25.00   8/6/23